W9-DDQ-847

SUSAN CLARK STUDER, PH.D.

THE TEACHER'S BOOK OF DAYS

Inspirational Passages for Every Day of the Year

PRIMA PUBLISHING

To Dad

© 1999 by Susan Clark Studer

All rights reserved. No part of this book may be reproduced or transmitted in any form or by any means, electronic or mechanical, including photocopying, recording, or by any information storage or retrieval system, without written permission from Prima Publishing, except for the inclusion of quotations in a review.

PRIMA PUBLISHING and colophon are registered trademarks of Prima Communications, Inc.

All products mentioned in this book are trademarks of their respective companies.

Library of Congress Cataloging-in-Publication Data

Studer, Susan Clark
The teacher's book of days : inspirational passages
for every day of the year / Susan Clark Studer.
p.   cm.
ISBN 0-7615-1700-6
1. Teachers—United States Miscellanea.
2. Education—United States Calendars.   I. Title
LB1775.2.S78   1999
371.1—dc21   99-15058
CIP

99 00 01 02 03 HH 10 9 8 7 6 5 4 3 2 1
Printed in the United States of America

How to Order

Single copies may be ordered from Prima Publishing, P.O. Box 1260BK, Rocklin, CA 95677; telephone (916) 632-4400. Quantity discounts are also available. On your letterhead, include information concerning the intended use of the books and the number of books you wish to purchase.

Visit us online at *www.primalifestyles.com*

CONTENTS

ACKNOWLEDGMENTS

The Teacher's Book of Days did not suddenly materialize in book format; rather it was the cumulative result of many years of teaching, learning, inspiring, and being inspired by others. So many individuals have helped me along my path of student, teacher, college professor, and finally writer that, trite but true, there are far too many individuals to mention. Suffice it to say, this book could not have been written and published without the help of many people.

I have been blessed with a support group that motivates, encourages, and yes, brings me back down to earth when I need it. At the forefront of this group is a loving family that is led by a husband who has been a major part of my life since our high school days together more than three decades ago. Our growing family began with two wonderful sons of whom I am very proud, who inspire me and, perhaps more important, let me know how proud they are of me. Also included in my family support group are my parents, who have been instrumental in the writing of this book for at least two reasons: Not only did they instill in me a work ethic that keeps me writing when I would rather be doing something else, but also, long ago, they taught me a respect for teachers and education. In our home, school was a very important privilege *and* a responsibility.

Marriages have also brought several new people into my life. Many years ago I was privileged to marry into a family who accepted me from the beginning (or at least appeared to). This family included a mother-in-law who never believed in the term *in-law,* who introduces me to this day as her daughter, and who has taught me what a mother-in-law should be; and a father-in-law who passed away much too early in our relationship. More recently our family has grown to include two fine daughters-in-law and (so far) one grandchild, who gives us hope for the future, who will be going to school one day, and who could quite possibly be in one of your classrooms by the time you are reading this book.

Most of us have families who are supportive, but those of us who have significant friends and others who bolster us are doubly fortunate. In addition to my family, I have two good friends who are always nearby to pat me on the back and/or to kick my butt, depending on which I need the most. I met these two individuals while teaching, and both continue to work in the public schools today.

A book about teaching would not be complete without a word of gratitude to my students, who have come to me in many forms. Some came into my classroom as young people when I taught in public schools, others as pre-service teachers contemplating careers in teaching, and some as student teachers honing their skills and learning what to do and not to do while working with children and school systems. Many of my students are teachers who are enrolled in a master's degree program, taking time out of their busy schedules to continue their educations, to become more informed and thereby better teachers of today's young people. These individuals range in age from twenty-one to seventy-nine years old (yes, that's right, one of my students is seventy-nine years young), and many of the messages you are about to read have originated with these unique individuals, through discussion, observation, and preparing lessons to share with them. They have inspired much of what follows.

And finally, to the staff at Prima Publishing, who have been encouraging, helpful, and downright pleasant to work with, I thank you. I wanted to write a book that would inspire others, and you have made it a reality.

To the teachers who have taught me, to those with whom I have worked in public schools, private schools, adult education programs, and universities, and to those I now teach, this book is for you.

v

INTRODUCTION

WHEN I FIRST CONSIDERED writing this book, I thought that I had an abundance of information, good ideas, and a file cabinet full of quotes that I had collected over twenty years of teaching in public schools, universities, and in private settings. I had also raised two children of my own and participated in their educations as well. I felt that I had a wealth of information that might be of some benefit to others in the teaching field. But the problem, I realized from my own days of teaching, was not that the information would not be worthwhile, but that most teachers lead such busy, giving lives that few would have the time to read all of this information that could very well make their jobs easier. Therefore, I felt that all of this wonderful information needed to be presented in a very concise format, or no one would find the time to read it. I also discovered through my research that, although much has been written for teachers, very seldom is it compiled into an abbreviated form, nor published in one book so that teachers and other interested individuals can experience a "daily thought" that might just enhance their practice.

Although I felt strongly about the need for a daily reading for teachers, upon acceptance of my idea by the publisher, I have to admit that I panicked. My first thought was, "Do I really have enough information to motivate teachers positively for 365 (or 366) days?" Anxiously, I began to collect, analyze, and organize my "data" only to find (much to my relief) that I had more than enough ideas to fill a book (or two, or three . . .). The result is this book, *The Teacher's Book of Days,* presented to you as a collection of inspirational messages written by educators over the centuries and as classroom tips shared by experienced teachers from their everyday lives.

A question in some minds may be, "Why do teachers need to be inspired? Isn't the act of teaching a child inspiration enough?" And, for the most part, the answer is, "Yes." But I know from experience that although I enjoyed my job as a teacher, while "in the trenches" of teaching classes (that were too large) of junior high students who were thirteen years old one day and (seemingly) thirty-five the next, I often wished for a book just like this one to motivate me to get up some mornings, and to inspire me to do my best on others; a book that appreciated what I was going through each day.

I do not know how you are feeling today, or how your day is going, but I do know that when I taught in public schools, although many days were good, sometimes I felt as though I was fighting a losing battle—that no matter what I did, I simply could not win. There were also times when I felt as though I was the scapegoat for the world's problems, certainly for the parents' and often for the child's. Possibly the worst was every year at election time, when it seemed as though no matter what the party affiliation or who was running for what office, teachers and education became targets for party platforms. If elected, the candidate promised to "fix" my profession (whether it needed fixing or not).

Many times the joy of reading the morning paper was diminished by stories concerning teachers and educational issues that were necessary to report, but depressing nonetheless. These stories, occasionally about a teacher who was accused of molestation, often made me feel as though all teachers were being viewed with suspicion.

Also stressful were the yearly publication of test scores, complete with a headline such as "Are Our Schools Failing Our Children?" (always on the front page of the newspapers). Whether the stories reflected the subject I taught or the children (who might have had special needs) that we were teaching, it appeared to me that teachers were being blamed for students' poor test scores and for failing the young people entrusted to our care. According to the politicians and the journalists, it seemed as though these children had no other influences on their lives—no parents, siblings, society, media—nothing but their teachers to blame for their perceived failings, if any failings actually existed.

Yet, in retrospect, my years of teaching were all worth it. Whether published or not, for the educator who feels pressure to do the undoable, there is good news. Recently reported statistics have shown that, however negative the public's views may be toward education in general, Americans have positive feelings about their own neighborhood schools and toward the teachers who are educating their children. Studies, too, have found that, given the increased number of students taking SAT and other performance tests and the number of non-English-speaking pupils and children "at risk" in our classrooms, teachers (and students) are doing quite well (thank you very much). Among the findings of these studies is information that high school dropout rates are decreasing, Graduate Record Examination scores have risen significantly in the last few years, and that the "crisis rhetoric" of the last two decades, simply is not true.[1]

What is true, and what needs to be celebrated, is that many teachers are doing a fine job with limited resources and under difficult circumstances. We all know of wonderful things that are happening in our own schools and maybe even in our own classrooms. If we think back to our own years of schooling, many of us can recall at least one teacher who believed in us, motivated us, and whom we remember with fondness; the good news is that many of your students probably feel the same way about you. Most teachers have positive relationships with students, students who love them and in later years speak of them as being instrumental in their successes.

Although we may feel that sometimes the public and certainly the media do not like us, the truth is that we are doing a good job. Over 3,000,000 teachers in the United States alone teach more than 52,000,000 students to read, write, and accomplish a myriad of other important subjects every year.[2] One need only recall the popular bumper sticker from a few years back (which should be recycled at regular intervals) which read, "If you can read this, thank a teacher," to be reminded of the important work and service we provide to our society.

Maybe we are not all brilliant scholars, and we occasionally make mistakes (as most humans do), but we do our best under adverse conditions, working with children from a variety of backgrounds, with various cultural and familial influences, who in some cases have experienced oppressing circumstances, poor parenting, drug use, and who have been inundated with an onslaught of less-than-appropriate media images, movies, and television programming that hardly supports education or even appropriate moral behavior for young people. Coupled with these challenges, some of us are forced to work with hostile administrations and non-supportive parents and communities. For all that we put up with and accomplish, we should pat ourselves on the back and move on with the task at hand.

Although most of us may never win a "Teacher of the Year" award, or even receive a written thank-you note from a former student, rest assured, we have given our students our best. Some of us may question our lack of whatever it is that motivates others and ourselves. Some of us may be wondering what the "favorite" teachers have that we obviously do not. Some of us may even be questioning if good teachers are "born" with teaching skills or if it is possible to learn the craft through years of trials, tribulations, and, yes, errors. In an era of negative press, in which newspapers, magazines, television, movies, and politicians take daily potshots at teachers, and in which those who work in the field of education find it necessary to duck and weave to survive the punches, there is no doubt that a book that motivates professionals to continue, when there are days when it feels like everyone is against them, is a necessary addition to every educator's library.

This book, *The Teacher's Book of Days*, is designed to be a motivational and inspirational book for all individuals who are entrusted with young peoples' lives, whether in public or private schools or other organizations. It is a combination of informative and thought-provoking daily readings designed to encourage and help educators through their busy days. *The*

Teacher's Book of Days is divided into daily entries which include historical notes, inspirational quotes by leading educators from the past and the present, important dates in education, thoughts to savor, time-saving suggestions for use in the classroom, humor, and activities designed to promote diversity and to be fun. Each daily topic is briefly discussed and ends with a thought-provoking question for the reader's further reflection. Quotes, including citations for reference, help to make this a reference book for further instruction. Because it is not written for any particular year, and dates are generic, it is designed to be usable year after year.

We hear about the importance of teachers doing "reflective practice": taking the time to think about how the day developed and rehearsing in our minds what went well and what can be improved for the next time. These daily readings encourage reflective practice. To get the most out of this book, the reader should read each entry daily and take time to ponder what has been read. In doing so, and in answering the daily concluding question, you will discover personal answers that will enhance your practice.

Teachers are a very valuable resource, members of society who do not often receive the encouragement that they need. This book is designed not only to encourage, but to empower educators to become strong leaders of future generations of young people. Its message to teachers is that whether teaching in the elementary, junior, or senior high school, or running the local boys' or girls' clubs, you are needed and appreciated by the children, their parents, and the community in which you teach.

Teaching is a passion-filled profession. You have a passion for teaching, and I have a passion for the professorial role. I teach teachers daily, striving to motivate them to be reflective practitioners. But, more important, I feel strongly that it is part of my job to encourage teachers, assuring them that they are wonderful people, doing a wonderful and necessary job. This book allows me to reach a larger audience, to encourage and thank teachers for the role they play in young peoples' lives. As you read the daily readings I hope you agree.

AUGUST

August 1

I KNOW THAT AUGUST is hardly the time that you want to start thinking about going back to work, but if you can dedicate a little time each day to the upcoming school year, you'll find that the last few days before it begins will be a little less hectic, and you can begin the new year much more refreshed. This is not to say that you shouldn't be enjoying your well-deserved vacation; it is only to encourage you to remember that mental preparation is a large percentage of any job well done.

Some of you have already started school. Some readers who teach in year-round schools may be well into your new year. If that is the case, how is it going? Pretty good? I hope so, but if not, maybe you can use these ideas to help make the year better.

My last public school teaching position was in a junior high school that placed students on one of three year-round tracks. Although some of my colleagues began the year on July 1, my track always started on the first day of August, and just like today, it was always hot. But there were some advantages to beginning school in August, mainly because it felt like we were getting a head start on everyone else. Most of the students had no plans for the summer, their parents were working, and many were bored and missing their friends (junior high students are very social beings). Parents were happy to have their children in school because they were a little uncomfortable having their eleven-, twelve-, and thirteen-year-olds at home alone with nothing to do. Just about the time everyone else was coming back from their vacations, trying to get back into a scholarly mode after three months off, we were well into our new year and buzzing right along.

So, for those of you who have started school, have fun! And for those who have a month to go, keep enjoying your vacation. You probably do not want to think about going back yet, but you can mentally prepare for the new year and still enjoy your ice-cold glass of lemonade on your shady back porch with the sound of neighborhood children, or your own, laughing and enjoying the remaining days of summer vacation.

☙ WHILE YOU ARE *mentally preparing for the new school year, ask yourself, "What would I like my students to accomplish in the new year? What personal goals would I like to accomplish? How can I prepare for that to happen?" (And that is enough thinking for today!)*

AUGUST 2

IF YOU ARE LIVING in the Northern Hemisphere, then it is probably hot. Very hot. Hot, hot, hot! Which brings to mind a variety of sayings about "well diggers' destinations," and "Hades" (as in "Hotter than . . ."), to name only a few. Just the word *hot* when coupled with *outside* or *weather* reminds me of the Robin Williams movie *Good Morning, Vietnam,* in which he plays the character Adrian Cronauer, a disc jockey stationed in Vietnam during the 1960s conflict.

I have a friend who calls me on very hot days and either plays a tape from the movie or does a perfect impersonation of the Robin Williams character saying, "What's the weather like out there? It's hot, d____ hot, real hot . . . hot I tell you. . . . Were you born on the sun? It's d____ hot! It's hotter than . . ." and so on.[1]

Having my friend play this tape does not make the day any cooler, but it does bring a smile to my face nonetheless.

Friendships can also get you through the heated times in your classroom. They may not be able to change the situation, but friends can certainly lighten the load. I do not know how I would have made it through one particularly difficult year without my friend's sense of humor and his being there at the right times.

3

❧ DO YOU HAVE *a friend from school? Have you talked to him or her since school was out for the summer? Why not invite your friend for lunch or a chat?*

AUGUST 3

AIR-CONDITIONING! Isn't it wonderful! If you are sitting in an air-conditioned room right now, aren't you glad? And if you are not, are you sure that you want to read further? I am quite happy about the invention of air-conditioning, especially because I live in southern California, inland, away from the ocean breezes and in a desert-like part of the state. Because of this, I have air-conditioning in my house, my car, my office, and my classroom.

So many things, like air-conditioning, we take for granted. For example, indoor plumbing, good roads, the telephone, the computer, our jobs, and our health, and we assume that those around us have these, too. We assume that our students have the same amenities that we do, but do they? Some of your students may be living in very bleak environments, or even in cars.

We as teachers also have so many things that our predecessors did not have—computers, books, supplies. . . . Yet it is so easy to complain.

❧ WHAT DO YOU HAVE *that you take for granted?*

AUGUST 4

THE TIME BETWEEN the first of August and the end of September is known in baseball as the "Dog Days of Summer," a time when it is hot, the season has been going on since spring, and the end is still a good distance away. The Dog Days of

Summer is usually a time when players are getting nicks and bruises, more than a little fatigued (both mentally and physically), and sometimes even serious injuries. But it is also a time when good players rise to the top.

Schools have their Dog Days too, except that this time is more likely to be around March or May than in August. The "Dog Days of School" is the period when there are long spans of time without holidays or any special activities. Mental and physical fatigue set in for both students and teachers, and there are educational injuries as well. Yet, as in baseball, the Dog Days is the time when the cream rises to the top.

Maybe you think it's premature to discuss the Dog Days of School, but probably it's not. Now is the time to prepare for them, before the "fatigue sets in." You can prepare activities that will help the students and yourself through the Dog Days, activities that everyone can look forward to, like field trips, good behavior trips, contests, or a major activity unit such as "Gold Rush Days" complete with panning for gold.

What can you do *to prepare for the Dog Days of School during the Dog Days of Summer?*

August 5

The cornerstone of the Statue of Liberty, a gift from France to commemorate the centennial of American independence, was laid on August 5, 1884, on Bedloe's Island in the New York Harbor. Two years later, the 152-foot, 225-ton statue, designed by Frederic Auguste Bartholdi, was unveiled and dedicated by President Grover Cleveland on October 28, 1886.

Probably most adults have heard the beautiful poem, *The New Colossus,* which is most associated with the statue, and tells of people coming to America to be free. The poem was written by the American poet Emma Lazarus:

Give me your tired,
Your weary, your poor, your humble masses
    yearning to breathe free,
The wretched refuse of your teeming shore.
Send these, the homeless, tempest-tost, to me,
*I lift my lamp beside the golden door.*²

I love this poem because it speaks of other people who have struggled to come to *my* country to find independence and opportunity. I also think this poem can describe students as well. Students are tired, weary, poor, longing to be educationally free. They are, whether they know it or not, looking for independence and opportunity, a chance to be successful in their lives. They seek the freedom that comes from having knowledge. Education frees—all races, all ethnicities, both men and women, young and old.

❥ ARE YOU *a Statue of Liberty for your students? How can you be?*

AUGUST 6

WARNER BROS. STUDIOS began producing talking pictures on August 6, 1926, and they have continued producing movies ever since. Aside from pictures, as you probably already know, Warner Bros. also produces some of the funniest, longest-running cartoon characters known to audiences around the world. Warner Bros. produces the Looney Tunes characters, including Bugs Bunny, Daffy Duck, Tweety, and Sylvester.

It seems that everyone has a favorite cartoon character. My favorite is Tweety, and everyone who knows me—family members, students, staff, coworkers, and friends—all know this. When my birthday or some other personal celebration comes around, or just when they find something irresistible with

August

Tweety on it, these wonderful people buy a "Tweety present" and give it to me, and I just love it. Last week, after summer vacation, I arrived back at my office to find in my mailbox a writing pen with Tweety on the pocket clip, and I have used it ever since. I have asked around, and no one seems to know where it came from or how it arrived in my mailbox. (And they all say this with a smile.)

In my home I have Tweety salt and pepper shakers, a tea pot, and various other household utensils. At work, I have Tweety pens, pencils, a mug, and a stuffed Tweety from our wonderful education secretary, Theo. All of these items make me smile, because not only is Tweety a cartoon figure and therefore funny, but the thoughtfulness of the givers leaves a special feeling in my heart.

One of the reasons that I like Tweety is because he or she (I cannot tell which) has a little bit of attitude. Although small and a potential victim, she (or he) uses her (or his) cleverness to escape from dangerous situations, from that "mean ol' Putty Tat." I think there is a little Tweety in all of us.

My reason for keeping these items around is twofold. Not only do I like the character, but having Tweety in a professional office and at home adds a note of friendliness to the places where I spend the majority of my time. People come to my office with burdens that make the corners of their mouths droop, and suddenly, after looking around, their lips upturn. Though my students may come to my office having thought otherwise, I now am approachable. If nothing else, the items in my office are conversation pieces.

❧ Do you collect *something that can be displayed in your classroom to help alleviate tension, make you appear human and approachable, and break the ice for the student who is afraid?*

7

August 7

WHEN I THINK of summer, I often think of cool, icy beverages, whether iced tea, lemonade, soda, or ice water with a slice of lemon in it. There is nothing more refreshing during a hot day than a tall, cool drink.

If I have grading to do, lessons to prepare, or if I am doing my morning exercises, my container of water is close by. When my husband and I go for long drives, bike rides, or play tennis, we take recycled plastic soda bottles that are filled with frozen (but melting) water. In fact, as soon as a soda bottle is emptied, it is washed out, filled half-full with water, and put in the freezer. Whenever I want it, I pull the bottle out of the freezer, fill it the rest of the way up with fresh water to get the ice melting, and I am on my way.

I learned this frozen water trick when I was teaching at the year-round school. Our classrooms were very hot in the summer. Although they were air-conditioned, the system was on a timer that during the work week was only on between 8 A.M. and 4 P.M. The rest of the time (sixteen hours not including weekends) the rooms continued to be warm from the hot California sun. Although most of us kept our doors and windows open to let the hot air escape (which brought the wrath of the district upon us for wasting energy) it seemed to take most of the day for the air-conditioning to cool the room.

During these hot summer months, I got in the habit of bringing my frozen, water-filled soda bottle to school each day, and as the day progressed, and the ice gradually melted, I enjoyed a cool drink. What a refreshment!

People can be refreshing, too, like a tall drink of water.

꣎ IN THE HEAT *of the summer it is important to drink lots of fluids. Do you? How can you make sure you're getting enough cold fluids?*

August

August 8

THE SUMMERTIME can bring awesomely frightening storms that may be worsened by the area of the country in which you live. I have lived in southern California for several years and have found that, although California children may experience torrential rainstorms and mudslides, they do not experience the severe storms, thunder, and lightning that I grew up with in the Midwest. Anyone who has lived in the Tornado Belt knows what it is like to spend an afternoon in the basement or storm shelter during a tornado watch or warning, experiencing the stomach-turning fear of the greenish skies, the golf ball-sized hail, the high winds, and the eerie silence of being in the "eye of the storm." I just returned from Arkansas this spring, where I was reminded of these storms, the storm-warning sirens blaring in the middle of the night, and keeping tuned to the weather channel to track the storm and its proximity to the home where I was staying.

I have lived, too, in the lands of typhoons, and have listened to the radio as the winds increased and the warnings became more severe as the storm approached. I would tape my windows to keep broken glass from flying and would watch in relief as the storm path changed directions and we were saved from devastation.

I have also experienced, in my years in California, the earth moving. I would be shaken awake during the night as my bed moved, windows rattled, and items fell off shelves and dressers— with *no* warning. As an adult, I know that I am able to reason and get over the fear of nature and mortality.

But the reason I can "reason" is that I have had several people throughout my life who have helped me work through my fears. Many of these kind people were teachers who happened to be with me when fear-producing events were occurring. One was the third-grade teacher who told me to count between the lightning and the thunder so I could figure out how far away the storm was; if the numbers I could count to were increasing, she said, the storm was moving away from us. Another was the second-grade teacher who told us that thunder was only God

9

bowling with the angels. (This was comforting to me; I guess because it made it a game.) There have been many other "comforters" along the way.

In California schools, we have regularly scheduled earthquake drills in which we teach students to "duck and cover" during the drill, and, amazingly, they do it when the real thing comes along—automatically. (An amusing side note is to be with a group of teachers out "in the real world" when the ground starts to rumble, and you find yourself under the table with your fellow teachers in the correct "duck and cover" position.)

Teachers not only calm students' fears during real episodes with Mother Nature or during drills; their instruction saves lives!

⊃» WHAT POSSIBLE CALAMITIES *have you prepared your students for? What can you say to calm students' worries?*

AUGUST 9

SEVERAL YEARS AGO, on this date, I was preparing to begin my student teaching in social studies at a high school in Wayne, Michigan, when an event occurred that changed my way of thinking and made me question how I would teach about our government, our country, and the world to my high school students.

It was August 9, 1974, the day that President Richard Nixon resigned from the presidency of the United States. I hurt for my country and wondered, "How will this affect my teaching?"

I loved U.S. history, and I can remember that I wanted to teach it from the time I first studied about it in fifth grade. I loved my country even though we had just passed through the difficult period of the Vietnam era and I, like so many idealistic college students, disapproved of the U.S. involvement "over there." (I also disapproved of my friends, classmates, and husband being drafted to serve in such an unpopular war.)

Having survived those years of disillusionment, the Watergate issue was the last disappointment that I wanted to experience in that summer of 1974. With the lies and deception, my government had let me down one too many times. And, as I look back on it now, fortunately I continued to teach my classes with pride in my country and in being an American.

It appears that, in the last thirty years, whether as a result of these many disappointments of the 1960s and 1970s or of something else, we have maintained a disrespect, rightfully or not, for our country and its leaders. But it is still *our country* and our responsibility to make it what we want it to be.

I have come to realize that placing leaders (movie stars, sports figures, and other human beings) in the roles of heroes probably only sets us up for disappointment, because these people are only men and women just like us, only with jobs that have more exposure. President Nixon was not solely responsible for Watergate, nor have other presidents been free of all wrongdoing. In fact, Richard Nixon accomplished some good deeds while he was in office.

The question is not whether you will experience change or difficulties that will affect your teaching, but rather how will you deal with change? The question is, "Does change throw you or do you grow?"

꩜ HAVE YOU *had to deal with change recently? How did you deal with it? Was the outcome positive or negative? Why was it?*

AUGUST 10

AUGUST, IF YOU ARE NOT WORKING, is a time when you may take a vacation away from home, and deservedly so. Getting away from home can be refreshing and exhilarating, and can be that mind-expanding trip that jump-starts the rest of the year or

11

that mind-cleaning opportunity that clears the garbage out of your brain and lets you start anew.

However, if you are like me, it seems that no matter where you go on vacation, it is always good to be back home, sleeping in your own bed, wearing your "around-the-house" clothes and being in familiar surroundings.

One of the more positive aspects of a teaching career, short of motivating and watching young people grow, is the amount of time off throughout the year available for vacationing, whether a scheduled trip far away, a weekend to someplace nearby, or just a vacation trip you take in your mind—what I call "mental vacations."

Personally, I like short vacations, ones that last only a few days, and definitely for less than a week. I like vacations where I can fit everything into one bag and be on my way. But I also like vacations in my mind, so I frequently take a mental vacation—a day off here and there to read books that have piled up on my night stand, a spa vacation where I soak in the tub, a trip to a ball game or a day on the "greens," or a facial (free at most makeup counters), a manicure, and/or a pedicure. Simple, inexpensive pleasures that feel good.

It is important, when you are giving so much to others, that you also take care of yourself. Give yourself a vacation in your mind regularly throughout the year.

   ⁀ WHEN ARE YOU GOING *on your next vacation? Where, or how far, are you going?*

AUGUST 11

WHEN THEY GO ON VACATION, most people pack a camera to take pictures of the new sights they see, the family members they visit, or to remember the special times with family and friends.

August

When my father passed away this spring, I became the curator of the family pictures, most of them in black and white, taken with a Kodak Brownie camera, but also a few slides. I am so glad that my parents took pictures of our trips and of the family as we were growing up.

Have you ever thought of taking a camera to the classroom? The students would love it. Take some pictures of them at the beginning of the school year and then again at the end to see how they have grown and changed. (Don't forget to get yourself in the pictures, too.) If you do not want to keep the pictures, give them to the students to keep.

If you have a video camera, that is great too. If students get used to having their pictures taken, you will find that your students will begin to feel more comfortable being filmed and the camera can be used for speeches and other class activities, even if you tape over previous tapings. Working in front of the camera will be natural for them and for you. (You may want to check with your administrator about whether you need to obtain parent permission before photographing students.)

☙ Do you have access *to cameras? How can you use them with your students?*

August 12

ONE OF MY FAVORITE WRITERS, who just happened to write on the subject of education, is John Dewey. Dewey was born in 1859, died in 1952, and spent much of that time writing hundreds of works. During his long life he served as a professor at several universities, including the Universities of Chicago, Michigan, and Minnesota, and at Columbia University. He also founded the Laboratory School at the University of Chicago, which still instructs young people today.

Dewey frequently wrote of the importance of the school and the community working together to enhance learning. The following quotes are from Dewey's *School and Society*, written a century ago and still true today, and are typical of his writings: "What the best and wisest parent wants for his own child, that must the community want for all of its children. Any other ideal for our schools is narrow and unlovely; acted upon, it destroys our democracy."

Dewey continued, writing of the important role that school plays in maintaining the democracy Americans find so important: "All that society has accomplished for itself is put, through the agency of the school, at the disposal of its future members. All its better thoughts of itself it hopes to realize through the new possibilities thus opened to its future self."

Dewey believed that "only by being true to the full growth of all individuals who make it up, can society by any chance be true to itself. And in the self-direction thus given, nothing counts as much as the school."³

When you absorb the words that Dewey wrote, you realize that being a teacher is a great responsibility because the lives of young people are influenced by what you do. That is why it is so important that children be seen as individuals and that adults help them to discover their true potential. Children grow so that society can continue.

    ⟫ IF YOU WERE A PARENT *of the children that you teach, what would you want for your child? Are you providing that for your students?*

AUGUST 13

JOHN DEWEY BELIEVED that society benefited the most when the young people in its care were "induced by the mature members into the society." The best place for this to happen, according to Dewey, is in the school, a school that resembles and reflects the community surrounding it. A child also benefits when the school is a learning environment that reflects the community in which the student lives, where new knowledge presented fits easily into old concepts that are already familiar to him or her. The result of this cooperative effort is that the school and the society work jointly to maintain and enhance the community.

School is (or at least should be) the great equalizer, providing all children with opportunities and encouragement to ensure that everyone becomes a successful member of society. To allow, or provide, any less to those in our charge is, according to Dewey, "unlovely."

☙ WOULD YOU DESIRE *anything less for your children?*

AUGUST 14

AUGUST 14 IS V. J. DAY, a day which celebrates the ending of the war with Japan in 1945, when the Japanese forces signed a surrender aboard the battleship *Missouri*.

August 14 is also the date on which, in 1935, President Franklin Roosevelt signed the Social Security Act—what the historian Arthur Schlesinger calls "one of the most far-reaching pieces of legislation in American history"—a system that guarantees pensions to citizens who retire at age sixty-five. The Social Security Act, paid for by the contributions of both employees and employers, also provides financial assistance to dependent children, the blind and others.[4]

Social Security is, among other things, a provision for our old age, but it is only one provision. You may want to plan ahead to provide for yourself financially when that joyful time of retirement arrives. Years pass quickly, and many teachers and other

15

school personnel retire at what is still a young age, in many cases age fifty-five, with many years ahead of them. Do you have plans to provide for times of poor health? If you have good health, will you want to travel? Will you have the money to take the trips that you want to take?

Some teachers, depending on the district and the retirement system, do not have Social Security benefits, and state retirement payments may be meager. Now, no matter what your age, even if you are a brand-new and very young teacher, is the time to make preparations for your retirement years.

❧ WHAT ARE YOUR PLANS *for retirement? What are you doing to make the retirement dream come true?*

AUGUST 15

JOHN DEWEY WROTE, over one hundred years ago, that a child should be taught information that is practical *and* that coincides with what he or she is learning outside the school, in his or her home and community. The problem with education, according to Dewey, is that we try to fill the child with information that is not relevant, and the isolated bits of information do not fit together, with the result that the child has difficulty learning it. This prompted Dewey to write that teaching information that was unrelated and irrelevant was a waste, and that "all waste is due to isolation."

> The great waste in the school comes from his [the child's] inability to utilize the experiences he gets outside the school in any complete and free way within the school itself; while, on the other hand, he is unable to apply in daily life what he is learning at school. That is the isolation of the school—its isolation from life. When the child gets into the schoolroom he

August

has to put out of his mind a large part of the ideas, interests, and activities that predominate in his home and neighborhood.[5]

◈ As we look *at our new school year and subject organization, it is important to ask ourselves if the subjects we are teaching are "isolated from life." How can we make them un-isolated?*

August 16

One of the questions teachers are often asked in curriculum classes is whether they should be teaching children for the present time that they are living in or for some distant time in the future. John Dewey argued that, contrary to what was being taught in the schools of his day, subject matter should be for the present. Dewey believed that one of the problems with traditional education was that it was thought of as preparation, as acquiring certain knowledge that will be useful at a later date rather than at the present time. With this thinking, Dewey wrote, "The end is remote, and education is getting ready, is a preliminary to something more important to happen later on." The result is that childhood becomes "only a preparation for adult life, and adult life for another life... a preparation for something coming later."

But education should be for now, Dewey claimed, "The best thing that can be said about any special process of education... is that it renders its subject capable of further education.... Acquisition of skill, possession of knowledge, attainment of culture are not ends: they are marks of growth and means to its continuing."[6]

❧ Do you believe *that learning is for the present or for the future, or both? How does your teaching reflect your belief about this?*

AUGUST 17

ALTHOUGH EDUCATION is thought of by some as simply learning the facts and comprehending "the basics" (reading, writing, and arithmetic), an important yet often overlooked element of school is that it also facilitates a socializing process. Whether we choose to approach issues of social learning or morality in teaching, we know that these issues are present whenever we teach, in the manner in which we teach, in the modeling we show as adults, in the rules and regulations we choose to uphold, and in the positive and negative reinforcers that we utilize in the classroom. All of these elements speak of who we are personally as members of our society and what is our morality.

Whether or not we choose to think of ourselves as leaders, we are seen as such by the young people in our charge and by the community we serve. Although this may seem to inhibit us at times, it also gives us privilege. A wise teacher will think of this leadership role and how it affects the young people in his or her charge. A favorite statement of mine that John Dewey wrote nearly a century ago is, "The conception of education as a social process and function has no definite meaning until we define the kind of society we have in mind."7

❧ WHAT IS YOUR VIEW *of society? What kind of future society do you have in mind? How does your role as a leader of young people in the community reflect your view?*

August

August 18

On August 18, 1587, Virginia Dare, the first English child born in America, was born in Roanoke, Virginia. On this date in 1920, the Nineteenth Amendment to the Constitution was passed, giving women the right to vote. Isn't it interesting that it took nearly 150 years from the time of the Declaration of Independence for the country in which all men are created equal to give equality to over half of the population? Three hundred and thirty-three years from the date of the birth of the first child, a female, born in this new land? Isn't it interesting for those of us who regularly vote to imagine that our grandmothers could not?[8]

In our society we profess the equality of opportunity for all, and yet, in some areas, including in some schools, young women are not given the same opportunities and education as young men.

⟫ Do you treat *boys and girls equally? Are you sure?*

August 19

In 1994, Myra and David Sadker wrote a wonderful book entitled *Failing at Fairness: How Our Schools Cheat Girls,* for which they received much deserved acclaim. As a "fair-minded" teacher and supporter of equality in the classroom, I was amazed to discover when I was reading it that I was doing things in my classroom that could possibly be keeping girls from accomplishing what they were capable of achieving.

In their book, the Sadkers, who had researched gender issues for decades, wrote of a test that they give in their university classes at American University in Washington, D.C., and during seminars for teachers. During these lectures, they ask participants to list twenty famous women from American history, with a few restrictions. The list cannot include figures from sports or

19

entertainment nor presidents' wives (unless they are famous in their own right). How many can you write down? I have given this test many times to my college students, and unless they are history teachers, they have a very difficult time coming up with a list of twenty women.

According to the Sadkers, boys and girls, "sitting in the same classroom, reading the same textbook, listening to the same teacher . . . receive very different educations." Inequality is subtle, they write. If you think you are treating boys and girls the same, I recommend that you read this book.[9]

꙾ Now, *answer the question again, Do you treat boys and girls equally? Are you sure?*

AUGUST 20

LEST ONE THINK that the Sadkers have neglected boys in their study of gender bias in schools, they write in a chapter called "The Miseducation of Boys" that "gender bias is a two-edged sword. Girls are shortchanged, but males pay a price as well." The Sadkers claim that "while boys rise to the top of the class, they also land at the bottom." Boys tend to earn more labels than girls; they seem to be seen more "as problems in need of special control or assistance; boys are more likely to fail a course, miss promotion or drop out of school. . . . They dominate accident, suicide and homicide statistics." Where girls "suffer silent losses," boys' problems "are loud enough to be heard throughout the school."

The demands that are absent from a girl's school career, and which therefore keep her from achieving, are the very demands that a boy will experience as pressure, often resulting with the boy not trying, dropping out, experiencing aggressive tendencies, or in some other fashion rebelling against the school and possibly the home and society as well.[10]

❧ Do you demand *or expect more of the boys in your classroom? Do you make comments that imply that students have "rightful" places in society as men and women?*

AUGUST 21

THE IDEA of gender equity is not new to education, nor is it a result of the 1970s feminist revolution. John Dewey wrote in 1920 that the purpose of education "is to set free and to develop the capacities of human individuals without respect to race, sex, class or economic status." The test of the valuable teacher is "the extent to which they educate every individual into the full stature of his possibility."

"Democracy has many meanings," Dewey continued, "but if it has a moral meaning, it is found in resolving that the supreme test of all political institutions and social arrangements shall be the contribution they make to the all-around growth of every member of society."[11]

What Dewey wrote about almost a century earlier, the Sadkers expanded on in the 1990s. The question that Dewey was asking was, "How can schools teach democracy and not offer equality to all?" The question from the Sadkers is, "Are you really teaching equality?"

❧ What is the *moral meaning of school in a democracy and how does your answer reflect your practice?*

AUGUST 22

SINCE THE QUESTION was first posed in 1859 by Herbert Spencer, educators have debated, "What knowledge is of most worth?" Spencer answered, "Science." Dewey replied, "Geography." When I asked this question of my master's degree students, answers varied, with "Reading" usually coming out on top. Although this may seem an arguable and possibly unanswerable question, it is, however, a very important one. What you value, or give most worth to, determines what and how you will teach children what they need to know.

John Goodlad, author of *A Place Called School* and professor of education at the University of Washington, poses the question in a different form. In *The Future of Learning and Teaching*, he wrote that "the first educational question will not be what knowledge is of most worth, but what kinds of human beings we wish to produce."[12]

"I wish we had some kind of Hippocratic oath," Goodlad wrote a decade later, "to remind us always to keep solid principles of learning, teaching, and education at the center and to guide us in choosing what follows from them."[13]

When hired, most teachers recite an oath about upholding the laws of the country, but an educational "Hippocratic Oath" goes somewhat deeper; it expounds a moral obligation to young people—to define by our teaching "what kinds of human beings we wish to produce."

---

๑ EDUCATORS *throughout the last century and a half have asked the question, "What knowledge is of most worth?" Today's question is, "What kinds of human beings do you wish to produce?" Another question might be, "What is your moral obligation as a teacher to produce?"*

AUGUST 23

IF YOU WANT TO RAISE the hackles of school personnel, parents, and the community, bring up the issue of morality and the role that school plays in the teaching of it. Many people are a little nervous about teaching morals in the classroom or in having their children's morals taught there. The common question is, "Whose morals shall we teach?"

Yet, morals are taught in school whether or not we deliberately set out to do so. One cannot get around teaching morals, because what you *say* is encircled by what you *do*—and the *doing* is the morality you are teaching. Do you teach fairness? The Golden Rule? Cooperation?

According to Daniel and Laurel Tanner, whose well-known textbook, *Curriculum Development,* is often required reading in curriculum theory classes, "Moral education can no longer be regarded as mere moralistic preachments to maintain the status quo of the social order. Democratic social ideals require that the rising generation be equipped with the power of reason in attacking social inequities and iniquities, and thereby to make possible a better society." Where John Dewey spoke of the importance of education being for today, the Tanners write that it is important to teach for the future. "The schools of a free society are the chief agency for developing in the rising generation the power of reason so as to bring about the needed social transformation."[14]

☙ How do you *define "power of reason"? How do you teach it?*

AUGUST 24

MOST OF US like to think of ourselves as professionals. We are teachers. We have college educations. We have jobs. Many of us have years of experience in the classroom. Many of us are also concerned with the poor reputation that teaching gets from the media, which undermines what we do in the classroom. Some of us are concerned about the reputation teaching has as being less than professional. And, unfortunately, some of this bad press is deserved.

While most of us consider ourselves professionals, there are many things that some teachers do that affect the reputation of all of us, and one is the unprofessionalism that exists in every school. This may not be pleasant for some of you to read, but one of the things that used to bother me when I taught in public schools, and still does when I work with student teachers in the classroom, is the unprofessional manner and appearance of some of my peers. We have all walked into classrooms and seen teachers wearing clothes that should not be worn to work, possibly not worn out of the house: dirty, worn sweatsuits in the elementary schools, strapless tube tops, see-through blouses in the junior high and high schools, shorts and T-shirts on both men and women.

I don't disapprove of other people's taste in clothing nor am I a fashion snob or prude. I understand perfectly that elementary teachers often work on the floor with children and that the weather is hot in some parts of the country. But what I am saying is that, like it our not, we are judged by parents, the community, and others by the way we look as well as how we teach. As role models, we should at least be neat and clean.

Studies have shown that student discipline often correlates with teacher appearance. Studies have also shown that teachers who dress more professionally tend to have better behaved students and fewer problems. We often tell our young male student teachers who are experiencing student discipline problems to wear a shirt and tie, and they have seen dramatic results. Because I am short, I found when I substitute taught that wearing a higher heel helped. (Not that I am recommending high heels, nor do I ever want to wear them again!) The point is that students respond to your appearance, and the way you appear reflects on all of us.

❧ How does *the way that you dress appear to your students? How does it appear to the community?*

August 25

On August 25, 1916, the National Parks Service was created as a bureau of the United States Department of the Interior, to "promote and regulate the use of the federal area known as national parks, monuments, and reservations . . . to conserve the scenery and the natural and historic objects and the wildlife therein, and to provide for the enjoyment of the same in such manner . . . as will leave them unimpaired for the enjoyment of future generations."[15] As a result of the efforts of many individuals, some of whom are volunteers, we can now spend hours of enjoyment visiting national parks, forests, and monuments throughout the country.

Having just returned from a drive through Yosemite National Park, hiking the Bridle Falls, and dinner at the Wawona Hotel, I am personally in deep gratitude to those individuals who had the foresight to set aside land for future Americans to enjoy.

What always intrigues me in these wonderful places is the number of non-English-speaking people whom I run into in these parks, on the trails, and in the visitors' centers. People pay (a lot of) money to travel long distances to see all of the natural wonders that we take for granted.

If you have not recently (or ever) had the opportunity to visit a national, state, or even county park and enjoy the beauty preserved there, think about doing so. Bring back pictures, postcards, memories, and souvenirs to share with your students.

❧ When you think *of a national park, which one do you think of? Have you been there? How long ago was it? Is it time to go again?*

AUGUST 26

A DAY OR TWO AGO, we were discussing the importance of professionalism in teaching and, in particular, that how we look plays a part in how we are perceived as professionals.

But professionalism is more than just dress. The following *Teacher Tips* from veteran teachers give us more to ponder as we think about returning to school:

• One of my student teachers was impressed by her master teacher, who "always came to class full of energy and ready to start his day, even after twenty-six years of teaching." She claimed that he arrived at work every day an hour early to plan his whole day "so that he is not running around trying to get organized when the students are entering the classroom."

• In addition to dressing professionally, it is also important to keep the classroom neat and organized. You never know who will drop by to visit your classroom. "It models positive behavior," writes one veteran teacher, "*and* a respect for your students."

• It can also be valuable to attend school sports, games, and activities. Students need to see teachers participate in events outside of the classroom.

• "Don't forget that you will have almost complete control over selecting teaching techniques and learning activities," one teacher wrote. "Choose carefully."

• Be sure to model expected behavior for your class at all times. We cannot expect young people to follow the saying, "Do as I say and not as I do." This includes being polite, talking to students as you would an adult, and saying "Please" and "Thank you."

ᴐᴑ DOES THE WAY *that you look, act, and relate to students and adults show that you are a professional? Does your work area send the right message?*

August

August 27

MOTHER TERESA once wrote that "we cannot do great things on the earth. We can only do small things with great love." Born Agnes Gonxha Bojaxhiu on August 27, 1910 in Skopje, Macedonia, Mother Teresa epitomized in this short sentence the meaning of teaching. Known for her charitable work with the poverty-stricken, the sick, and the neglected in Calcutta, India, Mother Teresa accomplished great things on earth by doing small things with great love.[16]

Teachers and those who work with young people have hundreds of opportunities each day to do small things with love. From listening intently to a child's personal story to offering help with a problem assignment, a teacher may accomplish great things in a young person's life. Although we may not win the Nobel Prize as Mother Teresa did in 1979, or even the "Teacher of the Year Award" at our school, the teacher who pays attention to the small things wins the hearts of his or her students every day. An added prize for caring is the reward of a student who is willing to work harder for the teacher who cares.

‿ WHAT SMALL, *loving things can you do today to show your students that you care?*

August 28

IN THE NEW SCHOOL YEAR, one of your first responsibilities will probably be helping students to get organized. Their organization depends on yours. So let's get organized and think about how we will help our students do the same. The following are some *Teacher Tips* from veteran teachers to help you accomplish this:

27

- Depending on how you want work kept and turned in, provide clear directions for the students about your expectations. This may include showing them where and how to turn in assignments, and how and where you want them to put a heading on their papers (including name, subject, date, and so forth).

- On the first day, give students a list of the supplies that they will need for the year. You may want them to have a three-ring binder, two pencils, pens, an assignment book, colored pencils, or whatever. (Be sure to make provisions for those students who cannot afford the supplies.)

- For a well-organized lesson, write the daily agenda or objective on the board so the students can see it first thing as they walk in the room. This will let them know what they will be studying during the period, and it also lets them know that you have a plan. Some teachers have the students write down the agenda in their notebooks at the beginning of class time.

- Provide clear and concise instructions so your students know what is expected from them. You may have to repeat directions in various ways to ensure that they are understood.

- Be sure that *you* come to each class prepared. Be an expert in your area. Most experienced teachers *over*plan; in case the lesson goes too quickly, they are prepared with the next lesson.

❧ How can you plan *for student organization before the year begins? How do you want the details to be managed? What would make your day easier?*

AUGUST 29

ALONG WITH TEACHING your students organization skills, having an organized plan for teaching will help your students throughout the year. The following *Teacher Tips* may help your students this year:

• At the end of each day's lesson, during the last three to five minutes of each period, ask the students to write a summary of what they learned. This not only helps the students to organize the day's objective and gives them notes to keep, but it also helps you see if they understood what you were teaching.

• Before imparting important information, or showing a video or movie, give the students some form of study guide that requires student input. This may result in more students paying attention to the presentation and give them hints on how to observe and listen.

• Give specific directions for what you want. Always give over-detailed instructions on assignments. It is often easy for us to forget that we know how to do the assignment and the students do not.

• Have homework for the week posted in a specific area of your room and handouts kept in a special place for absent students. With a board designated only for assignments and due dates, the teacher relies on the students to handle their assignments on their own.

• Some curriculum developers recommend timing exercises to commercial breaks. They claim that some students are so geared to watching television that they need a break every ten to fifteen minutes to refresh and regroup their thoughts. When that time approaches, take a short commercial break and tell a joke or a story, infuse values, or simply begin a new lesson.

• Some teachers recommend that students have a different notebook for each unit and keep all work done in class, notes, handouts, quizzes, and so on in the notebook. This teaches the students to hang on to their work until it is no longer needed. (It also teaches them how to organize a notebook with a table of contents and an index.)

❧ WHAT OTHER *organizational tips will help your students begin a more successful year?*

AUGUST 30

ON AUGUST 30, 1963, a "Hot Link" was created between the United States and the Soviet Union, designed to promote talk rather than trouble during the Cold War years. Wouldn't it be nice if every class room had a "hot link" with the community, to dispel rumors before they begin, call home when trouble is brewing, or provide information between the two parties most influential in the students' lives—the parent and the teacher?

Come to think of it, a hot link does exist. It is called a telephone, and it provides the community and the classroom with vital information for peace and maximum student growth. Get in the habit of using the telephone from the first week, not only for bad news, but for good news, too. Make it a goal to talk to every parent or guardian at least once before the end of the first semester. You will be glad that you did.

❧ HOW WILL YOU *use the "hot link" to help your students succeed?*

AUGUST 31

THE BAD NEWS IS, summer is over; the good news is, it is time to return to the job that you have chosen, teaching young people. I hope that you have enjoyed your time off. And for those of you who have been teaching already, I hope that the new school year is running smoothly.

Charles Silberman wrote in (his somewhat negative book on teaching) *Crisis in the Classroom* that most teachers "are decent, honest, well-intentioned people who do their best under the most trying circumstances." I think we should add to that, that most teachers are bright, educated individuals who dedicate their lives (including a lot of their home lives) to the growth of young people and the continuance of society. Society owes a lot to you for what you are about to begin (again).[17]

May I leave you with a few remaining "words of wisdom" before you begin the new school year? This year, try to spend a little time with each student rather than a lot of time with just a few.

⟫ ARE YOU READY *to begin the new school year? What do you have left to do before it starts?*

Here we go!

31

September

September 1

Although preparing lessons, goals, and objectives for the year are arguably the most important items on your "things to do" list prior to the start of the new school year, there are other key elements that are important for ensuring student success. One of these elements is how students feel when they are sitting in your classroom. We know how we feel in certain settings, that certain places evoke feelings of happiness and light-heartedness, while others seem to make us feel tired or are downright depressing.

Have you ever looked around in the various environments you frequent throughout the day, and asked yourself, "Why did the designers of this room choose the colors that were chosen to be used in this place?" In stores? In nursery schools? Did you ever wonder why hospitals and doctors' offices are decorated in soothing tones that would be too tiring for our own homes? Why are kitchens often painted in warm tones? Interior designers make good livings coordinating walls and accessories for their clients' homes and offices.

Although you may have little choice in the colors or permanent objects in your room, if you have a room of your own, you do have choices in determining what will be on the bulletin boards, chalkboards, and hanging from the ceiling. You can also determine how desks are arranged and where in the room your desk will be situated. With a little color and the thoughtful placement of objects, you can make your classroom attractive and *inviting*, a place where students are comfortable and *want* to come and spend time.

Six hours of a child's day are spent with you in yours and other teachers' rooms. All of us have "served time" in rooms that were uninviting and barren (barren of possibilities). Colleges are the worst offenders—examples of sterile environments where intelligent thinking and discourse is expected to ensue. These classrooms more often suffer because of the high degree of traffic that moves in and out of the room and because no one instructor can claim ownership of the area. I know, I teach in such an atmosphere now—each course in a different classroom, each of which look dutifully alike. No pictures, no curtains, white walls, bright overhead lights, tables and chairs that make room arrangement difficult. Ugh!

Worse than barren rooms, however, is a classroom in which the *atmosphere* feels barren, one in which we sit, feeling like strangers, alienated from what is going on. A room in which we are not even guests. Such rooms display posters that have not changed for years, and walls that are covered with irrelevant information, or materials that the teacher likes but which are unrelated to the students' preferences or even what is being taught.

꙳ HOW DOES *your room look? Can you improve it?*

SEPTEMBER 2

ONE OF THE FIRST TASKS of the new school year is getting to know your students, having them get to know one another, and letting them get to know you. No matter how long I taught, meeting a class for the first time always made me a little nervous, because the first day can often set the tone for the whole year. First impressions are important. You may want to add the following *Teacher Tips* from veteran teachers to your list on getting better acquainted with your students:

• No matter how long you have been teaching at your school and/or how famous (or notorious) you are, don't forget to introduce yourself. I have had students who did not even know my name but who sat for a whole semester in my classroom. Probably because I never told them my name. (This is not to be confused with students who will call you "Mom" or "Grandma" as sometimes happens—and should be accepted with affection.) At the beginning of the first period with your students, write

35

your name on the board or overhead, and pronounce it for them. If you have a name that students like to get "playful" with, like Studer (Stutter, Studebaker), let them know that you have heard all of the various pronunciations before, and tell them how you would like to have your name pronounced.

• Along with introducing yourself, be sure to learn the names of your students and practice them. As someone who has a name that is consistently mispronounced, I urge you to ask the student's assistance in pronouncing his or her name correctly. Once you know their names, use them. It makes the child feel that you care. (If you have trouble with remembering names, as I do, a seating chart will help.)

• As a first task you will want to state your expectations clearly in a way that is palatable to your students. You will want them to know the rules, the consequences, and the requirements. But remember, there is a fine line between setting up expectations and appearing to be a tyrant.

___

⤷ WHAT OTHER *"first tasks"* do you need to accomplish *to get the school year off to a good start?*

___

SEPTEMBER 3

HAVING A ROOM look inviting, in John Dewey's words, "pregnant with possibilities," requires a little thought, a good amount of imagination, and a lot of love and understanding of your students. You need to be aware of their needs and comfort potential. The following *Teacher Tips* from veteran teachers may help you prepare a comfortable, yet inspiring classroom for your students:

• Keep live plants around the room. They not only improve the physical atmosphere by supplying oxygen and absorbing carbon dioxide, they add beauty to the area and help to make the room look alive.

September

• Display pictures of your family and/or your pets. This allows students to see that you are a real person and not just a teacher. Having pictures on your desk may even make students feel more comfortable about coming to talk to you, because they think that you are a caring person. Pictures in view not only help your students, they may help you. If you are having a difficult day, you can look at the pictures and remind yourself of why you chose to do this sometimes difficult job.

• Some teachers display their college diplomas and teaching credentials on their classroom walls. The idea behind this is similar to why physicians display their diplomas—it gives the individual professional credibility. Your credentials tell your students and their parents that you are an expert in your field. And, similar to the pictures you have in your room for yourself, looking at your credentials will remind you of how much work went into gaining this position, and the valuable job that you do.

• Before the new school year begins arrange the room so that you can walk freely around the desks, cabinets, tables, and other furniture. Have the room arranged so that it will allow you to have access to each student and give each student access to you. You need to be able to move around the classroom as much as possible, and students need to know that you are there and available to them.

❧ WHEN YOU LOOK *around your room, do you see any areas that can be, or should be, improved? What is needed to improve these areas?*

SEPTEMBER 4

ON SEPTEMBER 4, 1882, Thomas Edison's steam-powered central station on Pearl Street began supplying electricity in New York, changing the world thereafter. Can you imagine what it

37

would be like to live and work without electricity? Electricity is one of those "take-for-granted" items that was mentioned earlier.

Electricity lights our homes, runs our appliances, keeps our homes and workplaces comfortable, brings news and entertainment to us, and allows us to use videos, movies, overhead projectors, and computers in our classrooms. Our lives would be entirely different if we did not have electricity.

When we think (and grumble) about all of the work that we have to do, and the responsibilities that we have, what would it be like to have that same work and those same responsibilities and no electricity? We would cook on wood stoves (after chopping the wood), wash clothes by hand, hang them to dry, and teach children without all of the aids available to us today.

𝕯 HOW WOULD YOU *teach your students today if you had no electricity? (You may even want to try it.)*

SEPTEMBER 5

IF THIS IS THE FIRST Monday in September, then it is Labor Day. If it is not the first Monday, either Labor Day has come and gone, or it will be here within the next couple of days. Isn't it nice to know that we have all of these wonderful Monday holidays to take a day off, visit with friends, picnic, do yard work, or simply spend the weekend catching up on chores? Three-day weekends are lovely extensions to our typically overplanned regular weekends.

It wasn't always so, as most holidays are twentieth-century inventions. Labor Day, however, was proposed by Peter J. McGuire, a member of the Knights of Labor, sponsored by the Central Labor Union, and first celebrated in New York in 1882.

September

(Thank you, Peter.) Labor Day was set aside to honor labor and those who labored.

As a teacher, Labor Day was not necessarily a day that I looked forward to because it wasn't technically a day off. In the first district I taught in, school did not begin until the Thursday after Labor Day, so I reckoned that I would have had the day off anyway. But what Labor Day did signify for me, even as a child, was the end of summer and the beginning of a new school year, "pregnant with possibility." As such, it wasn't a restful day, but a suspenseful one.

> IF YOU ARE *truly experiencing a day off, enjoy it! What will you do today to enjoy the last holiday of summer?*

SEPTEMBER 6

ON THIS DAY, September 6, in 1986, I bought my first new home. Although this may not seem to you like a reason to celebrate year after year, suppose I told you that it took us almost twenty years to be able to do that? See how added information or perspective changes the way that we perceive issues? (Similar to the way the depth of knowledge you have about your students can help you better understand their needs and deficiencies in learning.) This home was so special, and long-awaited, that the first time I walked in, having signed what seemed like hundreds of papers filled with small print, and not knowing what I had signed away, that, in a moment of passion, I kissed the wall of my new home, leaving a big red lipstick print on the kitchen wall. A new, full-time teaching job had given me the opportunity to have a new home. Although we have lived here several years and, unfortunately, one overindustrious painter painted over it, if you come into my home today, I can show you where the lip print was located. You see, a home is truly a castle.

39

A place to be yourself, to be as you please, to be comfortable, to just *be*.

A classroom can be transformed into a home. A place for young people to be themselves, to be comfortable, *and* to learn. Many veteran (and new) teachers make their classrooms comfortable homelike atmospheres where children are comfortable learning and still maintain discipline. To give a classroom a "homey" touch:

• Occasionally, you may want to have classical music playing softly in the background. Some research on the use of music in the classroom has shown that an increase in memory retention has occurred when students listened to classical music.

• If space permits, some teachers bring in comfortable old furniture, such as a sofa or chairs, for reading. This is a good use for old pieces and makes the room comfortable—not too bad for your relaxation when students are not present, either.

• Some teachers suggest having desk lights available at each table, if possible. These lights, which are the type used in homes and offices, have bulbs with a softer light, helping those students who work better in different types of lights.

• If space allows, let students have their own space. Having room to spread out our work, without being encumbered or encroached upon by others, helps us organize our work and gives us room for comfort. I know it works for me!

✥ WHAT DOES *your room need to have a "homey" touch?*

SEPTEMBER 7

OBVIOUSLY, classrooms are more than just desks and furniture. Although the careful planning of a room arrangement includes adequate pathways to pencil sharpeners, room to gather, as well as room of one's own, walls are significant and perhaps are the most important extra space in a classroom. Of course, rooms vary as to the amount and type of wall space available. Some rooms, such as modular units, have four walls with bulletin board surfaces and chalkboards attached. Other, more traditional rooms have built-in bookshelves and display cabinets. Since most districts have at least some restrictions as to what a teacher can attach to a surface, careful planning should be made to ensure that walls are used to their maximum utility.

Although I have often admired the teacher who is gutsy enough to paint a mural on a wall, personally I feel that changeable displays are best, and the more often they are changed, the better. Walking into a room that for months has the same posters of sports heroes or music groups, however popular to the students, ultimately becomes boring. Besides, not all students like the same groups, so why should they be forced to look at these pictures day after day? To make effective displays, keep the following tips in mind:

• The best displays are colorful, seasonal, and relate to the subject being taught. Carefully selected background colors and choice of background is important. Bright colors such as yellow and orange, and or seasonal colors (for example, red and pink at Valentine's Day) add emphasis to the material attached. Coordinate colors on individual displays to keep the eye moving throughout the room.

• Use strong, clear lettering that is large enough to read from the students' desks. Many district offices have machines that will cut letters (and laminate them); these letters can be used over and over.

• Consider borders. Popular ones include corrugated, scalloped borders purchased at teacher supply stores. These can be purchased once and used year after year, especially if you keep color schemes simple. Borders give a finished appearance to your display, hide rough edges, and look professional.

❧ You are *going to spend approximately 186 eight-hour days in your room. Shouldn't it be an attractive place to spend your time? Can you think of any other tips for your walls to make them uniquely yours?*

September 8

Your students spend a significant part of their day in your classroom, too. Therefore, the room should reflect their presence. At least one area, if not more, should focus on the pupil's own work. Everyone's work should be displayed at one time or another. Seek out the work of a student who rarely has work worthy of displaying. Give every student the opportunity to star.

Involve your class in displaying work. Let your students help you design the walls and select colors for displays. After all, they are going to "live" here too. Students of all ages can be very creative. It may even help them with their rooms at home or their homes in the future.

Include an area for photos, newspaper items, school rules, upcoming events, and other information pertinent to the students' success. Most classrooms have a lot of space to fill—not just bulletin boards, but walls, windows, ceilings, and furniture sides and backs.

❧ What information *do you need to have available for your students? Where will you post it?*

September

September 9

Now that school has begun and the students are comfortably settled and back at work in your attractive, inviting classroom, it is time to evaluate the premises to see what is working and what can be improved upon. A room setting does much more than allow inhabitants to be comfortable; the setup of the classroom can help prevent potential problems before they begin. A veteran teacher will "use" the room to help with classroom management and, in the process, effectively control student behavior without the students' awareness. This may alleviate the need for negative punishment as the days progress. The following *Teacher Tips* from veteran teachers may help you to utilize your space more effectively:

• Locate key positions in the room. Find vantage points in the room that allow you to keep an eye on what students are doing and let them know your presence. This way, they will sense that you are watching the class without letting them know who, in particular, is being watched.

• Have a calendar displayed with the assignments, including homework, for the month as soon as due dates become known. It also helps to reproduce notebook-sized copies for each student to receive at the beginning of the month. This leaves little doubt as to when assignments are due.

• In an obvious location, have an in-box for homework or for assignments due at the end of the class period. This saves time in class because, instead of collecting the homework, students place it in the box as they walk out. If you teach more than one class, or more than one subject to the same students, it is best to have individual boxes that will keep class sets of papers together.

❧ What are *some other ways to organize your room for efficient classroom management?*

43

September 10

Somebody (possibly Hallmark) has ordained some time in September, around the second Sunday of the month, as Grandparents' Day. We celebrate Mother's Day in May, and Father's Day in June; we see the cards in the stores, but how many of us actually celebrate Grandparents' Day other than sending a card (if we remember)? And yet, where would we be without grandparents? They gave birth to our parents who gave birth to us. Grandparents gave us life. Yet, we know we can get away without celebrating Grandparents' Day because grandparents are so-o-o forgiving. They have lived through parenthood, and they have learned not to expect anything.

Let's change that this year. Let's do something nice for grandparents. After all, they love us (I know, I am a grandparent). If some of your students do not have grandparents, or their grandparents do not live close by, adopt some. Call a retirement complex and invite senior citizens to visit your classroom. Before they visit, have students talk about what is special about grandparents. What are some of the advantages of being retired? What are some problems older people may being facing? (Why might they be crabby?) What do grandparents do in their spare time? You and your students might be surprised that many older people are very active, athletic, and do many good things for the community.

Many other cultures have respect for the aged members of their communities. They seek the advice of their elders, and often many generations live in one household. In our country, we tend to segregate ourselves from the older generation. We find homes for them, visit occasionally, and if we think about it, buy them a card on Grandparents' Day. Inviting the older generation into your classroom may give students an opportunity to learn respect for senior citizens and vice versa.

ॐ WHAT CAN YOU *and your students do for grandparents or other senior citizens today?*

SEPTEMBER 11

STUDENTS ARE MORE LIKELY to respond in an organized setting and to be organized themselves when lessons have a clear plan, a purpose, and appear to be going somewhere. A lesson plan also allows you, the teacher, to know where you are going *and* when you have arrived.

When I teach methods classes to students desiring to become teachers, I like to introduce the unit on lesson planning with an excerpt from Lewis Carroll's *Alice's Adventures in Wonderland.* Often it is difficult to convince pre-service teachers of the importance of having a written plan, or that they will need to plan every year for many years to come. The "uninitiated" teacher often believes that lesson plans are just an assignment for student teachers and will not be necessary when they are "real" teachers. Unfortunately, they can always point to that rare successful teacher who has no plan and "wings it" day after day.

In *Alice's Adventures,* Alice, trying to find her way, comes across a cat in the tree and asks:

"Cheshire Puss, . . . Would you tell me please, which way I ought to go from here?"
And the cat answers, "That depends a good deal on where you want to get to."
"I don't much care where," Alice replies.
To which the cat responds. "Then it doesn't matter which way you go."¹

Although some teachers can be successful without plans, for most of us, planning is necessary. So this is probably a good time

45

to reintroduce the "Hunter Plan," with which you are probably familiar (no groans please), as one method for getting information to your students. According to Madeline Hunter, a lesson plan should include:

1. A review (where we look for a moment at the previous lesson)

2. An anticipatory set (to stimulate interest in the new topic)

3. An objective (which states explicitly what is to be learned)

4. The input (where we present new material)

5. Modeling (providing a demonstration)

6. Checking for understanding (monitoring student work for understanding)

7. Guided practice (periodically checking for understanding)

8. Independent practice (where students work on their own)[2]

Yes, there is debate on whether this plan works for all lessons. But it is a plan—somewhere to start. Hunter herself said that it was just a plan, never meant to be the only plan, and it is possible that it may not be accomplished all in one day.[3]

꩜ HAVE YOU MADE *a lesson plan for tomorrow or, better yet, for the rest of the week?*

SEPTEMBER 12

AN "ANTICIPATORY SET" introduces the lesson by drawing the student into the subject. This can be done in a variety of ways but seems to be most effective when it is fun or at least involves the students in the activity rather than beginning with a lecture. A method that I found to be very effective to begin the lesson for that day was to have a question on the chalkboard or

September

overhead projector as the students entered the room. This "focus question" was directly related to the topic we would be discussing and the material being covered that day. Students wrote their answers in journals that were collected each marking period. They were not graded on having the correct answer (because I had not taught the lesson yet), they were only expected to make an effort at an educated guess (practice critical thinking). For example, when we were studying nutrition, the question was, "Vitamin A is found in _____. It is necessary for healthy _____." Students then knew that "Vitamin A" was the topic for the day *and* that on a test they were expected to know in which foods it is found and which parts of the body need that nutrient.

An added bonus for using a focus question is that the students know that they are to be writing when the tardy bell rings rather than walking around the room and talking to friends. Because of the focus question, classes always began on time. (It also provided a few minutes for taking attendance while the students were answering the question.)

☜ How do you *get your class started at the beginning of a period? Does what you are doing set the tone that we are here to learn?*

SEPTEMBER 13

ANOTHER METHOD that teachers, especially reading teachers, use to begin their classes is SSR or Silent Sustained Reading. Students who enter their classes know that they are to have a book, open it, and read for a short, specified time. Although SSR is, as true with focus questions, a good time to take attendance, it is probably best in this case if the teacher is reading, too, modeling reading for his or her students. (You say you never have

47

time to read; this gives you a few minutes to read a good book yourself!)

Many years ago, I taught in a junior high school that required schoolwide SSR after lunch. The administrator of the school and the staff agreed that having that fifteen minutes after lunch and a brief recess period quieted the students down, getting them prepared for their afternoon studies. It worked.

An alternative to SSR is the teacher reading a book aloud to the students. Many years ago, when I was a student in seventh grade, I recall my teacher reading classic books to us for a short period each day. I specifically recall *Hiroshima* and *1984* being read with meaningful emphasis. These were books that I, at twelve years old, most likely would not have enjoyed had I been required to read them on my own.

⟫ How can you *fit reading into your lesson? Would your students benefit with a little SSR? Have you thought about reading a good book to your students?*

SEPTEMBER 14

IT IS THE RARE TEACHER, if there are any, who does not use handouts in the classroom, whether they are made on a copier or the long-effective ditto machine. (I never much liked using ditto machines, which always seemed to leave blue ink all over my hands, clothes, and often on my face—walking around all day without anyone telling me it was there. But I do like the smell of a fresh ditto! Are these machines still being used?)

Handouts are an important part of most teachers' lesson plans. Just ask any teacher whose paper budget has run out in December what she would like Santa to bring. I have known teachers who would trade a week of recess duty for a ream of paper by early spring! Here are some helpful *Teacher Tips* for using handouts in the classroom:

- Handouts should pertain to the lesson and be a necessary part of the instruction. Just because a handout comes with the textbook does not mean that your students need to use it.

- The handouts you design should be clear, correct, and free of errors. If you are a poor speller, have someone else proofread your handouts for spelling and grammatical errors. Remember, parents sometimes see these papers, too. It helps to make them visually attractive.

- Know the copyright infringement laws before indiscriminately copying works from books and workbooks. There is a fair chance that you will not get caught, but you are cheating that author and publisher, being a poor role model for your students, and breaking the law. There have been teachers who have been caught, and it is an expensive mistake. (If you are unsure of the copyright infringement laws, ask your district administrators.)

- Handouts should not take the place of good instruction. Teach your students in the most effective manner necessary for them to learn the information *and* "save a tree!"

---

᠑ TAKE A SECOND LOOK *at your handouts for the day. Are they clear, correct, and attractive? More important, are they necessary?*

SEPTEMBER 15

IT WAS BOUND TO HAPPEN sooner or later. The students become used to you, they are comfortable in the "homey" classroom you have prepared, and they are a little tired of the day-to-day routine of being back in school. If not today, then sometime soon the time will come when it is "Test the Teacher to See What We Can Get Away With Day." As an experienced teacher (and former student) you should expect it, but sometimes

49

it catches you by surprise. If you are a veteran teacher, I don't need to tell you that if you "lose it" with threats or other loud responses, you have lost it for possibly quite a long time. To keep this from happening, read, and memorize the following *Teacher Tips* from those who have "been there," and lived to tell about it:

- To get back on track, it is important that you regain the attention of the class without appearing to be doing so. This can be accomplished by Plan A: Try to do nothing at first, stop the lesson by standing still and saying nothing. Students will soon realize that something is amiss and wait to see what you do next. Or, Plan B: Take advantage of human curiosity. Begin doing something that students will want to watch.

- If one particular student is being disruptive, or simply talking, walk over to his or her desk and stand very close to the student, look at him or her, and *say nothing*. Do not begin the lesson again until the student stops talking. Every time the student talks, stop the lesson. For some reason this always seems to work.

- If you are having problems with one particularly difficult student, check with colleagues to see if they have found anything that works to quiet this student.

- If nothing works, begin effective discipline.

- Never, *ever*, get in an argument with a young person. Once you open your mouth, you lose. There is no discussion. Disruptive behavior keeps others from learning. It cannot be allowed.

Ꙅ ARE YOU EXPERIENCING *any continual disruptions in your classroom? Have you designed a plan for ending them?*

SEPTEMBER 16

I THINK IT IS NATURAL for all of us to want to feel that we are being treated fairly in life, that we will get what we work hard

September

to obtain, and that we will have an equal opportunity to be successful. Yet, many of us can recall the teachers that we felt treated us and others unfairly or those whom we felt had "teacher's pets." None of us knowingly try to give special treatment to certain students, but obviously we are human and we do. The following *Teacher Tips* from veteran teachers may help you become the "fairest teacher of them all":

• Have students write their names on the backs of papers rather than the front. Using this method keeps the teacher from what might be called "preconceived grading."

• Keep a container of popsicle sticks with each student's name written on a stick. When a question is asked or students are reading aloud, the teacher can pull out a stick for the next answerer/reader. Be sure to replace the stick each time, or the student who was just called on soon learns that he or she is "off the hook" and no longer needs to pay attention.

• Be careful when giving rewards to students who frequently misbehave. I know this goes against what you are taught in educational psychology classes, but rewarding a child with "student of the week (or month)" because they had one good week is unfair to those students who always behave well. Find some other reward and give it to the behaving students as well.

⤳ Do you treat *your students equally? Are you sure?*

SEPTEMBER 17

SEPTEMBER 17 is Citizenship Day, which marks the anniversary of the signing of the United States Constitution in 1787. Many countries have similar holidays to dramatize the importance of citizenship and the privileges and responsibilities of being a good citizen. This might be a good day to discuss what it means to be a citizen with your students.

51

During the discussion you may find that some of your students are actually citizens of other countries, or hold dual citizenship. This is a great opportunity to begin discussing culture and diversity, which we will look into more closely on other dates.

You may want to discuss what the requirements are for becoming a citizen in this country, the information needed for tests, and the ceremony that accompanies the granting of citizenship.

⚬ WHAT DO YOU *want your students to know about citizenship? How will you teach that?*

SEPTEMBER 18

BETWEEN SEPTEMBER 15 and October 15, National Hispanic Month honors the Hispanic culture, history, and contributions that people of this heritage have made to American life. Living in California, as I do, we have many reminders of the contributions that people of Hispanic heritage have made and are still making to our state. If your state does not have a large Hispanic population, you may need to study a little deeper to discover the role that people from Mexico and South American countries have played in our history.

Celebrating National Hispanic Month (or even Day) may be a good introduction to incorporating the heritage of many cultures into the classroom. A good beginning may include, if you have not already, finding out where your students or their ancestors originated. If there is time, your students can then complete a variety of projects about their countries. For example:

• After finding where their ancestors originated, ask each student to write a one-page paper explaining the sport that is most popular in his or her country. After each student reads their paper to the class, if there is time, play the sport.

September

- Ask your students to share photos (be very careful with them), family traditions, origins, and histories with the class.

- In discussing an event, whether current or historical, have students pretend to be a part of the event or take the side of their heritage. Ask them to write a letter to a family member, or in a journal, expressing the events and their feelings about them from their cultural perspective.

- Display a large map of the world. Have your students place a pin on their family's place of origin.

- Assign a family tree for students to complete. By doing so, students often learn interesting information, and necessary health-related data, about their ancestors.

Information that you gather about the various cultural representations that you have in your classroom may give you ideas for activities that are usable throughout the year.

ॐ HAVE YOU CHECKED *your own ancestral heritage? Why not do this project along with your students?*

SEPTEMBER 19

DO YOU EVER THINK about how difficult it is to sit in a wooden chair for long periods of time? Not only sit, but sit quite still and remain alert for, say, six hours? I can almost always pick out a teacher at a meeting, can't you? They are usually the ones who are standing, not sitting, in the back of the room, even in the college classroom. Think about that. Now think about this: We expect our students to sit still for five or six hours *every* day! Can you imagine?

If you think you can sit for five or six hours every day and be talked *at,* sign up for five or six college classes at your local university.

53

Think about giving your students a break, have occasional stretch breaks during an intense lesson, or plan for an occasional active-participant activity (emphasis on the word *activity*).

Besides, we all need exercise and movement in our joints and muscles. It is good for us.

⤷ How can you *bring some activity into your classroom?*

SEPTEMBER 20

How observant are you? How observant should you be? Being an observant individual can enhance learning and bring "alive-ness" to us and to our students. Help your students become more observant by asking them some questions (without the students looking) such as: What color is the face of your watch? Who is on the one-dollar bill? What did Jane or Bill wear to school yesterday? What was on the lunch tray today? And so on. Let the students ask you questions to see how observant you are.

Being observant is much more than remembering; it is "seeing" in the first place. Seeing requires quietly watching, observing, reflecting on what is seen, and being *aware*. So many of us spend our days in a blind rush, missing out on the beauty of the environment and the people around us.

⤷ Do you take *the time to "see" what is around you? How can you improve on this?*

SEPTEMBER 21

Sometime in September, the actual date depending on the year, Rosh Hashanah will begin the Jewish New Year and open

September

the ten days of penitence and spiritual renewal. The ten days of Rosh Hashanah close with Yom Kippur, the most holy day in the Jewish year, marked by fasting and prayer.

Not only do we have students of different geographical origins in our classrooms, we also have students whose families worship in a variety of different manners. Although we are taught to be careful, and even to not approach religious issues in school, these holidays, and others like them, give to us excellent opportunities to discover culture, diversity, and tolerance of others.

⠨ IS IT POSSIBLE *to celebrate the many holidays in an educational way in the public schools? How can you make this a positive learning experience for both diversity and tolerance?*

SEPTEMBER 22

ON SEPTEMBER 22, 1776, Captain Nathan Hale, caught while spying on the British troops who were stationed on Long Island, was executed. His famous last words reportedly were, "I only regret that I have but one life to lose for my country."[4]

What a remarkable display of courage, to be willing to die for something that you believe in, or for your country! And, although there are probably a few of us who would be so courageous today, we should honor those who are, or who have done so in the past.

Do you, as a professional teacher, believe in anything so strongly that you would at least be willing to fight for it? I am thinking, in particular, of the times when we do what we are told to do in the classroom rather than what we know is right for our students. A good example is the current debate over phonics versus whole language teaching in elementary schools. Often districts are quick to "jump on the bandwagon" when new research makes claims of effectiveness for students, and experienced

55

teachers, who know better, change what works for them and their students rather than fighting for what they know is right.

⟫ IS THERE SOMETHING *that you believe in that you are willing to fight for? How much are you willing to give for the cause?*

SEPTEMBER 23

IN THE AUTUMN, or fall, leaves drop from trees that were once lush with the greens of summer. With the falling leaves, graying skies, and frosty air, some people see fall as a dismal time, the end of summer, end of vacation time, and the beginning of the dreary winter days ahead.

But fall is not dreary. School has started, and it is a new beginning for students who are anxious to come back to school, to learn, and to be with friends who they have missed all summer. Yes, a dormant time is coming. It is getting darker, and the air is getting cooler. Daylight Savings Time will be ending, and we are reluctantly looking at shorter days with less sunlight than we would like. It is easy to get caught up in the melancholy of autumn without seeing that it has a good deal to offer.

Although falling leaves may be a nuisance and need raking, they can also be a joy to roll in, sweep up, jump on, and sweep up again. Fall colors, with their abundant earth tones, are often vibrant with colors that appear only during this season. There may not be the whites, pinks, and reds of spring and summer, or the blue skies and green leaves, but instead, in autumn we have oranges, yellows, reds, browns, and grays. Fall's colors include the brown footballs, the reds and yellows of maples and other trees, the black cats and the orange pumpkins of Halloween, and the harvest colors of Thanksgiving.

All is not dormant in the new school year either. Fall is not only resplendent with the myths of the season—stories of Hal-

September

loween and pilgrims being greeted by natives—it is alive with the excitement of the school year ahead. Sometimes what appears to be dormant is, in reality, quite lively. It could be the enthusiasm for learning that lies within a young child and that you can help bring to the surface.

❧ WHAT OTHER POSITIVE ASPECTS *of fall or autumn can you identify?*

SEPTEMBER 24

I HAVE A STUDENT in my graduate program who walked across the stage this summer to accept his master's degree in education. This is not unusual, except that he is seventy-nine years old. Seventy-nine! Obviously he is not planning to teach, but he could if a district will hire him, and if he wanted to. But he doesn't want to, because he enjoys his own successful real estate business. The interesting thing is that, after a lifetime of doing what he wanted occupationally, and at a time when most people are considering retiring, he has returned to our university, earned his bachelor's degree and continued on in his education to complete master's work. It will not surprise me if I hear that he has entered a doctoral program some day. He was truly a wonderful addition to our classroom experience with his personal history in education.

For his master's project this student wrote a book-long thesis on his experience with education beginning in a one-room school house in Nebraska that was built by his ancestors and staffed by his family members for the last century or more.

What I glean from the experience with this student is that somewhere, someone—a teacher—instilled him with the importance of being a "lifelong learner." It is my hope that I have instilled others with this characteristic, too.

57

> How can you *teach your students to be lifelong learners? How can you be a lifelong learner?*

SEPTEMBER 25

SEVERAL STATES now celebrate Native American Day on the fourth Friday of September. Here is another opportunity to celebrate culture and diversity. Besides studying the many tribes native to the United States, this may be a good day to celebrate the Native American's love of nature with a lesson on ecology. Perhaps you can begin with a lesson on Native Americans' oneness with nature: the idea of using the environment but only taking from it what is needed for one's own survival.

There are many wonderful books on Indian lore, in which, similar to *Aesop's Fables,* each story offers a lessons to learn. Including examples of Native American art and music can also make the topics interesting for your students.

> WHAT HAVE *Native Americans contributed to the subject you teach? How can that be utilized in your lessons this week?*

SEPTEMBER 26

TODAY IS George Gershwin's birthday. Alone, and with his brother Ira, George Gershwin composed some of the most memorable music written this century, including "Rhapsody in Blue," and the opera *Porgy and Bess.* Gershwin was born on September 26, 1898, and he died in 1937. In less than forty years of living he wrote music that has lasted out the twentieth century.

September

Do you use music in your classroom? So many of our students hear nothing other than their own favorite radio stations for a lifetime. They never experience Gershwin, Cole Porter, Glenn Miller, Patsy Cline, *The Music Man,* Mozart, or Puccini, or any other variety of musical works. Because administrators have reduced school budgets by cutting music programs, many children have never had an opportunity to experience music classes in their twelve years of schooling. I am most proud that in our home we had music of all varieties and for all ages. As a result, my children are at least music-literate.

☙ IS THERE A WAY *to infuse music into your classroom without it interfering with learning?*

SEPTEMBER 27

SOMETIME AROUND THIS DATE, on the fourth Friday of the school year, schools across the nation experience what is called "Fourth Friday Count," the day when all students are counted and schools are given money according to their ADA (Average Daily Attendance). This date is very important for school districts, because budgets depend on per student capita from the state, determining class sizes, number of staff hired, supplies, and other money being made available for expenses for schools in their area.

Some schools go to great expense to ensure that all students are in attendance, and teachers are asked to determine carefully who is, or has been present, and who has moved.

It seems funny, albeit necessary, to put a price on a child's head. I wish that we could have grand donations of money for schools and students rather than arguing over which districts set a figure of $2,500 on a student's education while others provide $8,700. After all, isn't education priceless? Isn't the price of ignorance much more expensive?

⌖ Do you put *a price on a child's head or is each child in your classroom a worthy investment?*

September 28

CONGRATULATIONS! In Confucianism it is Teacher's Day, the day that commemorates Confucius's birthday somewhere around the fifth century B.C. and honors the teaching profession. Have you ever heard of Teacher's Day? Nor had I. Maybe it is a well-kept secret.

Another well-kept secret is a document called the *Perspectives on Education in America,* a comprehensive study conducted by the Sandia National Laboratories for the U.S. Department of Energy and subsequently suppressed by the U.S. Department of Education, "delayed from publication for more than two years because so many of its findings ran counter to the allegations in *America 2000* and *Goals 2000.*"[5]

Using data collected from such prestigious sources as the National Center for Education Statistics, National Science Foundation, U.S. Department of Labor, U.S. Department of Education, U.S. Bureau of Census, College Entrance Examination Board, National Assessment of Educational Progress, and others, the Sandia Report findings showed that SAT scores, contrary to what we had been told, were actually rising, dropout rates were declining, the United States led the world in bachelor's degrees (including science and engineering), and that the United States was underinvesting in elementary education. In effect, United States students ranked high in many academic areas, even with the rise in the number of non-English-speaking immigrants in the classroom, the rise in children in one-parent families, or where both parents work.[6]

It is time to let the community know that, considering all of the possible obstacles we face daily, teachers are doing a good job. Pat yourself on the back and enjoy your day.

September

⁙ DID YOU KNOW *what a good job you and your peers are doing? Are there other positive reports that you are not aware of? What can you do to find out?*

SEPTEMBER 29

REMEMBER MY "lifelong learner" from September 24? The seventy-nine-year-old student in my classroom? Not only did he complete assignments during his degree program, but he often brought interesting notes and information to share with me or with the class. I could almost depend on at least one article or anecdotal story being slid under the door of my office at the college, waiting for my next arrival date.

On one occasion he typed a quote (he always used a typewriter) written by Haim Ginott, teacher and psychologist, and ran off copies for all of his classmates. It read: "I've come to the frightening conclusion that I am the decisive element in the classroom. It's my personal approach that creates the climate. As a teacher, I possess a tremendous power to make a child's life miserable or joyous. I am a tool of torture or an instrument of inspiration. I can humiliate or humor, hurt or heal. In all situations, it is *my* response that decides whether a crisis will be escalated or de-escalated and a child humanized or dehumanized."7

⁙ DO YOU REALIZE *the amount of power that you hold in your classroom? Do you use it wisely?*

SEPTEMBER 30

END OF THE MONTH, time to change the calendar. And *you made it* through the first month of school. How are you feeling about your class or classes? Is there anything that needs to be changed? Are your students into a nicely functioning routine?

Maybe it is time to reward them with a little positive reinforcement, a surprise for doing their work, being polite, and being good learners. Maybe you can tell a few stories, play a few games, or show a video. (All educational of course!)

All of us like surprises. Today, as I was working on this section, I got a surprise. I received a phone call from a florist who said that he had a delivery for me and wanted to make sure that I would be home. I waited twenty minutes for his arrival, wondering who the flowers were from, who would be so thoughtful to send flowers when it was not even my birthday, a holiday, nor anything special to celebrate. When the flowers arrived, they were beautiful, and from a special person (my husband) who wrote, "Stay on a roll!" Just what I needed to encourage me to continue writing.

ֆ HOW CAN YOU *surprise your students and tell them to "Stay on a roll!"?*

OCTOBER

OCTOBER 1

IF YOUR SCHOOL DISTRICT is like most, either yesterday or today was payday. Yesssiree! For some of us, this day reminds us why we do this job. For others, myself included, we love what we do, and payday is not the primary reward. But, do not misunderstand me. Paydays are wonderful additions to the blessings of employment that is enjoyable in itself—it's an added joy to doing what we enjoy doing in life.

For some of you, this may be your very first paycheck as a teacher; for others, who do not have twelve-month pay periods, this may be your first check since July. In either case, there has been a long drought of careful planning and perhaps concern as we wait out the time between the first day of the new school year and the end of the month.

Anyway, now you have it! And you probably do not need any *Teacher Tips* to tell you how to divvy it out. But I cannot resist the temptation and responsibility of telling you what to do with your long-awaited money anyway:

1. The first task is to pay what you have to ("Well, duh!" as the kids say).

2. Next, plan carefully for the month ahead.

3. Try to put some money away in a retirement plan. (Believe it or not, the time will be here before you know it. They will not let you teach forever.)

4. Finally, keep out some, if only a little, as play or "mad" money. It is important that we reward ourselves for the marvelous job we do for children, their parents, and society as a whole.

꙳ HOW WILL YOU *divide your money today? Have you set aside a few dollars for play?*

October

OCTOBER 2

ACCORDING TO MY friendly *Almanac* (which I pick up at the bank and which tells me when to plant my crops even though my crops consist of a postage stamp–sized lawn encircled by various colored flowers and assorted unidentifiable plants given by friends because they "looked pretty" in their yards. But, I digress. . . .) the first *Peanuts* comic strip appeared on this date in 1950, a half-century ago! Who has grown up and not become acquainted with the lives of Charlie Brown, Lucy, Linus, Schroeder, Pigpen, and of course Snoopy the dog? Do you remember when these cartoon characters first came into your life?

Sometimes people come into our lives quietly through invitation, and others enter our lives without being asked by you but by someone you love. I am reminded of this today because in two days it will be my daughter-in-law's birthday, and I did not ask her into my life. I did not pick her for my son nor ask her to take part in the personal trials and celebrations of our family. But one day she appeared with my son. Every parent knows how difficult it is to accept that your son or daughter is grown and to share him or her with a stranger.

But, once here, my daughter-in-law Jessica has become an important part of our family. A blessed addition. Finally, after years of being the only female, I found that, as a mother of sons, I now had a daughter. Better yet, one who was grown and whom I did not have to raise! Jessica has taught us many things and has given us a beautiful grandson, too. We are not alike, and we do not always agree, but that is OK.

Often into your classroom will come students whom, had you been given the choice, you might not have selected—you may have heard about them in advance from their previous teachers, or recognized problems from the first day. Remember that, given the opportunity, such a student may turn out to be a blessing to you. Teaching is not a one-way venture in which one person does all of the teaching and the other learns. Often we,

65

the teachers, learn from a student when we least expect it. Your change in behavior toward that student may be a turning point in that student's life.

 ❧ WHICH OF YOUR STUDENTS *came uninvited? How can you see him or her differently? Can you learn something from that student?*

OCTOBER 3

DO YOU REMEMBER the Golden Rule: "Do unto others as you would have them do unto you"? I imagine that we all have heard that biblical saying at some time or other. You probably first heard it in a way similar to the way I did a long time ago when I was very young. The scenario went something like this: Having just done something that was not very nice to someone, my mother (who, as most mothers do, seemed to know my every move) responded, "Now Susan (she always called me by my proper name when I was in trouble, which amazingly sounded sharply, like a bullet 'Su-zin'), you would not want someone to treat you like that, would you? Remember the Golden Rule, 'Do unto others . . .'"

Learning the Golden Rule probably kept me out of hot water many times in my lifetime. It taught me to treat other people like human beings, the way that I would like to be treated.

But somehow, the Golden Rule gets distorted when we are working with children, whether our own or those of others, and we forget that the Golden Rule applies to them, too. Remember, even though you are the teacher and an adult, children should be treated in the same manner as you want to be treated today, and how you would have wanted to be treated as a child. Doing so will demonstrate to young people what the Golden Rule really means.

- It means you must be consistent and fair. Give all students a fair chance to succeed.

- Be polite, by saying, "Please" and "Thank you," every chance you get.

- Don't make promises (or threats) that you cannot keep. (Children learn quickly who is sincere and who is not.)

- Teach and expect the Golden Rule in your classroom.

❧ YOU MAY OCCASIONALLY *have a student who does not know the Golden Rule. How will you teach it to everyone?*

OCTOBER 4

THROUGHOUT THE SCHOOL YEAR, there will be many times when you will need to begin teaching new topics, and (assuming that your students have mastered the previous topic) it will be time to move on, sometimes into what seems to be uncharted territory. Do you remember the tedium of your school days, sitting in classes where it seemed to be "the same old thing" only with a different teacher, or worse, a new topic with a new teacher who assumed that you had received the necessary background information from your previous teacher? Either of these situations can create problems in introducing a new topic to your students and achieving positive results from the instruction and activities.

One way to introduce a new topic and ensure a more successful outcome is to do what some experienced teachers do. That is, when starting a new topic, they have students fill in a "What I Know" chart. This is similar to a pre-test/post-test situation except that it creates less anxiety for those students who hear the word *test* and, even though the test is not graded, have an instant increase in stress. (Not a very positive way to introduce a new

67

topic!) The "What I Know" chart lists different subjects or terms that students may or may not know. The students fill in the charts by marking what they have seen, know, or do not know; the papers are collected, and you can evaluate where to begin the subject, how much teaching is needed, and how long the unit may take. Completing the chart is perhaps best done at the end of a unit, in the last few minutes of class, so you can have time to evaluate the students' charts and plan accordingly before the next day.

☙ WHAT IS THE SUBJECT *of your next unit? What questions do you want to ask your students ahead of time to evaluate their previous knowledge and learning needs?*

OCTOBER 5

I DON'T KNOW about you, but I personally *hate* doing grades. It has nothing to do with the amount of work involved in reading and correcting papers, scoring points, or recording the results (although that is no picnic either). What I dislike is *evaluating* learning. I know when a person has the correct answers on their paper, or writes a good paragraph; what I do not know is how far that person has come to arrive at those answers—how much he or she has actually learned.

Do you see where I am going with this? If a person knows very little about a subject, works very hard, and arrives at a correct solution, is that as valuable as the person who knew how to do the problem before the subject was introduced?

Another aspect of grading that troubles me is how a child's self-esteem gets tied into grades. In grading, the child who is not as mature and not ready to understand a concept is measured against those who are. The result is a failing grade or even a failing year, creating a child who is a failure because he or she is not ready. Furthermore, how many children who "failed" a grade in school have self-concepts of being failures as adults?

Although your time is limited for correcting papers, keep in mind that the grade at the top of the paper means much more to the receiver than it does to you.

> ⟫ HOW CAN GRADING *be used in a positive manner to reflect and encourage growth rather than create failure in students?*

OCTOBER 6

FOR SOME REASON, just the word *homework* makes me cringe, not only as a former student who despised doing it (and held particular fondness for any teacher who did not assign it), but as a teacher I disliked hounding students to do homework, and found that having daily exercises that were dependent upon work completed at home rarely made for a satisfactory lesson. Personally, I feel that homework is often abusive to students who should be allowed to rest after school, play with their friends, and participate in sports and family activities without worrying about getting home in time to do homework.

It is one thing for students to be required to finish work that they did not complete in school; it is another to assign lessons just because schools or districts have homework policies. I recall when my children were in elementary school we lived in a district that had a policy of one to two hours of homework per night no matter the age of the child. In the elementary schools they were six to eleven years old. When were they supposed to play or partake in sports, church activities, and scouts? As a parent, I also resented teachers who were determining the activity *I* would do

69

with my child during our family time. As did many schools, my children had teachers who were assigning to me, the parent, "Read to your child fifteen minutes every night." Maybe I had read to them since they were tiny infants and I would prefer to throw a ball with them or go swimming. I still resent the fourth-grade "build a mission" and "science fair" projects which, having lived in a "professional" neighborhood, became stiff competition between families to build wind tunnels and robotic hands.

Make your homework assignments meaningful or do not assign the homework. The following *Teacher Tips* from veteran teachers may help with making homework assignments that will enhance your "in-class" assignments:

• Ask yourself, "Is this homework assignment necessary or just busywork?" Do you plan to use it as a grade or in the next day's lesson? Isn't your students' after-school time as valuable as yours?

• Sometimes homework, especially in math, may be for practice. If you find that you do not have time to correct each individual's paper, ask yourself if the assignments are worth doing. Why ask your students to do homework if you do not have time to correct it?

• Also ask yourself, "If the student can show me in ten problems that they know how to do long division, must they do twenty?"

• If you have determined that the assignment is indeed worthwhile, but you do not have time to correct all of the papers, simplify your paperwork by selecting some papers for grading and some for completion points.

• Students discover quickly when a teacher does not give adequate time to correct homework papers. The result is that they often either turn in sloppy work, and/or they resent it. (Wouldn't you?)

October

꙾ ARE YOUR *homework assignments meaningful? Worth the students' time and effort? Worthy of the time it takes to correct and record?*

OCTOBER 7

IF YOU DETERMINED yesterday that your homework assignments are meaningful (and, I might add, this is a daily decision), worth the students' time and effort, and worthy of your time to correct and record the grades, then it is time to look into ways to save your time correcting and recording.

The following *Teacher Tips* from veteran teachers will help you to maximize the homework's potential and keep you from hours of grading and recording grades after school:

• Instead of taking precious classtime to collect and return homework, take a few minutes at the beginning of each class to walk past students' desks checking to see if the assignment has been done. Take your grade book with you and mark whether the student has done the homework assignment or not. Identify one or two problems that you can quickly spot for correctness. This saves time and indicates to your students that the assignment is meaningful.

• Do not collect homework every day. Instead, check to see if it was done, as just mentioned, giving credit. Then, have students turn in a notebook at the end of the quarter with all of the assignments, and select several assignments to correct thoroughly.

• Another alternative to grading homework is to distribute homework calendars to the students, either on a weekly, monthly, or semester basis, depending on the age and responsibility of the students. (In other words, how long are they able to hold onto the sheet before it becomes lost.) When walking around checking for homework completion, stamp the date on the calendar if the homework has been done. At the end of the week, month, or term, students hand in the calendar to be included in their grade. (Important—have a stamp made especially for this purpose, and make sure that the stamp is one that is not accessible to the students, or you will be astounded to discover that all of your students have finished all of their homework, every day. That is a lovely thought, and I hope all of your students do complete their work, but that it is accomplished honestly.)

• Keep a basket of worksheets available to be used as alternative assignments for students returning from an absence, for advanced students who may want something extra to do, for remedial students who may need more practice, or for students who want extra credit. (This is an excellent use for extra papers left over from previous years.)

◑ Now that you *have decided that your homework assignments are meaningful, what else can you do that will simplify the correction and recording of grades for these assignments?*

October 8

There appears to be a hierarchy in schools—of knowledge, subject matter, and who teaches the "most important" subject. It has probably always been this way, but more recently this hierarchy has been fueled by reports that suggest that, due to a lack of qualified people to teach certain subjects, more money should be paid to recruit individuals with expertise in these areas. When carried to the extreme, we have high school teachers who are more important (better than?) elementary school teachers, because they teach higher learning (to students older and more

October

apt to learn it), calculus teachers "smarter than" home economics teachers, and physical education teachers who spend all day outdoors, in the fresh air playing games.

Sounds like stereotyping to me. And the truth is, a calculus teacher is probably no more effective teaching first graders to read than the kindergarten teacher is in teaching physics. But that does not mean that the kindergarten teacher cannot do calculus or that the physics teacher cannot read.

We all have our skills and we hope that we are in the right positions, teaching what we teach best, working together for the whole child.

Jerome Bruner once wrote that, "intellectual activity anywhere is the same, whether at the frontier of knowledge or in a third-grade classroom." He later added, "In teaching from kindergarten to graduate school, I have been amazed at the intellectual similarity of human beings at all ages."[1] And that's the truth!

❧ Do you treat *all teachers, no matter what subject they teach, with respect? If not, why not? If so, how?*

OCTOBER 9

JEROME BRUNER, writing in *The Process of Education,* states that the curriculum of a subject should be determined by the most fundamental understanding that can be achieved by the underlying principles that are giving structure to the subject. Instead of asking whether a given subject matter is worth a child's knowing, he said, "We might ask, as a criterion for any subject taught in primary school, whether, when fully developed, it is worth an adult's knowing, and whether having known it as a child makes the person a better adult."[2]

So many of the things that we teach, we do so "just because." Because they have always been taught, or worse, because we are told to. How many times do you question information that you are teaching?

⠀

⠀⠀ARE THE SUBJECT *and lessons that you are teaching a child "worth an adult's knowing" or going to make the child "a better adult"?*

OCTOBER 10

SINCE SCHOOL HAS BEEN in session for a month or more, are your students possibly getting a little tired of the routine? Are you? Then maybe it is time for a minor change. Maybe it is time to invite a guest speaker to liven up the classtime. Guest speakers can enhance the subject matter with their knowledge or be a surprise break in the lesson. The following ideas may encourage you to seek out a guest speaker or speakers for your students, *soon:*

• When writing your parent letter at the beginning of the year, ask parents to write down on the letter any talents or cultural heritage they would be willing to share with the class, and to return the letter to you.

• Invite local musicians to come into your class to play or sing a variety of songs for your students. Maybe they will bring instruments for the students to try, too.

• Seek out artisans and craftspeople in the community to teach or at least explain their craft to the students.

• Have a career day for students. Ask parents and people in the community to come into your class and talk about their careers with students. Be sure to include people who are in nontraditional-gender careers (male nurses and hairstylists, female pilots and police officers, and so on).

- Ask a parent, librarian, older student, or senior citizen to come in to read to students.

- Check with high school, community colleges, universities, and local play groups to see if they will perform for your students.

🌦 HOW CAN YOU *include speakers in your classroom?*

OCTOBER 11

SHORTLY AFTER the turn of the 19th century, when educators were seriously discussing what knowledge is of most worth and what role the schools (especially the newly formed high schools) would serve for the community, a U.S. Bureau of Education Commission on the Reorganization of Secondary Education determined the school role for the people. In their famous document, *Cardinal Principles of Secondary Education,* they claimed that "in America, racial stocks are widely diversified, various forms of social heredity come into conflict, differing religious beliefs do not always make for unification, and the members of different vocations often fail to recognize the interests that they have in common with others." The result is, they concluded, that "the school is the one agency that may be controlled definitely and consciously by democracy for the purpose of unifying its people."[3]

Think of the importance of school's "purpose of unifying its people." What a grand commission. The problem is, how do you propose to unify people and maintain individuality? Is the unifying principle the knowledge that we are individuals?

Yes, we have differing religious beliefs, vocations, backgrounds, and ethnicities, but schools are unified in desiring equal opportunity for all children, teaching diversity and tolerance.

75

꩜ How do you *"unify" the individuals in your classroom? (Or do you?)*

OCTOBER 12

TODAY IS COLUMBUS DAY, the day on which Christopher Columbus arrived in San Salvador, on what date? When did he "sail the ocean blue"? That's right, 1492. Isn't it interesting that until just a few years ago, this date was a celebration of the founding of our part of the world. Brave Columbus and his three ships. What were they called? (The *Niña, Pinta,* and *Santa Maria.*) See, we all know the story.

A few years ago, the story of Columbus's sailing to America fell out of favor as we learned of his abuse of the natives he found and a myriad of other ugly details.

I find it interesting that stories change throughout history to fit today's standards rather than being kept within their historical perspective. Not that the original story was correct, but that both extremes find their paths into our understanding. In my lifetime, I have seen too many individuals go from hero to creep practically overnight. And both extremes are problematic. The problem is that we canonize the achiever until we find that he or she is not perfect, and then we belabor all of the person's faults, instead of just seeing her or him as an individual who had opportunities and rose to the occasion. A human being just like us, with failings, too.

꩜ WHOM DO YOU MAKE *a hero to your students? Is he or she completely worthy? Could his or her accomplishments be celebrated without portraying the person as more than mortal? Can we keep history in perspective and not judge it by today's standards?*

OCTOBER 13

WHEN COLUMBUS came to America he found a people whose beliefs and culture differed from his own. We read on October 11 that the *Cardinal Principles* report urged schools to be the "unifiers" of the people of this land; one way to unify people with various backgrounds and beliefs is to learn about those backgrounds and beliefs. The following *Teacher Tips* from veteran teachers may give you some ideas for teaching about diversity and tolerance with your students. To learn about other countries' beliefs:

• Study music from other cultures. Learn a song or folk dance from another culture. How did the geography influence the instruments built and the form that the music took?

• In discussing the elements on the periodic table, discuss how different elements were found in different countries. Who discovered it, and when? Place a small sticker with the discovering country's flag (available at stamp-collecting stores) on the chart.

• Discuss the importance of the sun in the production of energy, warmth, happiness, and the circle of life. Research how ancient and more modern cultures worshiped the sun.

• Schedule a "Culture Immersion Day," on which students will study how a specific culture has impacted our society. Consider the dietary origins of other cultures, including those who don't eat meat.

• Collect stories from other cultures. Compare and contrast the authors of many countries. What is the style? What influences the topic? Read, summarize, or dramatize stories or novels and evaluate them. Are there similar story themes in the stories of other countries? Select two poems from different cultures. Placing them side by side, and without telling your students where they are from, see if they can determine which poem came from which culture. What gave them a clue?

❧ WHAT DO YOU *want your students to know about other cultures? Why do you want them to know that?*

OCTOBER 14

CONTINUING ON OUR THEME of diversity, we know that different cultures have different feelings or beliefs about many things. Just as people within a country are individuals, countries are individual, too. In discussing this topic with your students, you may learn something that can be of value to your teaching as well.

An important part of getting along with others is understanding how various cultures feel about the following issues: social distance, touching, volume of voice, eye contact, timing of verbal exchanges, silence, gestures (such as pointing, thumbs up, moving a hand across one's throat, *V* for victory), posture, talking with your hands, or smiling. Learning about these differences may seem trivial, but it may make a difference in how your foreign students respond to you and others.

A fun topic may be a discussion on the history of language. Listen to the language and discuss how it evolved. (Be sure to include controversial dialects such as Ebonics, and maybe even "Valley girl," too.)

Collect artwork from various cultures. Compare two sculptures, paintings, photos, and other *objets d'art* of different cultures. How are they alike? How are they different? Ask your students to give their opinions about the meaning of art to the culture and how culture affects our understanding of visual images. Discuss the period of the artwork. What was going on in the culture during the time that it was made? Discuss how universal events or disasters (volcanoes, war, peace, famine) influence artists. Ask students to imagine how they might illustrate their feelings if they were living through a major event or disaster, and ask them to do that.

And, of course, the obvious lesson is to discuss holidays in various cultures. What is the occasion? Why is it important? How is it celebrated?

Whew! There are so many ways to look at and "see" other countries and peoples.

꩜ WHAT OTHER LESSONS *provide insight into the culture of a country?*

OCTOBER 15

IN SEPTEMBER, we discussed the importance of the look and "feel" of the classroom for making students feel comfortable and enhancing learning. We considered seating arrangements, the placement of desks, and the importance of being able to move around and see each student. Where each student sits in this arrangement is of equal importance.

Although some teachers allow students to sit wherever they choose, often placing the students on some sort of "good behavior" to maintain seats by their friends, I always found it beneficial to develop a seating chart from the beginning of the school year as a way of informing the students that learning, not socializing, is the purpose for being in my classroom. (It also informed them from the beginning that I was in charge.)

Whether at the start of the year you selected the seating arrangement for your students, or allowed them to select their own seats, school has been in session a month or more by now, and it is probably time to change seats, if for no other reason than to break the monotony of a classroom that always looks the same.

I disagree wholeheartedly with those of you who think that seating charts are unnecessary and so do not use them. Not only

79

do seating charts allow you to learn the students' names quickly, the charts are an absolute necessity for substitute teachers who may be called to a classroom with discipline problems and need to know each student's name. (Substitute teachers, I accept your applause graciously.)

The following *Teacher Tips* from veteran teachers will help in utilizing seating charts in your classroom:

• Change seating charts often. This helps break up or prevent cliques from forming within the classroom, which can lead to disturbances and discipline problems. Also, studies have shown that teachers often teach to and call on students in the center of the classroom. Changing seats gives all students an opportunity to be in this area and be called upon.

• Use different methods to change seat assignments. This can be done by placing the students in alphabetical order by last name or by first name, telephone number, or street address. Or, it may simply be up to your good judgment to determine what the best arrangement will be.

• Number the desks so that when you decide to rearrange the room, the students immediately know where they are supposed to sit by finding their number on the desk.

☙ HAVE YOU CHANGED *your seating arrangement lately? What method did you use for placing students? Did it work? Why or why not?*

OCTOBER 16

HAVING BEEN A SUBSTITUTE TEACHER for more years than I care to remember, this day is devoted to those individuals who help us when we are in need, whether we are attending a conference, staying home ill, having a personal crisis, or are just "sick of

October

teaching." Although we may complain about the job they did, how they did not carry out our plans exactly as we instructed, or that they allowed some infringement of our rules, where would we be without substitute teachers?

As a substitute teacher, I often felt underappreciated, disrespected by students and some staff, and at one point vowed that I would go on welfare before I would accept another call at 6 A.M. to supervise a class for a teacher who left no seating chart and a lesson plan filled in some secret code, if filled at all.

So, in order to celebrate what I have identified as "National Substitute Teacher Appreciation Day," today is a good day to thank those hardy souls who get showered and dressed at the last minute, maintain our classrooms without knowing the subject or our particular pet peeves, and who enter an atmosphere where it is "open season" for abuse. (You all know what I mean; you were students at one time, and you had substitutes. How were they treated by you and by others?) And on top of all of this, substitute teachers receive no benefits. A particular thank you to those who did not fall for the "She always lets us do such and such" routine (e.g., "She lets us go to the bathroom, chew gum, run around the room, and leave early, et cetera.")

The following *Teacher Tips* are from veteran "subs" (of which I have been one), to help make the day easier for the substitute teacher taking your place, and to ensure that everything is in order when you return:

• Leave plans written out in detail and all papers run off ahead of time. If a substitute is called late, he or she may not have time to run off papers before school. Have extra assignments in case the lesson does not take as long as you planned. (Even if you are not planning to be absent, before you leave each day your lesson plan should be prepared with the next few days' assignments and lessons run off, and in clear view on your desk in case of emergency.)

• Make sure that the lessons you leave are meaningful. Students can tell if an assignment is bogus and only assigned because they have a substitute. (Wouldn't you resent work that was a waste of time?) Unfortunately they will not resent you, but the innocent substitute teacher who is unwittingly wasting their time.

• If you have specific rules that you expect the students to follow, do not expect them to tell the substitute, and do not identify a "trusted" student and expect them to rat on their peers. They may do this for you, but it puts them in an unfair, perhaps dangerous, position.

• An up-to-date seating chart should be readily available. Although it may seem unfair, I used to pencil stars by potential problem students who needed to be watched closely.

• If you know you are going to be absent, prepare the students ahead of time. Tell them how you expect them to behave toward the "guest" who will be coming the next day. Inform them of the possible rewards for good behavior and the consequences for behavior that is inappropriate.

• There will come that day when you need a substitute due to an emergency or an unexpected illness, and you left school unprepared. To ward off potential chaos, have a substitute packet always on your desk with activities that, although they may not be related to what you are studying, will give the students a meaningful and enjoyable lesson to complete. The packet should include a seating chart, rules, and assignments.

☙ HAVE YOU PREPARED *your "substitute packet" today? What can you do for a substitute teacher to thank him or her for the job that he or she does?*

OCTOBER 17

ALBERT EINSTEIN was born in Ulm, Germany, on March 14, 1879, and he died in Princeton, New Jersey, on April 18, 1955. On this day, October 17, in 1933, Einstein, having fled Nazi Germany, arrived in the United States. Perhaps best known for his theory of relativity, having completely revised the existing concepts of fundamental, universal laws and paving the way for the atomic age, in March 1953 he devised a single mathematical formula that included the laws of gravitation, electromagnetism, and relativity ($E = mc^2$).

It is easy to tell students that old story about Einstein being a poor student, but that misses the point. In reality, relatively speaking (excuse the pun), Einstein saw education as an important element in a child's life and in the life of the society. In his autobiography, Einstein wrote, "Sometimes one sees in the school simply the instrument for transferring a certain maximum quantity of knowledge to the growing generation." Where, in actuality, "the aim must be the training of independently acting and thinking individuals who," he added, "see in the service of the community their highest life problem."[4]

Rather than informing students today that it is OK to do poorly by holding up Albert Einstein as a model, it is better to encourage students to strive toward genius and extol the virtues of education.

☙ ARE YOU ENCOURAGING *your students to genius with the aim of training them to act independently and think? If not, why not? If so, how are you doing this?*

OCTOBER 18

IN A PERIODICAL for educators called *Education Week,* an article about a seventy-four-year-old teacher named Naomi

83

Duncan appeared in the "People" section. What is so unusual about this teacher? (Other than that most teachers have long since retired by that age, or at the very least, cannot match Ms. Duncan's fifty-six years of teaching?) It is that, in fifty-six years of teaching, "she has *never* missed a day of school, not one."

For the last forty-four years, according to the article, Naomi Duncan has taught art to junior and senior high school students at Woodland R-4 School in Marble Hill, Missouri, *and* at the time of the article, had no intentions of quitting. Her determination to keep a perfect record, the article said, "may have stemmed from the fact that during her days as a student, she never missed a day of school" and "she said she has been lucky not to have had any major illnesses."[5]

Now that is dedication!

ഇ BEFORE YOU GO *adding up the number of sick days Naomi Duncan has accumulated in fifty-six years, ask yourself this: "Although I may have missed a day of teaching here and there, in what other ways am I as dedicated to my job?"*

OCTOBER 19

IF YOUR SCHOOL has been in session for a few weeks, then it is probably time to evaluate your students' progress. Your school may even have a policy of sending progress reports home around this time. Although I appear to contradict what I said earlier about finding grading to be very troublesome, evaluation for progress reports is a little different and therefore justifiable. Evaluation does not necessarily mean grading a student; it quite simply evaluates whether each student is on target with your (or more likely your district's) expectations for a student in your grade and subject. Progress reports can give your student, parents, and you an indication of what the student has accomplished and therefore his or her ability to move on to the next subject, and what needs to be further explained or worked on. In any case, the following *Teacher Tips* from master teachers may help you in preparing these reports:

• Send home weekly progress reports rather than waiting until the middle of the marking period. It is much easier to catch up when you are a week behind noting your students' work than six weeks. Weekly progress reports also keep parents posted early so they can help sooner. This eliminates surprises at report card time and may limit the number of parent phone calls you will have to make when report cards arrive home.

• Send progress reports that require a parent's signature. Although students may sign these papers themselves, or have a friend sign them, at least you have documents with a signature when parents claim that they did not know that there was a problem.

• Remember that progress reports are for the student as well as their parents. Design the reports so that students understand the areas in which they are deficient and what is necessary to arrive at satisfactory progress.

• Also remember that progress reports are for you. Giving progress reports requires that you keep up with grading so that you know where each student is. This may be a lot of work, but it has at least two benefits: a) When parents call with questions about their child's work, you have the information readily available; and b) It makes it easier to plan lessons when you know your students' current progress.

᠍ KEEPING ABREAST *of student progress, as you can imagine, is not an easy job. How can you simplify grading and recording grades in order to make the job easier? Is there a way to keep aware of student progress other than grading?*

85

OCTOBER 20

JOHN DEWEY, who some educators refer to as one of the greatest educational philosophers of our time, was born on October 20, 1859. In many of his works, Dewey wrote of the importance of the classroom as a microcosm of the society as a whole. In *The School and Society* (1900), Dewey wrote that "when the school introduces and trains each child into membership within such a little community, saturating him with the spirit of service, and providing him with the instruments of effective self-direction," the result is that "we shall have the deepest and best guaranty of a larger society which is worthy, and harmonious."[6]

Teaching children harmonious living can only occur when they are enmeshed in an harmonious environment. The teacher who models the spirit of service and encourages self-direction is providing society with a student from whose membership in the larger society we will all benefit.

꩜ ARE YOU PROVIDING *your students with the elements necessary for them to become a benefit to our society?*

OCTOBER 21

THE PROLIFIC WRITINGS of John Dewey also include a beautiful little piece called, "My Pedagogic Creed." Published in 1897, this work stated outright Dewey's beliefs for education, teaching, and learning. In it he wrote, "I believe that education is a regulation of the process of coming to share in the social consciousness; and that the adjustment of individual activity on the basis of this social consciousness is the only sure method of social reconstruction."

"I believe," he continued, "that the teacher is engaged, not simply in the training of individuals, but in the formation of the

October

proper social life." And, he concluded, "I believe that every teacher should realize the dignity of his calling; that he is a social servant set apart for the maintenance of proper social order and the securing of the right social growth."[7]

A pedagogy is, by definition, the "art or science of teaching." It is, in Dewey's model, a belief system in how he perceives the importance of school and the teacher as keepers of society, and all that is good, to introduce the child into the membership of the community and the future.

❧ WHAT ARE *some of the beliefs in your "pedagogic creed?"*

OCTOBER 22

JOHN DEWEY'S "Pedagogic Creed" continues with the subjects of civilization, social consciousness, and race, topics that we have been looking into this month. Dewey believed and wrote that "all education proceeds by the participation of the individual in the social consciousness of the race. . . . Through this unconscious education the individual gradually comes to share in the intellectual and moral resources which humanity has succeeded in getting together. He becomes an inheritor of the funded capital of civilization." The child, no matter who he is or where he is from, is entitled to partake in the benefits of the society. The capital is education.

"I believe that the only true education comes through the stimulation of the child's powers by the demands of the social situations in which he finds himself," Dewey continued. "Through these demands he is stimulated to act as a member of a unity, to emerge from his original narrowness of action and feeling and to conceive of himself from the standpoint of the welfare of the group to which he belongs." The child is not only an inheritor of

87

the capital but carrying an obligation of this inheritance for the welfare of the group.[8]

❧ EDUCATION IS *a right, and carries a price. How will you share this information with your students?*

OCTOBER 23

THE LATE Teachers College Professor of Education, Lawrence Cremin, author of the large, three-volume series *American Education,* which contains a wealth of information about how Americans have been educated for the last four centuries, also authored a variety of other books on the history of education in America that should be read by all teacher education students.

Similarly to Dewey, Cremin writes in *Traditions of American Education,* that, "Schooling—like education in general—never liberates without at the same time limiting. It never empowers without at the same time constraining. It never frees without at the same time socializing." Although we may want to think of school and education as being the great liberator of the masses, the problem is that, in the process of educating, we are doing the educating in a social atmosphere that has boundaries and limitations. And, ultimately the child becomes an adult in a society that has boundaries and limitations.

Cremin continues, "The question is not whether one or the other is occurring in isolation but what the balance is and to what end, and in light of what alternatives."[9]

❧ HOW CAN YOU *educate your students and liberate them at the same time?*

OCTOBER 24

UNITED NATIONS DAY commemorates the founding on October 24, 1945, over half a century ago, of this world organization dedicated to peace, security from aggression, freedom of choice, and equality among nations and people.

Although it may seem ineffective at times, as we have had wars, conflicts, and atrocities in the last fifty years, the United Nations offers, at least, an opportunity for people from different nations and beliefs to sit down and at least try to talk about situations before they escalate. Yes, it is not perfect, but communication is happening.

A fun activity, depending on the age of the students you teach, might be to have a mock United Nations today. As part of your lesson you can discuss the goal of the organization, the good that it does for children (UNICEF) and adults, and the importance of communication and discussion in settling differences. If you have time, students can select a country, study it, and represent that country in a debate on a current worldwide issue.

⟫ WHAT CAN YOUR *students do to better understand the purposes and importance of the United Nations?*

OCTOBER 25

ALONG WITH YOUR students participating in a mock United Nations debate, there are a variety of other ways that they can understand the purpose of the organization and what it does to help maintain peace in the world. The following *Teacher Tips* may be useful if you desire to continue this discussion:

89

- If your students are older and understand government, you may want to discuss the governing body of the United Nations organization. Who is allowed to sit in what assemblies and why?

- Younger students may want to learn about the United Nations Children's Fund and how it helps needy children throughout the world. (UNICEF has a catalog and stores in various parts of the country with excellent sources, calendars, books, and information for elementary grades, with proceeds going to the fund.)

- Students in geography classes can learn the countries which are members of the UN and why they choose to be a part of the organization, who are the current officials and representatives.

- All students can benefit from conflict resolution processes.

➲ WHAT OTHER LESSONS *can we learn from the United Nations?*

OCTOBER 26

SOMETIME THIS WEEK, maybe today, depending on the year you are reading this, Daylight Savings Time will end, and most of us will turn our clocks back to Standard Time. In some ways, ending Daylight Savings Time and returning to Standard Time seems like being asked to give back an award or a gift that was given by mistake. We get used to sunny evenings and longer days and then, just as it is getting darker naturally as winter nears, we are required to give back the extra hour as well. With the return to Standard Time, it is now getting darker earlier, much too early, and the lighter start of the day is little consolation.

Losing Daylight Savings Time takes its toll on students as well. Now there is little time to play outside before it turns dark.

For some students, it is almost dark when they get home from school. Outdoor activities change to indoor play. Students may benefit with more time outside during their school days.

🐌 WHAT EFFECT *does the return to Standard Time have on your students? How about on you?*

OCTOBER 27

NOT ONLY IS IT around this time that progress reports are expected, but parent conferences will be scheduled as well. Parent conferences are an excellent opportunity to get to know the parents of your students, a very important element in your effectiveness as a teacher. Therefore, it is important that the meeting is a positive opportunity to introduce yourself as a professional. The following *Teacher Tips* are suggestions from veteran teachers *and parents* on how to get the most out of these sessions:

• To begin with, you have to encourage the parents to come to the meeting. This may require a little creative scheduling. Expecting parents to take time off from their work so that you don't have to spend time after school is not the most effective way to schedule a meeting. Some parents are paid hourly wages; others are employed in situations where they are not allowed personal time off. Try to be flexible.

• Encourage students to invite their parents to come to conferences. Maybe you can reward them (as long as you are not penalizing those whose parents cannot come).

• Be professional. Dress like a professional, look like a professional, talk like a professional, and act professionally. Parents want their child to be taught by a good teacher; appearances are important.

- Be on time. Be respectful of the parents' time, both those whom you are talking to, and those who are waiting to talk to you.

- Be prepared. If you are a parent yourself, have you ever gone to a conference or open house and felt that the teacher did not have a clue who your child was? Know the children and what their progress has been.

Parents are an important part of the teaching and learning process. Take advantage of this opportunity to build a good relationship.

WHAT ELSE can you do to ensure that your meeting with parents is a positive one?

OCTOBER 28

WHETHER YOUR parent/teacher conference is a planned visit or an unexpected surprise drop-in by a possibly irate parent, there are several things that you can do to ensure that the outcome benefits the child, the parent, and yourself. We already discussed the importance of looking and acting professional. The following *Teacher Tips* from those who have been in these awkward situations may help you when the time arrives:

- If there has been a problem, do not be defensive. Caring parents often want what is best for their children. They have only heard one side of the story from their child. Now is the time to share the other side.

- Have your facts ready. Do not answer a phone call from an irate parent. Tell whomever answers the phone to take the number and you will call the parent back. Gather your information and then call back as soon as possible so time does not increase their anger.

- Know whom you are talking with. Is this a parent, legal guardian, grandparent, or older brother? You should only discuss this child with the person who has legal custody. (And call them by the correct name. Do not assume that the parent has the same last name as the child.)

- Do not discuss any other student, parent, or teacher in your conversation. Only this situation, at this time, is relevant.

- Arrive at a solution that is positive and comfortable for all parties.

- Try to end on a high note and encourage the parent to call again when they feel it is necessary.

Dealing with parents can sometimes be difficult, but it is the difficult parents that you need to have on your side for the child's sake.

↭ WHAT OTHER STRATEGIES *can you think of ahead of time to prepare yourself for working with difficult parents?*

OCTOBER 29

PARENTS CAN ALSO BE an asset *in* the classroom setting. Although many teachers are uncomfortable when parents and adults are in their classrooms, if a teacher can get over this, an extra set of hands is often a blessing. Elementary teachers tend to have more opportunities to utilize parents in the classroom, but secondary teachers can also benefit from parent volunteers. The following *Teacher Tips* may help you with adults in the room (and, who knows, you may just learn to like it!):

- Remember, even though these parents who volunteer may not be employed outside the home, their time is important to them. They have given you a valuable resource, their time. Do not waste it. Have things prepared for them to do and a place for them to find out what they are doing so it is not disruptive when they arrive.

• Don't assume that they are only capable of cutting construction paper and making copies. When I volunteered in my children's classroom, I had taught and was completing a master's degree. I would have preferred reading to the children to cutting out pink bunnies.

• Don't be sexist. Dads can volunteer the same as moms. *And* they should not be treated any differently. I recall, as a volunteer in my son's kindergarten class, that one father came in once a week to work with the children. I also remember that he had most of the fun, child-centered activities. But the topper was the last day of school when the teacher gave him a special "Super Dad" T-shirt and other gifts, as the rest of us female volunteers looked on. This is still sexism.

• And, speaking of appreciation, thank your volunteers with notes, a token gift, something to let them know you are grateful for all of the help they have been. Think of all the time and money they have saved you and the impact they have had on your students.

---

꧰ IN WHAT AREAS *could a parent, or other adult volunteer, be of help to you in your classroom?*

OCTOBER 30

DEVIL'S NIGHT. I grew up in Michigan and therefore knew, as all Michigan youngsters know, that the night before Halloween is Devil's Night (or maybe "Devils' Night" is more correct), when seemingly innocent children become monsters and do evil things to neighbors, such as toilet paper their trees or soap their windows, more often than not, in fun. Although I will not admit nor incriminate any of my friends by admitting to any shenani-

October

gans of this sort, I will admit that whatever was done was done to a friend and was an, albeit demented, way of saying we liked him or her.

Fortunately, I learned when I moved to California, Devil's Night was not a "holiday" here, and few people I mentioned it to even knew what I was talking about. So I would not recommend informing your students about this practice. But there are other ways to have demented fun during the week of Halloween, depending on the ages of your students. One fun activity might be to have your students write their own scary stories. When the assignment is due, divide students into groups of four, read each other's stories, and select the best one from the group to read to the class. On Halloween, turn the lights down or off, have a pumpkin available, and use a flashlight to read the stories.

WHY NOT READ *a scary story you select, or better yet, get in the fun and write your own? What is your scary Halloween story?*

OCTOBER 31

HALLOWEEN, the day (and night) of jack-o'-lanterns, ghosts, witches, goblins, and devils. The day when students, having spent the last week selecting just the right Halloween costume, whether scary, funny, or the latest Disney cartoon figure, go door to door begging for candy. Do you remember? Wasn't it great?

I think my first recollection of Halloween was second grade, when we were able to put on our costumes, have orange and black cupcakes and apple cider, and watch as our teacher's husband carved a pumpkin (this was a long time ago and pre-liberation). I could not wait until it got dark to go door to door. I lived in a big neighborhood and I always came home with two shopping bags full of goodies, root beer barrels being my favorite.

Halloween can be a fun time for students and an educational one as well. Although Halloween is thought of as pagan ritual, it is believed to have originated from Celtic practices that marked the beginning of winter. Originally called All Hallow Even and Hallowmas, it is traditionally associated in some countries with old customs such as bonfires, masquerades, and the telling of ghost stories.

Because this date is sometime associated with the Day of the Dead, it may be fun to have students discuss eulogies and epitaphs. What will they want to be known for after having lived a long life? How will their tombstones read? What is the significance of pumpkins and bobbing for apples? What other games did their ancestors play before modern conveniences? Why celebrate before winter?

Of course, your activities will depend on the age of the group you teach. Particularly scary activities may not be appropriate for young children. And it is always important to stress safety at Halloween time. (Watch for cars who cannot see you while trick-or-treating, carefully check candy before eating, never go out alone, et cetera.) But for teachers, probably the scariest part of Halloween is the students' behavior the next few days after having eaten too much sugar. Talk about goblins and devils!

What activities would your students enjoy that have not been done in other classes?

NOVEMBER

NOVEMBER 1

ALL SAINTS' DAY, November 1, is the day that follows Halloween. And maybe you are feeling like a saint today, working with students who partied as ghosts and goblins in your classroom yesterday, are full of candy from the previous night's trick-or-treating, and who are having difficulty focusing on the classroom activities you have planned for them to accomplish today.

The celebration of All Saints' Day as a festival originated in the early seventh century with Pope Boniface IV, to celebrate the transformation of the Roman Pantheon into a Christian temple and its consecration to the Virgin Mary and the martyrs. Today, as its name implies, All Saints' Day is a day that is set aside to honor the departed saints and to honor those who have died during the previous year.

In his book, *When Teachers Face Themselves*, Arthur Jersild, who was at the time of its writing a professor of education at Teachers College, Columbia University, wrote of the need for teachers to know who *they* are before they can begin to understand the children who are in their classrooms. Jersild writes in his book that too often teachers play the martyr routine by believing that they must give an all-out effort to help others without demanding any rights for themselves. "There are some who tolerate acute discomfort without feeling that they have a right to see their own comfort . . . who think that they should go out in love to all creatures but that it is not proper for them to ask for love, or to seek it, or to demand it."

Jersild continues, "A teacher who tries to go out to others but who cannot come home to himself and experience emotion *in his own right* may be noble, but he is not actually realizing his potentialities as a teacher."[1] Being a martyr to your students, children, spouse, whomever, may be admirable, but who wants to live or spend any quality time with a martyr?

November

⟫ WHEN YOU FACE *your day are you striving for sainthood or are you an approachable human being like the rest of us? What can and will you do, however minor, for yourself today?*

NOVEMBER 2

YESTERDAY WAS All Saints' Day, and according to the calendar, today is "All Souls' Day," the day on which the Catholic Church commemorates all the faithful deceased. Now, students are not all saints, but they are not dead souls either. They are young people who are alive with souls that need to be nourished and prepared to live today and in the future.

Unfortunately, teachers often treat students as lifeless when we coldly correct assignments and return them with little care as to the recipients' feelings when they receive their grades. If a teacher believes that a paper is worth assigning (as all papers should be), it is equally important that he or she respond in kind, by accurately assessing the pupils' work and including possible suggestions for improvement.

The following *Teacher Tips* from veteran teachers are important suggestions for analyzing, accessing, and responding to students in your classroom:

• Prepare and share your marking criteria with your students. What is often identified as a "rubric" is a list of achievement requirements that the teacher will be using to identify whether the student has correctly completed the assignment. Students should not need to guess about what a teacher is looking for in an assignment. Students should know what is expected and, if possible, given item percentages or point value to the steps necessary for a good grade.

99

• Keep clear records by grading and recording often. Not only is it fair for the students to know how they are progressing, it is good for the teacher to know which students are ready to move on to a new unit and to identify those who may need extra help. Keeping timely, accurate records is also important for selfish reasons. Believe me (do you hear experience speaking?), if you want to increase your stress level, be sure to wait until the last minute to grade papers, and spend the last few weekends of a marking period or semester, or worse yet, the school year, with baskets full of papers to correct and return.

• Give regular and positive feedback. This does not mean that a child who did not complete the assignment correctly or who failed to give the assignment appropriate time and effort should be given a positive grade. It means that it is important for students to receive feedback on what they finished correctly *and* which part of the assignment was incorrect. Even bad news can be given in a positive, growth-producing manner.

• Be aware of the student's feelings when returning papers. Some students fail to separate *self* from the work completed. It is important for a student to understand that the work may have been completed incorrectly and that the grade is not as an indication that the teacher does not like him or her. Self-esteem is a dubious thing. It is important to be careful with check marks and to respond to students' feelings about the grading.

• Give students the opportunity to redeem a poor grade. The purpose of grading is to give students the opportunity to clarify how well they understood the subject. Sometimes students may know, or be on the border of understanding the subject matter, but they may not have understood how you wanted them to complete the assignment. Again, preparing a rubric clarifies for the students how the assignment is to be done.

☙ HOW CAN YOU *let your students evaluate their learning in a manner that is meaningful for them?*

November

November 3

AROUND THIS TIME every year, especially if it is the first Tuesday of November, America comes alive with political rhetoric and campaign slogans, and without a doubt, there is an election taking place somewhere in the United States. This should come as no surprise. We do not wake up on the first Tuesday of November to a surprise newspaper headline which reads, "So-and-So Decides to Have an Election Today: Please Get Out and Vote." We know the first Tuesday is Election Day because we have been inundated for weeks or months with information on who is running and which issues are at stake.

Certainly voting is a privilege and a responsibility that we take for granted in our country, even though we probably should not (that is, take the privilege for granted). We do a great service to our students and society by teaching young people the importance of keeping aware of political issues and voting in as many elections as possible. An educated public is vital to making wise, educated decisions.

If you are unclear on how to teach the subject of politics and elections to your students, the following *Teacher Tips* may help you:

• Follow the elections with the help of newspapers, magazines, television, and local debates. Help students become aware of who is running and what the candidates' platforms are.

• Have a mock election with your students, following actual voting procedures. You may be able to obtain actual voting ballots and equipment. Explain how a voter must register before he or she is allowed to vote. If possible, and especially if your students are of voting age, have registration cards available.

• Elections are wonderful opportunities to understand political rhetoric and satire through television shows, political cartoons, and election advertisements. These give the students an opportunity to evaluate "political-ese," to identify candidate "selling" techniques, and to encourage students to be critical of campaign promises and accusations of those vying for political office.

• Political and campaign lessons can be used at times other than election time. Students can run for various classroom or school elected positions, or they can read and prepare for meaningful debates on current topics. Lessons with political focus also give students an opportunity to bring in and use the newspaper and other media for information and varying views.

How do you *teach students that rights* and *responsibilities are two sides of the same issue?*

November 4

Yesterday we discussed campaigns and voting, so, while we are on the subject of elections, November is a wonderful time to devote to government issues, politics, and democracy, no matter what your students' ages. Students will be voting members of our society in the not-too-distant future, voting on issues that will affect all of us as we grow older. And, however scary this thought may be to you, some of the young people in your classes may even be ruling our country one of these days, making decisions about our senior years. (I know that one particular student must have just popped into your head, because I almost heard you gasp and mutter, "I hope not.")

Because November is filled with American themes, such as elections, Thanksgiving, and Veterans Day, it is a good month to focus on these issues of democracy and everyone's rights as citizens. To continue with *Teacher Tips* for the month of November:

• To give your students an opportunity for humor and to understand the place of the political cartoon in history and today, when the class has studied a specific historical period, place a political cartoon on the overhead projector and ask your students to analyze the meaning of it. What might the various cartoon figures and drawings in the cartoon symbolize? Why do we use elephants for the Republican Party and donkeys for the Democratic Party? Where did these symbols originate?

• Ask students to write about the many roles that they are expected to fill in their lives. For example, they may be a son or a daughter, a student, a brother or sister, baseball player, band member, and so forth. Encourage students to list as many roles for themselves as they can. During the discussion of the various roles individuals play, point out that the president plays many roles as leader of the country, and he or she also has some of the same roles as your students.

• This discussion can be continued by asking the students to write about which role they would most like to assume if they were elected president of the United States, and why. Which role would they least like to assume, and why?

• Ask students to list the qualities and qualifications they believe that all candidates who are running for the presidency of the United States should have, and why.

• Discuss the importance of *image* for the president as a leader of the nation and as a representative of the nation to other countries. How is image important in our own lives?

∽ GUIDING YOUNG PEOPLE *to become responsible adults is an important role for all of us who have achieved adulthood. What can you do to encourage students to become responsible adults?*

103

November 5

LIVING IN A DEMOCRACY gives citizens of the United States rights and responsibilities. However, if the community is to function communally, it also includes written and unwritten rules of fairness toward all people. Democracy means government by the people, with equality of human rights, equal opportunity, and fair treatment of all ages, all ethnic groups, and both sexes. In order for young people to learn what democracy is, what it means, and how to maintain it, there needs to be an element of democracy within the classroom, used as a model for the students to understand the concept and learn to follow.

Yet it is common for teachers to ask, "How can my classroom be a democracy when I have to be in charge, when I know what is best for my students, or I have directives to follow? If I leave decision making up to my students, won't there be chaos?"

Democracy is not chaos. Nor does democracy allow everyone to "do their own thing" at the expense of others. Democracy is for the good of all, not only for the good of the individual. When we think of our lives as citizens of the United States, in addition to the benefits we reap, there are many rules that we are required to follow (and thank goodness for those rules). We cannot physically harm those who upset us, nor take other people's property; we cannot even drive on the left side of the road. There are plenty of rules to ensure that everyone has freedom, and that everyone's freedom is protected.

While many teachers feel that allowing democracy into the classroom will bring chaos if we allow students to make decisions about classwork, there are many areas where students can be encouraged and given opportunities to see democracy in action. Students can be given options for completing an assignment (notice I did not write options *of* completing an assignment, although that too would be democratic); students can have elections and make policy (with the benefit of your direction); and they can serve as supreme court justices in cases where class rules have been broken.

November

Too many times (and believe me, I have taught this way too), we adults enjoy the benefits of living in a democracy and yet we teach our students as though we were dictators, the only people with enough knowledge to know what the student needs.

☞ IS THERE AT LEAST *one area of your teaching domain that you can turn over to your students? What is it? How will you complete the transition of power?*

NOVEMBER 6

WRITING AND PASSING LAWS in your classroom, and allowing students to make decisions, however noble it may seem, is no easy matter. In order for the system to work smoothly and fairly in your democratic classroom, you will want to ensure that all students are given equal opportunity to have a say in the process and to vote without feeling intimidated by others. Although it may demand more of your involvement than you feel comfortable with, after an election or two, you will want to encourage students to make sure that everyone has an opportunity to fill at least some position (perhaps by appointment, if winning an election seems hopeless for some students).

One way to show students that even adults have difficulty agreeing on some matters is to ask the students if they have ever tried to get a large group of people to agree to have a party, to see a movie, or to go out to dinner. Ask them if this was an easy or a difficult task. Remind students that Congress acts on the same premise, with the exception that there are 535 individual members (or at least a majority) who must agree to work together to bring about legislation, write a bill, or to pass a law. Since it is unlikely that all members of Congress will agree on legislation, those in the minority must at least agree that "the majority rules."

It is also important to show your students that although a majority wins and a minority is overruled, those in the minority still have their rights that cannot be infringed upon by the majority.

☙ DOES EVERYONE *in your classroom have a "voice," that is, an opportunity to be heard without feeling intimidated by other students, or by you?*

NOVEMBER 7

IN ORDER TO understand democracy, politics and the country, it may help to give students an opportunity to recall information about our government by learning the geography of the United States. While certain classes, such as American government, history, and geography will focus on this subject in more detail, fun times can be structured in other classes to promote the recall of facts about our country, in the forms of "Trivial Pursuit–type" games or team contests. Some of these activities may take only a few minutes at the end of a class period when there is time remaining and the students have completed the day's tasks, while other forms of recall may take longer. It is also a good idea to leave a list of these kinds of activities in your "Substitute Folder" for those days when you are absent.

• Ask your students to write down the name of a state, historical leader, flower, animal, or your choice of subject, for each letter of the alphabet. Even younger students may be able to do this activity if done verbally, sounding out letters, and matching words for simple objects.

• Ask students to match states and their capitals, countries and capitals, or countries and their leaders. If students have difficulty with this activity, allow them to work in groups.

• Divide the class into teams. Have one member from each team standing by a map, preferably one that has no identification marks such as the countries' names on it. Say out loud the country, or the country's capital, and see which student can point to the country on the map first.

- A variation of the previous activity would be to use a U.S. map, say out loud the capital, and have the students point to the state.

- In a group or individually, say the name of a famous individual, and ask the students to match the person with the incident or activity that made them famous.

What other fun activities impart information that might otherwise need to be memorized?

NOVEMBER 8

IN SPRING 1998, in celebration of one hundred years in publication, *Time* magazine began a series of issues on political leaders, events, entertainers, and other people who had influenced Americans over the last century. The June 8 issue, on "Artists and Entertainers of the Twentieth Century," wrote about the men and women whom the *Time* editors agreed had impacted the world by their contributions to culture and the arts. John Dewey's *Democracy and Education* (1916) was credited, along with nine other books, in an article titled "Required Reading," as a book which, according to the author, "changed minds and lives."[2]

In *Democracy and Education,* Dewey expands on his idea that school is the place (along with the home) where young people are taught to become members of the community. The school is a part of the community and vice versa; the community should be part of the school, to ensure that there is nothing to break the learning that is necessary for students to become members of that community.

In order to maintain this school-community relationship, the two entities must become supportive and encouraging of one another. "The scheme of a curriculum," Dewey writes, "must take account of the adaptation of studies to the needs of existing community life; it must select with the intention of improving the life we live in common so that the future shall be better than the past."[3]

Often it is easy to see the community, and especially parents, as "them" and our school as "us," setting up an adversarial situation (as in "us versus them"). One begins to see, when reading Dewey's works, that he believed that it was important that the duality of the "versus" be replaced by "and." Therefore he wrote *The School and Society, The Child and the Curriculum,* and *Democracy and Education,* to name only a few of Dewey's well-known writings.

৶ IS THE COMMUNITY *involved in your classroom? Have you invited "them" into your classroom experience? How can you include them in your planning for the benefit of the students (and your classroom)?*

NOVEMBER 9

ON NOVEMBER 9, in 1620, the pilgrim ship *Mayflower* landed on Cape Cod, Massachusetts, and its sea-weary inhabitants disembarked into this new territory. Two days later, on November 11, the Mayflower Compact was signed, providing for a "civil body politic" to make all the laws for the new land. The Mayflower Compact remained the Plymouth Colony's basic charter until 1691, when the colony was absorbed by Massachusetts. Interestingly, although the inhabitants planned to "plant the first colony in the northern parts of Virginia," in actuality their landing and subsequent settlement was outside of the area of the Virginia Company.

The Mayflower Compact was intended to "covenant and combine ourselves together into a civil body politic for our better ordering and preservation ... and by virtue hereof to enact, constitute and frame just and equal laws, ordinances, acts, constitutions and offices from time to time ... for the general good of the colony."[4] Working together, not only for fairness, but as a necessity for basic survival.

When I think of how easy it is to drive across our country today, through the mountains, the deserts, to traverse rivers and lakes, or that one can take a pleasure cruise with fine food, leisure, and activity-filled days and nights, I am filled with respect for those who made the first journeys to these unknown places, whether it was across the ocean on the *Mayflower*, or across the continent on foot or in covered wagons. What a debt we owe to these brave people who sought out a new land for religious freedom and individual justice "for the general good of the colony."

☙ ARE YOU EXPLORING *new ground with your students? What risks are you willing to take? What will be the benefits that your students (and you) will gain? Will your journey pave an easier road for your students?*

NOVEMBER 10

A DEMOCRATIC CLASSROOM—are you still thinking about that idea? What a scary thought! Students running around doing whatever they want. Chaos. "No way," you say. Well, if that is the way you feel, then the time has come to consider what democracy in its purest form represents and how it can work for you and your students in your classroom.

To begin with, democracy requires discipline. In a democracy it is expected that citizens will be responsible, will be caring about others, and will work to ensure that the community and the freedoms continue. (Is this beginning to sound a little more reasonable?) In order for your classroom to be a democracy, students must realize that they have to be responsible, caring, and working members of the culture of the class. They must agree to follow "agreed-upon" rules, complete necessary work, and all the while show kindness to classmates. Sounds pretty good, doesn't it? Remember, democracy is not forced; it is agreed upon.

In 1900, John Dewey wrote in *The School and Society,* "A society is a number of people held together because they are working along common lines, in a common spirit, and with reference to common aims. The common needs and aims demand a growing interchange of thought and growing unity of sympathetic feeling."[5] Notice how many times he used the word *common,* the root of the word "community?" The society he was writing about was the school.

ℜ IN WHAT WAYS *can you encourage your students to work "along common lines, in a common spirit and with reference to common aims" (such as learning)?*

NOVEMBER 11

NOVEMBER 11, Veterans Day is a national holiday in the United States that recognizes and honors all of the men and women who serve and who have served in America's armed forces. Originally established in 1926 as Armistice Day, the day was set aside to commemorate the signing of the armistice that ended World War I in 1918. The name was changed to Veterans Day on June 1, 1954.

Whether we call today Veterans Day or Armistice Day, November 11 is the day we thank all of those men and women

November

who offered to give up their lives, and many who did die for us, so that we could partake in freedom and a democratic form of government. For those of you who are veterans, we thank you. For those readers who "also served" as the spouse or parent of a serviceman or servicewoman, we know that you also sacrificed.

Most schools have a holiday on Veterans Day (while, I might add, many veterans, and certainly servicemen and servicewomen, typically do not have the day off), yet few of us take the time out of our busy schedules to discuss the importance of this day. Even though we may disagree with some of the military confrontations our country has experienced in recent years and which may have soured us toward the government, the fact still remains that we probably would not want to be without our servicepeople and the personal protection they provide to us and our country.

⤳ IN YOUR *classroom today, how can you thank our veterans and current servicemen and women ?*

NOVEMBER 12

HAVE YOU EVER HEARD of the "Stupid Buffalo Award?" I recently visited a student teacher in a first-grade classroom after the children had gone home for the day. At the desk where I sat was a large adorable stuffed animal, which appeared to be a buffalo that a student may have forgotten to take home with him or her as the day ended. (Remember, early primary students sometimes bring their toys to school to share with others.) When I made a positive comment that it was a cute toy, the student teacher replied that it may be cute, but it was, in fact, the "Stupid Buffalo Award": an "award" placed by the master teacher on the desk of the child who asked a "stupid" question. I was, at first, dumbfounded, then appalled, and finally incensed that an "award" for being inquisitive was given to openly humiliate a six-year-old child. How sad! But wait, it gets worse.

The next day when I arrived for the actual observation of the student teacher, the "award" was still on the first grader's desk. And, not surprisingly, the child was absent. I asked my student if he thought that there might be some relationship between the award given and the child's absence. He replied that he had not thought about it, but it could be.

Maybe we need a "Stupid Buffalo Award" for this teacher and his master teacher.

This incident brings several questions to mind:

1. How many of us have asked "stupid questions"? If I was given an award for the many stupid questions I have asked, and continue to ask, I would have to move out of my home because my house could not hold all of the stuffed buffaloes. Some of these trophies would have been "awarded" quite recently!

2. How many times have we heard and told students that the "only stupid question is the one left unasked"? I wondered how many students in the classroom that I was visiting do not ask questions because they are afraid of being humiliated by being labeled "stupid"?

3. Shouldn't school be a safe place where curiosity is awarded, where questions are encouraged, and students are helped to find the answers?

4. How many times have we given "unseen" buffalo awards to students by our impatient response, or the tone of our voice when responding, or when we give a facial frown that indicates to the student that the question he or she has just asked was already answered or was inappropriate.

5. Worse yet, how many questions go unanswered, and how many times is questioning squelched by the fear of humiliation? (Or are the questions I just asked, "Stupid Buffalo Award–winning" questions?)

November

⍤ How do you *respond to students who ask a question concerning something you feel they should know about already, or that you feel you adequately discussed recently?*

NOVEMBER 13

ALL OF US who teach young people know that there are pre-existing goals and objectives that our school or our district expects us to fulfill. If you are contemplating the question of how to fulfill these requirements *and* maintain a democratic classroom, you have arrived at the right date. Inspiring students to inquire, solve problems, and complete tasks (and is it too much to add, do so joyfully?) is a good way to encourage them to accomplish the goals you and your district have determined to be necessary for the completion of your grade level and the maintenance of a democratic classroom. Why? Because the democracy does not necessarily come in letting them decide what they need to know (although that has certainly been argued by some educators); it lies in giving them options to select *how* they will learn what they need to know. The following *Teacher Tips* from veteran teachers may give you some ideas on how to motivate students to *want to do* the assignments you have selected:

• Preferred Activity Time, or "PAT," as it is commonly referred to, is a method used to encourage students to complete an assignment, most often a long-term task. At the beginning of a new unit, ask students to think of an activity that is educational but fun. When the assigned goal is successfully completed, students are rewarded by being able to do the fun activity.

• A variation on this positive reinforcer, used by some teachers, is to use PAT as a weekly basis for discipline. Students earn so many minutes of PAT time by exhibiting good behavior throughout the week, for example, five minutes for each hour of good behavior. The minutes are recorded daily, added up, and are "paid" on Friday with a fun activity.

• Gentle "attention-getting" methods encourage students who have moved off task to return to the assignment they are doing. Rather than a disciplinary measure, the method is a reminder to stay on task. One gentle method used by some teachers to get the students' attention, or to quiet a class when necessary, is to use a rain stick, which can be found in most nature stores. The stick, when turned up and down, makes a gentle trickling sound and sends a message to the students that they are getting too loud, or that they need to stop talking and get back to work.

• Certainly, a democratic method for keeping students involved in the classroom is to allow students to establish the class rules and the consequences for not following them. Although this is a good "first day" activity, it can be revisited throughout the year as necessary. By developing their own rules, the students feel that they have ownership of the classroom and a voice in what is going on there. Having been in classrooms with rules created for them in the past, students are always able to come up with the same rules that most teachers would make for them to follow (and sometimes even more), and they seem to have less difficulty following them. If you feel your students have overlooked some rules or you are concerned that an important rule is being deliberately avoided, discuss the importance of at least considering the need for the rule. After the students vote on the rules and agree to follow them, post the rules in clear view in the classroom. An additional advantage to this method is that students get a first impression of the teacher as a caring individual who entrusts them to be mature enough to make and follow their own rules. (Another example of the "hidden curriculum" at work. Not bad, right?)

• If students are going to be allowed to make decisions, they need to be given a variety of choices. Obviously there is no "one way only" to complete a task. Giving alternative assignments motivates students by letting them believe that they are in charge of their learning.

⊅ In what areas *can you give further "freedom of choice" to your students?*

November 14

When living in a democracy, citizens learn not only to respect the other person's rights, but, one hopes, to respect the person as well. As teachers, we often believe that we should expect or demand respect from our students as a condition of the position we hold. The logic of this thought pattern is, "Teaching is a respected position: I am a teacher; therefore I will be respected." Although that analysis may make sense to those of us who grew up respecting teachers and other elders, and we may be assuming our students and their parents were taught the same, a problem occurs when we find out that our assumptions are incorrect and we try to *demand* respect rather than earn it. While we may be a respecting person, taught to be respectful of our elders and our teachers, that does not mean that our students have been taught to believe the same thing.

A sure way of gaining the respect of students is to earn it by believing that they, too, are members of our society, however young, and deserve to be treated with respect. The following *Teacher Tips* may help create an atmosphere of mutual respect between you and your students:

• As often as possible, provide face-to-face feedback to your students concerning their progress in class. Discussing student strengths and weaknesses helps the students understand, gives them the opportunity to ask questions about what areas they may not understand, and provides you with the information needed to further assess their growth or areas where problems may occur.

• Decide what to tell an individual in private and what to share with groups. Certainly, any information that is personal or may embarrass a student should be told in private.

• If possible, always begin and end your conversation with a student on a high note. Humor may even soften a blow as long as it is not sarcastic or hurtful to the student.

• Look for feedback from the student that will help you to understand where the student is having difficulty, or why he or she is unable to do the work. There may be a situation that the student is in, such as a family problem, which is prohibiting him or her from completing the work.

• And, remember that cultural rules sometime dominate private conversations. For example, some cultures do not allow children to have face-to-face eye contact with their elders. Try to learn as many of these cultural uniquenesses as possible so that the discussion can provide important feedback to the student and the cultural rules not inhibit the process.

❧ BEING SEEN AS *a caring individual can encourage students to perform more positively in your classroom. Think of at least one situation you can change that will help you gain the respect of your students. What is it and how will you change it?*

NOVEMBER 15

A TEACHER WHO RESPECTS his or her students also helps the students to respect themselves. One way of encouraging self-respect is to help students learn to feel good about themselves. Generally, students who are successful feel better about themselves than those who do not. (This is probably true about adults, too.) Teaching is much more than presenting material; it is helping students to learn the material presented. To help make information more memorable, it is important to keep it in view of the students until it is learned. Expecting students to recall information they read or that you said only one time may work at the college level, but it will not help your students remember important information for further use. (And, by the way, I can tell you that it does not work at the college level either.)

To help students experience success in your classroom:

• Make packs of tagboard cards, similar to flashcards, of information that needs to be learned. Students can quiz each other or themselves to see how many facts they know. For information that has some order to it, dates for example, have teams of students race to put the cards in their correct chronological order.

• If you are studying vocabulary, have students write down as many vocabulary words as they can remember. Check for spelling.

• Write ten or fifteen scrambled words on the chalkboard or on the overhead projector from current and previous vocabulary lists. Ask students to unscramble them.

• Write a sentence on the chalkboard or the overhead projector. Ask the students to diagram the sentence, labeling verbs, nouns, prepositions, and other parts of speech.

• Write a sentence or a paragraph that is incorrect on the chalkboard or the overhead projector. Ask the students to fix whatever they can find that is incorrect: grammar, spelling, or content information. For variation, use incorrect sentences from the students' work (without identifying any student, of course).

• Ask students to write down five questions that they think would be fair questions to include on a test. This is not only a good method for reviewing information, but it clarifies any misinformation the students may have learned.

- Before beginning the lesson for the day, ask the students to write down three points that they remember from the previous day's lesson. This will not only set the tone for the new information but will check to see if the students were paying attention yesterday.

WHAT OTHER TECHNIQUES may help your students remember information and feel successful about their learning?

NOVEMBER 16

OK, BEFORE YOU BEGIN to believe it, I am not completely naive. Nothing is perfect, and especially when dealing with children (and adults) the "best laid plans...." Sometimes you do everything right in your democratic classroom, and some student does not buy into it and problems ensue. I will be the first to encourage both new teachers and those who have been around for a while not to put up with any unacceptable behavior. It only gets worse.

Democracy is wonderful, but remember that it is best when the democracy is inhabited by disciplined individuals. Sometimes, we need to remind our students to be disciplined, and to discipline those who choose to be undisciplined.

You know, but it bears repeating, that when disciplining students it is important that a teacher be fair and consistent, create a well-established rule system by establishing common rules for the common good, and remember that we are punishing the behavior of the student and not the student herself. We have discussed the importance of student input in making rules, but once the rules have been decided upon, students will be reminded that they are to be followed. (Even in our democracy we have rules that we have to follow.) Having said this, remember:

- It is important to deal with any misdemeanors before they become major problems. In order for students to follow rules, they first need to know what the rules are and to understand the consequences of disobeying. Rules need to be posted in a visible area so that students can see them. (Copies should also be run off for students' notebooks and for parents to see.)

- It is important to establish what the sanctions will be for transgressing the rules. Broken rules should have consequences, and those consequences should be known ahead of time by the students. The consequences should be fair and sequential. For example, the first infringement of the rule may be a warning or a conference with the student; the second, a detention; the third, a parent conference; and so on.

- By discussing general classroom procedures as well as the rules, you can avoid unnecessary interruptions in the classroom routine. A tricky but often problematic situation is the use of restroom passes or other passes to leave the room. Assuming your school allows students to use the restrooms during class periods, you may want to have students be responsible for their own use of the pass. You are not trying to control the students' bladder habits, but you do need to ensure that students are not abusing the privilege and leaving the room to visit friends or do some dastardly deed. It is often a good idea to have a system in place where students are limited in the number of times that they can leave the room. This works well in rooms where teachers give bathroom passes that are worth points. Each student is given a certain number of passes per quarter to use without question. If a student has managed to save the passes until the end of the quarter he or she can turn them in for extra credit points or to "buy" treats.

- Another interruption to the class period is that of students who are packing their bags several minutes before the class period is over, and while you are still talking. In most cases it is unnecessary to pack up early and rude to do so.

Certainly, the more rules you have, the more difficult it will be for students to remember all of them unless they are logical and fair. Do your students understand the importance of each of your class rules? Are all of your rules fair and logical?

NOVEMBER 17

ALTHOUGH WE ALL probably agree that students need to learn how to read, write, and compute before they leave school, one of the most, if not *the* most important objective of getting an education is to teach children to become "critical thinkers," able to make appropriate decisions as children and when they are adults. All of us are called upon to make decisions in our lives; some of these decisions are trivial, some come at a moment's notice, and some can actually be life-threatening. To be able to make decisions that will enhance one's life is critical to becoming a mature adult.

We often talk about critical thinking skills in school and make attempts to teach students how to acquire these skills. Being able to analyze possibilities is an important step in critically arriving at an answer.

The following *Teacher Tips* may give your students techniques for becoming thinking students and, in the future, wise adults:

• Teach your students how to organize, using some form of graphic organizers as a study tool. The ability to organize information allows students to categorize data and develop and enhance the relational aspects within subjects, as well as with other subjects.

• Practice difficult situations your students may encounter. Teach them to say, "No."

• Teach your students to think, arrive at opinions, and support their opinions. Teach them the positive side of emotions and intuition. (If a situation feels wrong, it probably is.) If you have access to a slide projector and art slides, show slides of paintings with the projector timed for intervals of twenty or thirty seconds. While viewing the slides, have students write down their feelings of what they feel the painting brings out emotionally, whether sadness, joy, loneliness, anger, or some other emotion. Students should be able to respond to the question of what it is about that picture or painting that suggests that emotion.

• A similar technique is to show the paintings and ask the students to respond in writing what they believe the artist intended to communicate to the viewer. Ask the students to use descriptive language to communicate the image.

• Our senses can have an influence in our powers to analyze. One activity that requires the use of the five senses is to pass out an object, such as a flower, and ask the students to describe the object through each of their five senses (or as many senses as applicable).

• Last, but certainly not least, the use of "brain teasers" as class openers, or during those times when the lesson runs short and there is time left, gives students an opportunity to dig a little deeper into their minds and think. (Working with another student can add to the enjoyment of this activity.)

ᘯ WHAT ACTIVITIES *would encourage your students to think more deeply today?*

NOVEMBER 18

ACCORDING TO my trusty *Almanac,* the third week of November is American Education Week, designated as such to "honor the public schools of America." Now I have never heard of American Education Week, nor celebrated it, but the *Almanac* does not lie (farmers have depended on it for centuries since Benjamin Franklin's *Poor Richard's Almanac* was launched in 1732. According to the encyclopedia, a British museum actually has an almanac dating from the time of Rameses II, 1292–1225 B.C.).[6]

So let us assume that this really is American Education Week and we are honoring the public schools of America. This requires that we ask the rhetorical education question: What is schooling? What does it do? And what does it look like?

In order to arrive at the answer, we need to keep in mind what schooling is not, that is, it is not a building (noun) but more likely a verb. We are not honoring public schools as buildings. We are honoring what is going on *inside* these buildings we call "schools." And, in actuality then, one could admirably argue that "schooling" could be experienced in places other than schools. (Lawrence Cremin, in his wonderful three-volume series *American Education*, has a well-written argument that newspapers, museums, libraries, and other media have been an important part of our educational heritage.)

(And by the way, thank you for being a part of the schooling process of our young people—this week honors you, too!)

So, HOW DO YOU *answer the question(s)? What is school(ing)? What does it do? What does it look like? And then ask yourself, "Is it me?"*

NOVEMBER 19

AS MENTIONED EARLIER, students are better able to follow rules and procedures when they understand that there is a purpose for the rule or procedure. But, in addition to knowing the purpose, it is also important for the student to know exactly how these rules and procedures are going to be interpreted. An understood rule informs everyone that there is no question of how the function should be carried out. No matter what age group you teach, to limit the unnecessary discussion of whether a rule was infringed on or not at a later date, it is best to visibly show the students how you want procedures accomplished and what you want. This is true for classroom procedures, too.

For example, a teacher may want his or her students to return their scissors or microscopes to a specific area, but also want them lined up so that they all fit in the cabinet and not be thrown on top. The teacher most likely will want the students to carry the scissors or microscopes in a certain way to protect themselves, those around them, and the equipment. The best way to teach your students the procedures you want them to follow is to show them the correct way to do so. Students can watch the teacher carefully picking up the equipment, keeping the points of the scissors down, or possibly placing one hand underneath the microscope, while the other hand holds on to it. This way there is no question as to how the procedure is done, and the students and the equipment are safe (or at least safer).

Your reason for asking students to make the rules of the classroom is very similar to your reason for wanting procedures to be clear. Prior to the activity of democratically writing rules, students can be told that rules are made to protect three things: themselves, those around them, and the school's equipment. When making rules, have the students ask themselves, "What rules protect me, or others (both physically, such as no running in the room, and emotionally, such as no put-downs) and the equipment (such as returning it to its proper home)?"

⠀ Do you have *a class rule that students seem to misunderstand or violate often? Could your students understand the rule better if it was visually presented to them?*

123

NOVEMBER 20

WHEN HELPING STUDENTS learn new information, it is often easy for the teacher to get discouraged. How many times have you thought that you covered the information in detail, maybe you were even proud of the assignments that you had made, and the students continued to do poorly on the examinations? After all of your hard work, they still did not "get it."

It is important to remember that your students may know the information, but may not understand the question that you are asking. (Isn't that certainly one of the problems with standardized tests?) If students are not familiar with the method used for testing (for example, how to write an essay test answer when their experience is with filling in the blanks) or how you wanted the work shown, or the essay developed, or how many reasons you wanted written in an explanation, then how can they be expected to do well on the exam? As in writing everyday assignments, students can benefit by being given hints (rubrics) as to *how* you want the question answered.

A second suggestion for helping students successfully learn material, and therefore complete tests, is to plan lessons that reach all learning types. It comes as no surprise to hear that we are not all the same. Some of us learn better visually, some auditorily, and some kinesthetically (to name only three types of learning). Plan your lessons to reach all of your students by developing lessons that reach all types of learners.

And last, remember that "learning is an ongoing process, not a product." Learning is not an "all or nothing" situation. It is best described as being on a continuum. It is the teacher's responsibility to find out where the students fall on the learning continuum of the subject that is being taught.

When you look at the last unit you taught to your students, where do you think they fell on the continuum? Were most of them far enough along to continue on to a new topic, or would it have been better if you remained with the old topic for a little while longer? Would you have reached more students if you had taught the lesson to reached a variety of learning styles?

NOVEMBER 21

THE IDEA OF EDUCATION being focused toward the possible future needs rather than the present needs of the students is not new. Educators have debated, no, argued, for over a century on whether the purpose of schooling should be to teach students what they need to know now (such as reading, writing, or computing), or whether a child's education should include those skills necessary to be competitive in the adult work world (such as punctuality or vocational trade skills) at a later date.

Robert M. Hutchins, who served as the president of the University of Chicago, believed that the answer to this question was "Neither." "The ideal education is not an *ad hoc* education," he wrote nearly four decades ago, "not an education directed to immediate needs; it is not a specialized education, or a preprofessional education; it is not a utilitarian education." But what is important is that young people are given "an education calculated to develop the mind."

Hutchins added, that although he was "in favor of the three R's and the liberal arts . . . trying to understand the greatest works that the human race has produced," and that he believed "that these are necessities," students also need to be given "the intellectual tools that are needed to understand the ideas and the ideals of our world."7

Teachers are going to be influenced by their own beliefs about what students need, and they are going to teach their students according to those beliefs. If a teacher feels that it is important for students to understand the basic skills necessary for the lives they are living today, then lesson plans will focus on those basic skills. On the other hand, the teacher who believes that it is important to prepare students for the future will include information that will help students with making later choices.

Hutchins may have been correct when he said that the answer was "Neither." But maybe the correct answer is that it is really "Both." Students need to be taught fundamental skills for today, sprinkled with important information for tomorrow. And, in all areas, to *think*.

ᗞ DO YOU TEACH *your students for today or tomorrow (or both)? Do you teach them to think?*

NOVEMBER 22

EVERY YEAR, on this date, the question is asked, "Do you recall where you were and what you were doing when you heard the news that President Kennedy was shot?" And yearly, people reminisce on the event that impacted so many lives. But, as years go by the percentage of people doing the reminiscing gets smaller and that of those who were not yet born in 1963 continues to grow. John Kennedy, thirty-fifth president of the United States, was shot and died on November 22, 1963. And in order to remember what one was doing on that fateful day, the individual doing the reminiscing would have to be nearly forty years old or older.

Your students do not have recall of the same events that have impacted your life as a young person. This came to light for me a

November

few years ago when, in an attempt to use the Vietnam War (excuse me, "Conflict") as an example to students in order to make a long-forgotten point, the example went right over their heads. They had not been alive at the time of the Vietnam War, they could not understand the conflict the nation was in, or the heightened feelings of those of us who were young, or what we had felt during the time. It was at that moment, that it made sense to me that this must have been what my parents felt when discussing World War II with their children. We could not understand the seriousness or the sacrifices that they had been called upon to make at that time.

But, what is important is that, although your students do not have the same recollections of crisis events that have impacted our lives as we do, they have their own examples to draw upon. A situation such as the Gulf War may have been less traumatic for those of us who are older because we had lived through similar situations earlier and survived. These same situations may have been very stressful for our students, who may have had family members—brothers, sisters, mothers, or fathers—who were serving in the military in dangerous areas.

Similarly, what may appear to the teacher as a trivial daily situation (such as a student who felt that you treated them unjustly) may be embedded in the student's mind for decades to come. Remembering this reminds us that our relationships with our students can be very fragile. To ensure that we make lasting positive memories, it is important to be, as the Zen practitioners remind us, "awake and aware" of the way that we treat others.

☙ DID ANY SITUATION *occur today between you and a student that might be remembered by him or her for years to come? Was it positive? If so, why? If it was negative, how could it have been turned into a positive experience?*

NOVEMBER 23

ROBERT HUTCHINS, like John Dewey, also wrote not only about the needs of students, but of the importance of recognizing that the school is a part of the community in which it exists, and that the school system must be responsive to the community's desires. Hutchins wrote, in 1968, that, "no educational system can escape from the political community in which it operates. . . . The system must reflect what the political community wants it to do."

He added, however, that although the educational system can be instrumental in a change for the betterment of the society, "the system can set out formally to change the community only if the community includes change of this kind among its aims."[8]

An educational question (similar to what came first, the chicken or the egg) has long been, "Who is in charge?" Who decides what children should learn? Should society direct the school or should the school teach children to better society? So we leave today with you making the decision.

○ SHOULD SOCIETY *have a say in schools and/or should schools have a say in society?*

NOVEMBER 24

A DEAR FRIEND sent a joke to me over the Internet this morning. She is a dear friend because we encouraged each other, supported one another, and both survived the doctoral program together. (And anyone who has completed a Ph.D. program knows that it is a *dear* friend who continues to help you through it after you, the candidate, have verbally and emotionally abused, and possibly alienated, family and other friends.)

The joke read, "I went to a bookstore and asked the saleswoman, 'Where's the self-help section?' She said if she told me, it

November

would defeat the purpose!" Think about it. How many times do we make similar comments to our students? We want them to help themselves, but we do not help them learn *how* to help themselves. The difference in the joke and the conversation with the student is that sometimes we are less direct. Instead, the reply to the question sounds like this:

- "I already told you what the assignment was."
- "You figure it out."
- "You weren't listening."
- "Go look it up."

None of this is to imply that we need to do the students' work for them, or make them dependent upon us to learn. But it is important to, in Lev Vygotsky's words, "build a scaffold" for the student to help them to get from one rung of success to the next. Then, only when the students are more sure of themselves, do we gradually take the scaffolding away. Students need to be shown where the "self-help" section is before they can find the answers to their questions, or be expected to. (This will be discussed in more detail later.)

While I was finishing my coursework, my dissertation, and my written and oral exams, my friend was not doing the coursework for me, she was encouraging and supporting me to finish it on my own, and helping me to find answers. I had a safety net to help me if I fell.

ꙫ How can you *build a safety net that will help your students without making them dependent on you?*

November 25

It is interesting that in November, when we celebrate Thanksgiving, and we ensure democracy by voting for our leaders,

129

that an observance called "Religious Liberty Day" also occurs. "Religious Liberty Day" has fallen on November 25 since the 1981 United Nation's declaration of religious liberty became a fundamental right for the people of all nations.

It should come as no surprise to Americans that everyone has the right to worship (or not worship) in whatever form he or she chooses, while citizens of other countries have not experienced the right to practice their religion of choice. Yet, how many of us encourage others to have their own beliefs when that belief is different from our own? How free are we if we do not allow others to have their own beliefs?

Although it is common for schools to practice a separation of church and state, when it comes to school celebrations, it is common practice for many schools to focus on only those holidays of Judeo-Christian origin, alienating students from other countries or whose families practice other forms of worship.

On the other hand, the denial of religion, practiced by schools who forbid Christmas parties and Easter bunnies, and who schedule "Spring Break" coincidentally at Easter time and "Winter Break" between Christmas and New Years, also denies our students opportunities to learn about our own heritage and background.

Schools should not forbid Christmas and Easter, nor should they exclude Hanukkah, Kwanzaa, or Buddha Day. Religion offers beautiful examples of storytelling, moral reasoning, and celebrations of life. Why not allow students to read of the various beliefs of our individual cultures rather than separating the community from the student? Why not allow students to learn about religion by having students research various holidays and having everyone celebrate them on the dates when they occur?

⟫ WHAT CELEBRATIONS *can you think of that would enhance learning and support diversity for your students?*

November

NOVEMBER 26

IN 1789, a Congressional resolution established November 26 as the first national Thanksgiving Day. The original proclamation, made by George Washington, offered thanks for the U.S. Constitution. It was only later that Thanksgiving celebrations grew to include pilgrims, the *Mayflower*, and a religious offering of thanks to God for the blessings that we had received during the previous year. It is also interesting that the original establishment and proclamation of the holiday was actually opposed by the Antifederalist Party, who maintained that Washington's proclamation violated the states' rights.[9]

Although November 26 no longer serves as *the* Thanksgiving Day, nor solely for the offering of thanks for the U.S. Constitution, the last Thursday of November is a day set aside for families to gather, eat (too much) food, and to reflect upon the benefits and freedoms that this document provides. If you have had the good fortune to travel in other countries, you have probably had an opportunity to rejoice in the fact that you are a citizen of this beautiful country. Although it has become common practice in the last four decades to see the negative side of the United States and of those who lead it, it is important to remember that, at least in this country, we have a say, and can voice our dissatisfaction about what we see as being wrong.

Being teachers, we also have the privilege of teaching the next generations of Americans, to ensure that the rights and privileges written in the U.S. Constitution continue for the generations that will follow.

➣ IS YOUR LIST *of things to be thankful for identical to last year's list? Try to think and thank a little deeper this year. What did you add to your list this Thanksgiving?*

131

November 27

When you were making your list of people and things to be thankful for at Thanksgiving time, did you remember to give thanks for the parents and guardians of the students you teach? (What? Am I crazy? Absolutely not!) Sometimes it is difficult to think of parents in a positive way because we may feel, or know for a fact, that they do not support us or our programs. In fact, we may honestly believe that they are our adversaries rather than our friends. And, sometimes they are.

Parents and teachers come to the parent-teacher relationship in much the same way partners join in a marriage—by mutual interest. Both of you have a similar interest in a young person that you are teaching in some way, and you hope that you both want what is best for the child. But, just as in a marriage, each individual party comes into the relationship with a previous life that might bring with it emotional baggage that requires the sympathetic understanding of the other person.

In some cases, you may encounter a parent who has had a negative school experience in their own past or with their child's previous teacher. He or she may be a stepparent who is having difficulty with the child who is your student. Some parents are intimidated by teachers even though they are no longer students themselves.

An important piece of information I often tell my student teachers is that parents can be your greatest cheerleader or your worst nightmare, and whichever it is, is often up to you. Reaching out to the wary or difficult parent may be burdensome, but it may also mean the difference between their subversion or their support.

It is also important to remember that you come to this parent-teacher relationship with baggage from your past, too. You may have had a negative experience with the parent of a former student, or you may sense that a student does not like you and has convinced the parent to feel the same. Whatever the feeling, put it aside, reach out, and see if it makes a difference.

November

⨀ IN WHAT WAYS *can you reach out to your students'*
parents to invite them into your classroom and/or encourage
them to support you?

NOVEMBER 28

THANKSGIVING TIME brings the story of the pilgrims, their
trip on the *Mayflower*, and their subsequent hardships in the new
land to new students every year. Every November, teachers recite
the story of the hungry first European inhabitants of New
England, their encounter with the Indians, replete with the big
meal, turkey, and all of the trimmings, and the generosity of
those natives to our ancestors. Then, what is interesting, and sad,
is that the story changes from the Indians as our friends to the
savages who had to be annihilated or defeated and sent to reservations across the American West.

Thanksgiving may be a good time to continue the story of
Native Americans as people, not savages worthy of extinction.
Continue the Thanksgiving story by discussing their history, their
beliefs, their myths, and their relationship with the land, which is
natural and often quite poetic. One way to help students to understand the history of Native Americans (and other minority cultures) is to have the students draw a time line of the United States
based upon the views of the minority people. Pictures can be
drawn at the appropriate date to mark significant events in both
cultures, which can be followed with a discussion of the dates, focusing on their importance to the minority group. Students can
also discuss the impact of the European Americans on the Native
Americans and vice versa (avoiding the stereotypical good cow-
boy/bad Indian image). The lesson can conclude by discussing the
problems that are faced by Native Americans today.

Often we are taught in history classes to think of America as
a melting pot where various cultures are assimilated into the

133

existing majority culture, when in actuality our nation is better seen as a patchwork quilt where colors maintain their uniqueness, yet are pieced together to create a beautiful covering of warmth and originality.

⚹ DO YOU HAVE any Native American students in your classroom or people in your community who can talk to your students about their beliefs, history, and lives?

NOVEMBER 29

TODAY IS Louisa May Alcott's birthday. Alcott was born on November 29, 1832, in Germantown (now a part of Philadelphia), Pennsylvania, and was brought to Boston, where she grew up. Best known for her novels, *Little Women* and *Little Men*, Alcott published her first book, *Flower Fables*, when she was twenty-two years old. Louisa May Alcott was fortunate to be able to grow up in a family that encouraged learning, supported her, and was surrounded with literary giants, including Ralph Waldo Emerson and Henry David Thoreau. What a life she must have lived!

How many of our students have opportunities to be encircled by encouraging family members who have literary friends? Probably not too many. As teachers, it is part of our job then to become models of learning and encouragers to the young people in our classes. Introducing young people to great works of literature, art, music, and information is an important opportunity to encourage the Louisa May Alcotts of the next century. (And, I might add, it is important to introduce male *and* female artists to our students, so all students will have role models to follow.)

☞ How do you *encourage your students to write, draw, sing, or pursue some other artistic endeavor? If not, how could you?*

November 30

Last, but not least, as November and our theme of democracy and equality comes to a close, it is time to take a look at the silent, undemanding, reposing, or shy student that we all love to have in our classrooms because he or she is quiet, does the assignments without argument, and rarely, if ever, creates any problems for us. And, sadly, they are sometimes the students whose names are forgotten simply because they cause us no grief.

It is easy to lose track of these quiet, good students because they do not raise their voices or make themselves heard. While some of them are quiet because they are mature and do not see the need to make their voices heard, sometimes these young people make no noise because they are students who do not believe in themselves, or they have tried to be heard in the past and been silenced by the insensitive or unintentional but unaware teacher who encouraged their good behavior over their desire to learn. For those quiet students it is important that we teachers give them opportunities to use their voices and encourage them to grow.

There are times, however, when we will encounter one of these quiet students who may be shy, may need your help to find his or her voice, and may have an emotional side, too. These are the students who will allow others to take advantage of them or who will cry when a paper returned to them has a low grade. With these students, it is important that they be allowed to express their emotions and encouraged to feel whatever they are feeling. Being a sensitive person allows the child to appreciate the effort you make to encourage their learning. I know, I was one.

> DO YOU HAVE *any quiet, shy, or sensitive students in your classroom? How can you encourage them to speak out, gain confidence, and feel more self-assured?*

DECEMBER

DECEMBER 1

JOYCE EPSTEIN, a leading researcher on families, communities, schools, children's learning, and parent involvement, writes in her report, *School and Family Partnerships,* that there are six progressive steps by which families get involved in schools. According to Epstein, this involvement, if sought by school personnel, helps fulfill shared responsibilities between the parents and the community for children's learning and development.

The first and most obvious step in this relationship, Epstein writes, is the family's acceptance of their responsibility for providing health, safety, and basic childrearing necessities for their children. The second step affirms the school's responsibility for keeping the parents of their students notified of information that enhances a child's learning or of special activities that are about to take place. In step three, parents are invited to become volunteers at the school site, helping teachers and administrators in the classroom and where needed. In steps four and five, the parents get even more involved in decision making, governance, and advocacy for, and at, the school site (the parents move from minor "token" or "rubber stamp" membership on a committee to an actual leadership or power position for making decisions). The sixth step requires the school to allow an equality of exchange between the school, the parents, the community, and its organizations.[1]

In other words, according to Epstein, parents are encouraged to move from merely providing the basics for their children's well-being to having an active role in the school. Some schools are very open to allowing parents to play decision-making roles, while others are content with parents staying at home.

 ⟫ AT WHAT STEP *are the parents of your students involved? Has anyone at your site encouraged them to become more active?*

December

DECEMBER 2

IN THE PAST several months we have looked at various educators and their views on curriculum." Today we look at Alfred North Whitehead, English mathematician, philosopher, and Harvard professor, who was born in 1861 and died in 1947.

Whitehead wrote in *The Aims of Education* that "pedants sneer at an education which is useful. But if education is not useful, what is it? Is it a talent to be hidden away in a napkin? Of course education should be useful, whatever your aim in life."[2] So if education is to be useful, then the curriculum should give the student information that is useful, right?

The problem with an answer such as this is in deciding what is useful. When I was in high school, shorthand was considered useful, at least for girls, and auto mechanics for boys. Although I never learned shorthand, and I don't know if it would have been helpful in college or elsewhere, I do know that I could have benefited many times from auto mechanics. Today, however, with new cars having more and more computerized parts, one could reasonably argue that this information would not have any modern value. If we teach students today on Apple 2E computers (that is, if the equipment that they are learning on is already obsolete), is that valid?

When I look back at my high school years, I have to say that the two most important classes for me were typing and band. One semester of typing made my college days easier, allowed me to work for a few years as a typist before becoming a teacher, and certainly is valuable to me at this very moment, as I type this book. Why band? Band taught me discipline—"practice makes (almost) perfect"—and gave me friendships that have lasted for decades.

☙ IS THE SUBJECT *you teach useful for your students? If so, how? If not, why not? How can it be made more useful?*

DECEMBER 3

IN SEPTEMBER we discussed the importance of having a classroom that is pleasant, and how various displays around the room can help make the environment colorful and homey. Bulletin boards give us a great opportunity to provide useful information to students while making the room a comfortable place in which to learn. The following *Teacher Tips* from veteran teachers may help you enliven your room with visual information and enhance learning:

• Keep your bulletin boards up to date. If you have had the same bulletin boards up since September, it is time to change them. Carefully take down your old displays and pack them away for another time. It is time to go up with the new!

• Designate one bulletin board for your students' achievements, such as sports, arts, and awards won in activities they participate in outside of your classroom. Encourage students to bring in newspaper articles and information about awards that they have won.

• Display student work on bulletin boards so students can see what quality work looks like. This will also create a sense of pride for the work that each student has completed.

• Some teachers keep a special bulletin board for students with baby pictures and current pictures of each student. They call it a "Look How Far We Have Come" board.

• Be sure to include displays that are relevant to the current subject and that may clarify learning for your students. For example, pictures of world leaders you are studying, or the theater at Avon if you are studying Shakespeare. And remember to get your students involved in the displays. If you do not have access to pictures, ask your students to try to find them or draw them. (I once asked my master's degree students to help me find a large picture of John Dewey for a display, and one did!)

◈ WHAT WILL YOU *be studying this month? How can you make a display that is relevant?*

DECEMBER 4

BOY, OH BOY, what would December be without food? I think that if a poll were taken about which month had the most food eaten, or the most activities that focused around food, December would win, hands down, for obvious reasons—the holidays.

Food is an important part of our lives. We cannot live without it. But it is also a very social part of our lives. My friends generally do not call to ask me to go for a walk, bike riding, roller skating, to the library, or anywhere else that requires physical work, but they do call several times a week to ask me if I can go to lunch with them. If your home is like mine, family members are more likely to come to visit on weekends if there is a cookout or special festivity to celebrate. Again, food is an important part of our lives.

Food is fun in the classroom, too. One method of studying other countries or diversity is to ask students to research and discuss the mealtime habits of other countries. How does the structure of the country's meals influence its lifestyle in general? (For example, what is the purpose of a siesta after lunch?) How does a country's climate and geography affect the foods grown, or the economy? Why not bring different foods to class, or ask students to bring foods to sample? The many times I tried this in my classroom, I was amazed at the number of students who had never tasted lettuce (and this was in high school!). What about kiwi, papaya, or bok choy?

One of the best food lessons I can recall happened when a quiet, lonely, special needs student had her mother make gumbo for her classmates. Not only was this a new food for most of these California kids, it also made a special experience for this lovely young lady. I think she gained some friends from that lesson. She certainly had a smile on her face for the rest of the classtime.

Who doesn't like food?

꙰ How can *the incorporation of food into your subject make it fun?*

December 5

Studying cooking and food can be further used during this time of year to enhance the learning experience of your students. Have students compile a recipe book with the foods they bring in to share or study from a country or culture other than ours. Note how other cultures gain nutrients from the basic four food groups in a manner different from our own. You may also want to discuss what American foods come from other cultures (spaghetti, pizza, stir-fry, et cetera). You could also include a discussion on the ingredients and methods used to cook these foods. How do they differ from the American way of cooking? How are they alike? Sample some of these foods.

Copies of the cookbook your students compile, decorate, and bind can be given as gifts for the holidays celebrated this month or used as a fund-raiser to buy supplies for the classroom. This is a great project for the computer and, while you are at it, have your students use a greeting card program to make cards for the gift.

꙰ How can *the study of foods be further used in your classroom?*

DECEMBER 6

SOMETIMES IT'S EASY to forget, but it is important to remember that you teach *students,* not a subject. As their teacher, you have the responsibility of determining what students need to know in order to become successful, functioning adults; imparting this knowledge may be more important than teaching a mathematical theorem or a foreign language. In other words, don't be afraid to let real life into the classroom once in a while—for this is where your students will get a glimpse of why they are in school.

What students need to know to be successful is often best taught by example. The following *Teacher Tips* may help you in this role as a mentor to your students:

• When someone goes out of their way for you (or even if it is not out of their way) by doing something nice or helping you in some way, be sure to send a thank-you note to them stating how much you appreciated what they did.

• Genuinely love all students. Even the youngest students can tell if you do and more important, if you do not.

• Reassure all students that they are bright, capable, and important individuals in your life. (After all, they are. Without them you are unemployed.)

꙳ HOW CAN YOU *make your classroom more "real" for your students?*

DECEMBER 7

WHEN MANY PEOPLE think of December 7, they think of that day in 1941 when Pearl Harbor was bombed by the Japanese, catapulting the United States into World War II. A vacation in the

143

beautiful state of Hawaii is not complete without a visit to the Pearl Harbor monument, which includes a boat ride to the ships that were sunk so many years ago. Anyone who has been to the monument built to honor those who died leaves solemnly. The visit is a memorable experience: you cannot soon forget looking into that clear water, seeing the submerged battleships covered with seaweed and beautiful fish. It makes teachers wish that they could educate their students with whatever information was necessary so that there would be no more need for war.

Nineteen vessels were either sunk or severely destroyed in the harbor on that fateful Sunday in 1941. Over 2,390 people lost their lives, an additional 1,350-plus were wounded, and 960 individuals were missing. Is there no better reason to do away with war?

⸮ DO YOU EVER *teach the subject of war to your students? What do you say? Is it possible to teach peace?*

DECEMBER 8

DO YOU HAVE SOMEONE in your life, or someone you know who is a good person, nice to know, and almost too good to be true? I do. My husband Paul and I met when we were in high school, a very long time ago. I was lucky to have met someone at a very young age and luckier still that our marriage has worked out so well. Today's *Teacher Tips* focus on what it takes to be a really nice person to your peers:

• Be willing to say, "I am sorry," or, "I was mistaken," when you have made a mistake or hurt someone, whether a student or another staff member. Even if you feel that the other person was equally or even more at fault than you, get over it and get back to business.

- Get to know the personnel at your school and in your district, such as your secretary, clerks, aides, custodians, and maintenance people. These people provide a major service in helping your day run smoothly, and often on a much smaller salary than yours. If you are nice to them, they are more likely to help you when you have special needs. Tell them how important they are to you and your students.

- Be fair and supportive of your administrators; their jobs are not always easy either.

- Greet your classes with a loud cheerful "Good morning," or "Good afternoon," and see if the students respond with a return greeting in a loud cheerful manner. Stand at the door between class periods to say hello to each child individually as he or she enters.

- Respect other teachers and staff members. Do not discuss your peers with the students nor allow your students to malign a staff member. (Remember that teaching is not a popularity contest.)

- Invite parents to visit your classroom as often as possible. Make parents partners in the education of their children.

One of the many positive attributes of my husband, and one that I could benefit from developing, is his extreme friendliness to everyone. Nobody is a stranger. The result is that he is well liked everywhere he goes.

❧ ARE YOU *a friendly person? Can you be friendlier?*

DECEMBER 9

IN DECEMBER in most schools around the nation, the theme for the month is Christmas, even though some of our students, and maybe their teachers, celebrate different December holidays.

The month of December is the ideal time for students to discover how different cultures and religions celebrate the season and to learn the origins of the various holidays. Even within Christianity there are a variety of ways (and dates) to celebrate the Christmas holiday.

A good lesson for this month may be to allow students to work singly or within groups to research a holiday that they have selected, allowing each group to present their report in some interesting, creative fashion (story, play, video, and so on). The grand finale can be to celebrate the reported holidays on their dates. Holidays may include (but are not limited to): Hanukkah, Christmas, Kwanzaa, Ramadan, and others. (Maybe your students can recommend more December holidays.)

⟫ WHAT OTHER *holidays are observed in December?*

DECEMBER 10

ARTICLE 26 of the Universal Declaration of Human Rights was adopted by the United Nations General Assembly on December 10, 1948. Although this document is over a half-century old, we should note that the rights have not changed. The document reads:

(1) Everyone has the right to education. Education shall be free, at least in the elementary and fundamental stages. Elementary education shall be compulsory. Technical and professional education shall be made generally available and higher education shall be equally accessible to all on the basis of merit.

(2) Education shall be directed to the full development of the human personality and to the strengthening of respect for human rights and fundamental freedoms. It shall promote

understanding, tolerance and friendship among all nations, racial or religious groups, and shall further the activities of the United Nations for the maintenance of peace.

(3) Parents have a prior right to choose the kind of education that shall be given to their children.[3]

Not only is education "free" and a "right," it is compulsory. Education is also for "the full development of the human personality." Young people, who are required to sit in classrooms for a good share of the day, have the "right" to be educated and developed. Often precious minutes are consumed by tasks that do not enhance learning.

---

೨ Do you make *the most of the time you are allotted with your students?*

December 11

On December 11, 1946, the United Nations Children's Fund, or UNICEF, was founded as a part of the United Nations Economic and Social Council to provide for the well-being of children throughout the world. On October 25 we looked at some of the materials the Fund provides. But what else does it do for children?

For openers, UNICEF provides food and supplies to underprivileged families around the world. Although we know that some children in our country are nutritionally and emotionally deprived, children in some parts of the world suffer extreme deprivations that are unthinkable in our culture. Perhaps having your students "adopt" a child from another country through a reputable organization may make a meaningful lesson. What better time of year to give to the less fortunate than at Christmas time?

147

❧ WHAT ELSE *does UNICEF provide to the children of the world?*

DECEMBER 12

FOR SOME PEOPLE, the Christmas season can be a depressing time, especially for those who are lonely, who have no family or close friends, or who have suffered a severe loss, such as the death of a loved one or the loss of a job. For others, ourselves included, the hustle and bustle of the holidays may be overwhelming, as we try to do too much for too many people, trying to make the holiday celebration too large. It is easy to get depressed because we eat too much, experience too much excitement, and then feel a letdown after Christmas is over.

But both problems—suffering a loss or feeling let down—can be solved by putting the two together. Maybe the holiday celebration needs to be smaller, cost less, and thereby be much more enjoyable. Try to give the best gift possible to others—the gift of yourself, and the gift of your time. And, if you can, find some time for those who have real problems in their lives.

Let's not let the hustle of the season overwhelm us again this year. Sit back, meditate, enjoy the time, and especially enjoy the time off.

❧ ARE THERE SOME PEOPLE *whom you know who are less fortunate than you are, or who are going through a crisis in their lives? What can you do to help? What can you give up in your own celebration to have more time for them?*

December 13

HAVE YOU BEEN LOOKING for the *perfect* gifts for those around you? Christmas, Hanukkah, and other gift-giving December holidays often tax our patience as we try to find the best gifts for the people who we care about. But there are many appreciative ways to tell a person that you care about them without spending a lot of money and time driving from shopping mall to department store to find that certain "something."

The following *Gift-Giving Tips* from veteran gift-givers may help make your shopping (and holiday season) easier:

- Give the gift of baby-sitting. One year when my children were very small, my mother-in-law gave us a coupon book agreeing to watch our children one weekend a month. What a great gift for a busy mother and father!

- Agree to do typing, filing, or substitute teach for a friend on your prep period, or do bus duty for a coworker. One principal I worked with (not *for*) at an elementary school agreed to take each of her teachers' classes for an afternoon on the teacher's birthday. I took that afternoon to have lunch and a special activity with one of my children, a "gift" for both of us.

- When you cook a casserole, make two. Save one for yourself and freeze the other to give to another harried coworker so she (or he) can get her (or his) shopping done, too.

- Give tutoring coupons to friends, agreeing to help their children with their studies.

- Take someone to lunch. At the university where I work, my close associates and I take each other out to lunch on various celebrations, not as a group, but one on one, for undivided attention. (Sometimes a birthday can get you two weeks of free lunches!)

- Give the gift of time. The gift I would appreciate most from my friends is a walk through a park, on a hiking trail, or through a botanical garden, and conversation. Time is so valuable for all of us; it is truly a gift to share it with another.

149

꩜ THERE ARE MANY WAYS *that we can give the gift of ourselves to others. What gifts can you give to those closest to you?*

DECEMBER 14

ON DECEMBER 14, 1774, Paul Revere gave a special gift to his countrymen and women. By making his famous "ride," he warned a group of Massachusetts militiamen, led by Major John Sullivan, of the British plan to station troops at Portsmouth, New Hampshire. Thus warned, the militiamen were able successfully to attack the arsenal at Fort William and Mary, capturing arms and ammunition without the loss of any lives. Paul Revere's act was a selfless gift to many who were unknown to him.[4]

We, too, can give to many who are unknown to us, and in a much less dangerous way. Giving to the homeless, used clothes to various charities, and your own blood to a hospital or blood drive can be an inexpensive and very much needed gift to the less fortunate. But, since many people give at this time of year, how about making a coupon for yourself, promising to donate at some other, less charitable time of the year, and tucking it away in a calendar?.

Do not forget to give to yourself, too.

꩜ WHAT CAN YOU *give to the less fortunate?*

DECEMBER 15

ON THIS DATE IN 1791, the United States government ratified the Bill of Rights, causing the first ten amendments to the United States Constitution to go into effect. These ten amendments, to which seventeen were added throughout the two subsequent centuries, gave Americans the freedoms of speech and press and the right to bear arms, along with other freedoms that we take for granted. I know there are times that we feel that the document is not perfect, such as when children bring guns to school, and pornography floods the Internet, but would we want any of our rights to be taken away from us? For a document to be over two hundred years old and still so fresh and up to date is nothing less than amazing!

Many of your students may not have had access to information concerning the Bill of Rights, yet they should know about the privileges that it protects.

⊃⟫ HOW CAN YOU *teach young people about the Bill of Rights?*

DECEMBER 16

BOY, DECEMBER JUST SEEMS to be the month for early American history parties. We already looked at Paul Revere's ride and the party "given to the British soldiers at Portsmouth," then we celebrated the ratification of the Bill of Rights. Now, for another "revolutionary" December party:

On December 16, 1773, in Boston, Massachusetts, a group of revolutionary activists, in what became known as the "Boston Tea Party," dumped 342 casks of tea off a ship and into Boston Harbor. Prior to the party, approximately eight thousand Bostonians had met in Old South Church to hear Samuel Adams, chairman of the gathering, receive the news that Massachusetts Governor Hutchinson would not allow the ships to leave the harbor without the payment of duty on the tea. During the night, a group of activists disguised as Mohawk Indians boarded the tea ships, and the rest is history.[5]

American history is filled with stories of courageous individuals such as the "partygoers" of the Boston Tea Party. To celebrate this significant event, let's raise a cup of tea to those brave individuals.

⟫ WHAT OTHER *"parties" were given for our benefit? What parties can or do we give for the benefit of others?*

DECEMBER 17

AT SOME TIME during the month of December (depending on the year), Hanukkah will be celebrated by Jewish people throughout the world. The first day of Hanukkah is the Festival of Lights instituted by Judas Maccabaeus in 156 B.C. to celebrate the purification of the Temple of Jerusalem, which had been desecrated by Antiochus Epiphanes three years earlier. On the first day of Hanukkah, in Jewish homes throughout the world, a candle is lit, and others lighted on each successive night of the eight-day festival.

To all of our Jewish friends, teachers, and students, Happy Hanukkah!

⟫ HOW CAN YOU TEACH *the celebration of Hanukkah to your students? What will be your key point in doing so?*

DECEMBER 18

OK, SO YOU are still working too hard for the season. Not only do you have to do shopping, decorating, cooking, wrapping, and partygoing, you are a teacher, which means holiday plays, presentations, and gift exchanges at school, and the shutting down of your classroom for the end-of-the-year vacation. Then, if you are really organized (compulsive?) you will have your room decorated for January before you leave for the winter break.

If I have not talked you into slowing down yet, here is my last attempt. Calming the hectic pace of the holidays can be done with a little Zen practice. Do all of the things that you have to do, but take a moment during each day to stop, relax, breathe, and focus on something else (entirely) than what you are doing or have to do. If you find it helpful, meditate, stare at a candle, listen to peaceful music, close your eyes, put up your feet, soak in the bathtub, or better yet, do all six!

Oh, and be sure to eat healthy food in between parties.

🔊 WHAT WOULD SEEM *peaceful to do right now? Can you do it right now?*

DECEMBER 19

ONE OF MY FAVORITE POEMS is Robert Frost's "Stopping by Woods on a Snowy Evening." Do you know it? Do you have parts of it in your memory? In his poem, Frost writes about stopping in the woods one evening and watching it "fill up with snow," but unfortunately he is called away because he has, "promises to keep . . . and miles to go. . . ."[6]

I love this poem and think of it often during the holiday season, especially if it is snowing outside. When you read it, especially aloud, you can almost feel the snow falling peacefully, covering the ground in a landscape of white. When I was a student in junior high school, a very bright teacher gave us the opportunity of a lifetime—taking us to hear Robert Frost recite his poems shortly before his death in 1963. Many audio bookstores

153

carry cassettes of authors reading their own poems. This poem is on one of them.

Maybe your students could draw, or act, or in some other form benefit from hearing this poem.

❧ DO YOU HAVE TIME *to play this poem, or others, for your students? Is someone appearing locally who may offer your students a golden opportunity if you make arrangements for them to see him or her?*

DECEMBER 20

THE HOLIDAY SEASON offers so many opportunities to read or hear meaningful stories in the classroom. One of my favorite Christmas time stories is O. Henry's *The Gift of the Magi*. Earlier I discussed the junior high teacher who read great works to us on a regular basis. Often he read works by O. Henry and James Thurber.

The Gift of the Magi is the story of two young newlyweds who have no money to buy gifts for each other at Christmas, and each sacrifices their most valuable possession to buy a gift for the other. She cuts her beautiful long hair to buy a watch fob for her husband, and he sells the watch to buy combs for her beautiful long hair.

Giving, not receiving, is what the season is about, and this is a beautiful story to teach that.

❧ WHAT OTHER STORIES *of the season have worthy morals for young people? Have you read any of these classic stories lately?*

December

December 21

No doubt about it, winter is a long, cold time. Even in what we consider to be the warm states, like Hawaii and those in the Southwest, winter can be a cold and wet time of year. The school year seems to get quite long during the winter months. The days become shorter. Some of us leave for work when it is dark and arrive home shortly before the sun sets. Most of our home time is spent with the lights on and the doors closed.

"Where is the sunshine?" we ask. And although the days seem shorter and shorter, they are actually lengthening, minute by minute, day by day. Longer days are coming, however slowly it seems. Just like learning. Sometimes it is minute by minute, sometimes day by day, but nonetheless, it is there. Minute by minute your students are growing daily. Sometimes, like the extending of daylight hours as spring nears, we don't see it happening, and at other times we do. Sometimes it seems to suddenly appear. Then we ask ourselves, "How did it get so light?" "When did the light appear?" "When did the light go on?"

꙾ Do you see growth *in your students? Have you looked for it?*

December 22

On December 19, we read Robert Frost's poem, "Stopping by Woods on a Snowy Evening," about an individual on a sojourn into a wooded area that was owned by someone else, how beautiful the walk was, and how (reluctantly) the individual convinced himself to move on and take care of important tasks.

Have you ever walked in a wooded area on a snowy evening? I may be living in California now, but I grew up in the cold

Midwest and remember with fondness the many times I trekked through snow, sometimes without any specific place to go. If you have lived in a cold part of the country, you know that there are different kinds of snow: the wet snow that clings and chills, and the dry crunchy snow that makes your nose and throat hurt when you breathe too deeply if your face is uncovered. There are also some times when the snow falling is more appreciated than other times. It makes a difference if you are waking up to a heavy snowfall, cleaning off the car to drive to work, or running out in the first heavy snow flurries of the year in the middle of the night.

DURING THIS BUSY SEASON, *take time to see, feel, and taste the snow. When was the last time you made a snow angel?*

DECEMBER 23

REMEMBER THE SONG, "The Twelve Days of Christmas," or Clement Moore's poem that begins, "'Twas the night before Christmas . . . ?" Who doesn't know this famous song and poem that we hear again and again through the holiday season?

As a child, did you and your friends spend hours making up your own renditions of these two holiday works? I still remember the version we had of "The Twelve Days of Christmas." We would draw out, "F-i-i-ve tubeless tires!" and roll around in shrieks of laughter. We were so clever, and funny (or so we thought).

Your students can have fun, too, creating their own versions of either of these two pieces. They could even make it relevant to the subject that you teach. (For example: "'Twas the night before Christmas and all through the lab. . . .") Why not give it a whirl?

December

֍ DID YOU MAKE *your own version of either of these two holiday pieces? If so, can you remember how it went?*

DECEMBER 24

YOU ARE PROBABLY on vacation by now, at least from school, but have you settled down from the hustle of the season? Are you ready for tomorrow?

For me, one of the most peacefully quiet and calming traditions of the season is to take time on Christmas Eve for candlelight services at a local church. I never seem to tire of this ritual, and I look forward to it every year: driving in the dark, joyfully greeting everyone, friend and stranger, with a sincere, "Merry Christmas," the lighting of candles, the singing of carols from memory, and the quiet procession out of the church into the cool, starry night.

Whether we are able to attend these services or not, we have always taken a nice walk after dinner, out in the fresh air for one last look at the Christmas lights, decorations, and the stars twinkling down on us.

֍ DO YOU HAVE *a calming ritual to end the harried season? If not, can you think of one?*

DECEMBER 25

IT IS HERE, one of the most, if not *the* most, popular holiday of the year in our country—Christmas! Whew! I hope that you are spending the day with your family and friends, even if you do not celebrate the holiday. And the good news is, you probably

157

still have some days off between now and the new year before you go back to work.

If you had a good, peaceful month, and you managed to escape the stress of the season, you may want to make a mental note for next year of how (and why) you did it. If you did not escape it, you may want to make a note of why not, and think about what you will do differently next time.

I hope Santa was good to you! And Merry Christmas!

☞ IF YOU FOUND *the holidays stressful (again), what will you do differently next year? (Write your suggestions down and tape them on the December page of your new year calendar.)*

DECEMBER 26

KWANZAA IS CELEBRATED from December 26 through January 1, and is a seven-day celebration of African American values and traditions and continued vitality. In Kiswahili, *Kwanzaa* means "first fruits of the harvest."

December 26 is also a celebration in England, Canada, and other Commonwealth countries. Boxing Day is celebrated on the first day following Christmas and was named for the Christmas boxes given to postmen, errand boys, and others who deliver packages.

So many holidays! So many events to celebrate in December!

☞ HAVE YOU EVER *celebrated holidays other than your own? Wouldn't it be fun to surprise everyone with a Kwanzaa feast or a special Boxing Day box?*

December

DECEMBER 27

IT'S OVER: CHRISTMAS, the preparation for the holidays, the excitement. Time to relax, and reevaluate. Was it worth it? All of the shopping, wrapping, cooking, celebrating, visiting, and partying? I hope so.

But today might be a good day to sit back, put your feet up, put some relaxing music on the stereo, and watch the kids play. It might even be a good day to sit down with that book you have been wanting to read. Does that seem selfish? So what, you deserve it! It may be just what is necessary to revitalize your energy and your physical and mental well-being.

Whatever you choose, enjoy!

---

๑ WHAT (APPARENTLY SELFISH) ACTIVITY *can you do today to revitalize your energy and make all of the previous activity seem worthwhile?*

DECEMBER 28

YOU THOUGHT we were finished with the Christmas season, didn't you? No, sorry, you don't see the lights down yet, do you? There is one last particular that we need to tidy up before we leave this topic and move into the new year.

I hope that you have enjoyed the season, and that you have rested and are beginning to feel your old self again. Now is the time to answer the question of how you can make the celebration of the spirit of Christmas last all year. Now, don't panic, I did not say, "make Christmas last all year." We are simply talking about celebrating the *spirit* of Christmas all year. The wonderful *giving* spirit should not be brought out at just one time of the year (or on schedule in December). It is a spirit that is necessary the rest of the year, too.

159

❧ How can you *make the spirit of Christmas last all year?*

December 29

Have you taken down the lights and decorations? Is everything packed and stored for the year? It seems like most people enjoy the decorating for the season so much more than the tearing down of the ornaments and other seasonal symbols. At least that is true at my house. Decorating the tree and the house is a family event; everyone has their job, it goes smoothly, and the decorating ends in a celebration (more food). My husband levels the tree and arranges the Dickens' Village and Bedford Falls structures. The tall sons string the lights, hang the upper ornaments, and place the angel on top, and my mother-in-law loves to put the icicles on "correctly" (one at a time). My job is to get the ornaments out of their boxes and decorate the rest of the house with seasonal items.

But, when it's time for the tree to be taken down, everybody seems to be much too busy to get involved. Where is everybody? I un-decorate the tree and the house by myself. Fortunately I don't mind, because I do enjoy getting the house back to its "rest of the year" look.

Putting Christmas stuff away can also be a good time for cleaning out those items that you have not used and only think of when you are trying to find room for the Christmas boxes in your storage areas.

❧ Can you *eliminate any clutter in your storage area?*

December

DECEMBER 30

LAUREL AND DANIEL TANNER, in their classic textbook, *Curriculum Development: Theory into Practice*, write in detail about the beliefs of major educational theorists throughout the nineteenth and twentieth centuries who attempted to answer the questions of "What knowledge is of most worth?" and "What ought the curriculum be?" The Tanners conclude with their own answers to those questions. They write, "In effect, the school curriculum is presumably designed not only to inculcate each member of the rising generation in the best elements of knowledge, systematically organized or codified since the dawn of civilization, but to enable each member of the rising generation to utilize that knowledge to improve the life of the individual and the life of society." In a vein similar to John Dewey's, the Tanners write that education is for the continuance of society as well as for the individual receiving the education. "From such a definition of education," the authors give the following definition of what the curriculum should be: "that *reconstruction of knowledge and experience that enables the learner to grow in exercising intelligent control of subsequent knowledge and experience.*"[7]

ॐ HAVE YOU THOUGHT ABOUT *whether you are providing your students with the knowledge and experience that will enable them to "grow in exercising intelligent control of subsequent knowledge and experience?"*

DECEMBER 31

FOR MANY PEOPLE, New Year's Eve is a time for reflection, when we look at the year that has passed, where we were, how far we have come, and what has happened to us. Newspapers and television programs spend several days at the end of the year writing and talking about what happened in the previous year, who married, gave birth, died, won sporting events, won elections, and so forth.

Thinking about the past, the future, and the present is what reflective practice is all about. Yet we relegate it to one day a year. Why not resolve to practice reflective thinking all year long?

☟ WHAT ARE YOUR HOPES *and dreams for the new year? (No fair including diets and breaking bad habits.) What do you hope to accomplish in your classroom? How do you plan to do that?*

JANUARY

JANUARY 1

NEW YEAR'S DAY. Happy New Year! A new day, a new year, a new beginning. Isn't it a wonderful feeling, New Year's Day? Having reflected on the old year last night, today we can start fresh with an opportunity to create a year (a life) all over again.

If you are like most people, you have made a list of things you are determined to accomplish (this time). Maybe your list includes losing weight, quitting a bad habit (such as smoking, biting your nails, not allowing yourself enough time to get ready in the morning, or keeping up with grading papers), or being more patient with those around you.

Like most people, I make New Year's resolutions, too. However, unlike in earlier years, I have found that as I get older the list of New Year's resolutions is getting shorter. Having a shorter list does not mean that I accomplish all my goals each year and scratch them off the list, or that I have few areas of my life that need changing. But rather, as I get older, I know which goals are reachable for me and which are not. It does not mean that the goals I forego are impossible to reach; it only means that I have learned that I simply do not wish to expend the effort it would take to accomplish some resolutions.

I have learned that the problem with resolutions that remain unfulfilled is that they go into a garbage bin in my head marked "failure . . . again!"

So the solution, as I see it, is twofold: 1) Only set goals that are most likely achievable; and 2) make each day what it really is. That is, each day is a new year, open to possibilities, and opportunities to fulfill *daily* goals. Ask yourself, "What New Year's resolution can I accomplish on this New Year's Day?

In 1900, in a speech before the National Education Association's (NEA) Department of Superintendence, Nicholas Murray Butler, then president of Columbia University, spoke, saying, "The skies do not change when a century is ushered in, or the thunders roll when it passes out. . . . Imagination however, gives to the century an objective reality and feeling welds our thoughts to it. We do well to resign ourselves to the spell of these creations and learn . . . to know our centuries."[1]

For many of us, January 1, New Year's Day, is the beginning of a new year, complete with the possibilities of new challenges, new successes, new hopes, and perhaps a list of resolutions which may or may not be accomplished. However, it is, in reality, only the day after December 31 and the day before January 2. What is more important is that the similarity of January 1 (even when it ushers in a new century) to every other day is not that it diminishes the potential of that day, but rather it reminds us of the importance of celebrating that the other 364 days are equally pregnant with the possibilities of challenges, successes, hopes, and fulfilled promises.

What successes will this year bring for you and your students?

❧ LOGICAL QUESTION *for the day, isn't it? What New Year's resolution can you accomplish on this New Year's Day?*

JANUARY 2

ALTHOUGH WE TALKED about getting organized in August, the new year just seems to lend itself to the topic of organization, doesn't it? We think of organizing as a New Year's (possible) resolution; now that you have had a few months in the classroom with these students, you may be finding that things are not working out as well as you had originally hoped, and a change in organization (what we call in teaching, "tweaking") may be just what you need to get the new year rolling.

One of the biggest time-wasting, albeit necessary, tasks for teachers is taking roll. Now, I am not going to tell you not to take attendance; I am telling you not to *waste* time taking roll. Unless your school administration requires attendance to be turned in each period, attendance does not need to be taken the minute the

165

bell rings. Get the lesson going, then take roll. There are a variety of time-saving techniques to do this. The following *Teacher Tips* from veteran teachers may be worth your implementation:

- Laminate a copy of your seating chart or enclose it in a plastic liner. Then, as your lesson is progressing, mark the "empty" seats with a wipeable grease pencil. Record absentees while your students are working individually.

- Develop a system similar to the time cards used by businesses. Pull the cards of the students who are absent, or, better yet, have students turn in their time cards, and note whose cards are left.

- If students use folders or portfolios for your class, after the folders are distributed, leave the leftover folders on your desk until the end of the period, or a time when students are working independently. Then mark whose folder was not picked up.

- Or, as mentioned on September 12, have the students write a focus question during the first five minutes of class. This gives you the time to take roll in your record book (especially useful for those teachers who work in schools that require roll sheets to be turned in each period).

- A teacher's aide can also be helpful for this activity, but some schools will not allow students to take roll.

☙ THERE ARE MANY WAYS *to take attendance in the classroom without wasting precious instruction time. What other methods can you think of to fulfill this important task?*

JANUARY 3

HAVE YOU EVER HAD a student in your classroom who is just so special that you wished that all of your students were like him

January

or her? Today is my eldest son's birthday, and although Paul may not have been that perfect student to the teachers he had over the years, he just seemed to be one of those children who did everything (OK, most things) right. Now that he's an adult, I find him to be sensitive to other's needs and feelings and a real joy to be around.

I have had students like Paul in my classroom over the years, those who, on days when it could seem otherwise, make the job of teaching all worthwhile. Not only do they sit, behave, and do whatever you assign (usually with more care and work than you were actually expecting), but they build the teacher's ego by paying attention, raising their hands to answer questions (usually correctly), they smile at you from their desks, and some actually *tell* you that they like what they are learning in your classroom.

Although there may be some people who feel that these young people are *too pleasing,* they sure make the day pleasant. And, they have also learned people skills that may help them in their futures.

---

෨ DO YOU HAVE *some of these student "pleasers" in your classroom? What can you do to show them that you appreciate what they do for you?*

JANUARY 4

ON JANUARY 2, we looked at organization, and today we will continue to do so. Today's *Teacher Tips* are designed to make your day easier and give you more free time in the new year. (Was "find more time for myself and my family" one of your resolutions?)

If you are teaching a subject that requires your students to use equipment that could get "lost" or "misplaced," there are ways to keep track of such equipment:

- When lending or passing out calculators, scissors, or other accountable items, use a laminated seating chart and mark an X when a student borrows something. When the item is returned, erase the X.

- Build a "tool bin" that has the same number of slots as pieces of equipment. When the slots are filled, the class is dismissed. If students know that class will not be dismissed until all equipment is accounted for, they tend to find missing items quickly. (A math teacher I worked with sewed a calculator "wall hanging" with numbered pockets for each of his numbered calculators. A sewing teacher had a block of wood with holes for each of her pairs of scissors.)

- Assign equipment to students, and if a student misplaces an item they cannot have another unless they provide "collateral." (Many teachers accept house keys as collateral, but I am uncomfortable with this. What if the student forgets to turn in the item and gets home to find that he or she has no key to get into the house? Also, do you want to be responsible for someone's key?)

☞ DO YOU FIND *that equipment gets misplaced or "lost?" How can you manage your equipment better?*

JANUARY 5

ALONG WITH organizing equipment and administrative details, keeping instructional activities organized can also provide extra time for you away from your classroom duties. Here are a few more *Teacher Tips* to help you begin the new year saving time:

- There will always be students who are absent for one reason or another, but your time does not need to be taken up by those individuals. Although most teachers feel it is the student's

January

responsibility to make up work, we all know that students often need help with this responsibility. One way to help these students, and save time, is to schedule all makeup tests and labs at the same time, for all returning students. (For example, after school on Thursday.) And, as mentioned earlier, keep a file of worksheets available for students to make up.

• One way to save time, supply money, and a tree, is, instead of running photocopies of tests or readings for all students, reuse papers by numbering them and asking the students to write answers on their own paper. If you number the papers, it is easier to account for them and they are much more likely to be returned to you when the students are finished.

• Save samples of all of the lesson plans, handouts, and other ideas that you have used in an organized, labeled notebook or folder. This makes the following years easier. Make notes of activities that worked and those that did not. I found that a notebook, labeled by class or subject, in which I added each day's lesson was a great way to manage lessons. If I added something new, I took out the old lesson and filed it in a file cabinet. (I may want to use it on some future date with students who would learn better with that lesson.)

• Keep weekly management "ideas folders." You may want to label them by the days of the week (Monday, Tuesday, et cetera) or in some other fashion. As you are planning the week or as ideas come to you, insert the ideas and materials into the folder for the appropriate day.

The idea of organization in lesson planning is to seek improvement not reinvention.

☙ How can you *organize your lessons to make each year easier, thereby seeking improvement, not reinvention?*

169

JANUARY 6

WAS ONE OF your New Year's resolutions of a more personal reflective nature, such as a reflection on where you are in your life, where you are going, or where you would like to be? Maybe for some of you who are now teachers, teaching is not the career that you plan to have for your whole working life. Or, perhaps you aren't planning to leave education, but you may be looking to the day when you will move on to work as an administrator in a school, or in one of the many decision-making positions at the district level.

If it is your plan to move into an administrative position, now is not too early to begin gathering the information necessary and beginning the steps to do so, even if you are planning to teach for the next few years before moving on.

Even if you are not planning to move to another position in the near future, the day may come when you are recommended for a mentor or department chair position, or possibly a teaching award. Whatever the reason, it is best if you have kept your personal paperwork organized along with your lessons. The following *Career Tips* may help you in these areas:

• Keep your vitae (or resume) and portfolio up to date. Whenever you achieve an award, are sent a letter of appreciation, receive a good evaluation, or anything else that you feel should be added to your resume, put this information into a file and add it to your resume when you are updating it.

• Be sure to maintain your appearance. If you always look and act professionally, you will be seen as a professional, and will not have to convince others that you can be. Trying to act professionally for one day because you want a new position is much more difficult than *always* being professional.

• Begin to plan your own career. Decide if, and what, classes you may need to take to get the position that you want.

• Begin to build a network of people in and around the positions you seek. *Actively* volunteer for district and administrative

January

positions such as superintendent's advisory, curriculum council, school site plan, or mentor.

❧ HAVE YOU THOUGHT *of changing careers one day? What are you doing now to plan for that day?*

JANUARY 7

ONE LAST NOTE about organization for January before we move on to a new "New Year" subject. Helping students with their organization will simplify your class work and help your instruction time be more productive. The following *Teacher Tips* from veteran teachers will help your students be a help to you:

• If resources are available, provide a tape recorder for each cooperative learning group in the classroom. When it comes time for students to do group work activities in which students are expected to work together and interact, a tape recorder placed in the center of each group to record the conversation that takes place not only provides you with information on group dynamics and who is doing the work, but it keeps the students on task when they know they are being taped. The teacher can then review the tapes to see if students were able to stay on task and if everyone was involved.

• Restroom visits can be disruptive for classroom instruction and can also be abused. But few teachers want to be in control of other people's (their students') personal habits. To eliminate potential problems, create a well-established system for restroom passes that makes it difficult for students to abuse the privilege and yet allows for necessary visits. (Ideas for bathroom passes are discussed on November 16.)

• If you are assigning a research project, have your students use a file folder to organize the project. Staple the project to the

171

inside of the folder so that when opened it can "stand up" on a table or be displayed like a poster on a bulletin board.

❧ IN WHAT *other ways can you organize your students' work to help you with organization?*

JANUARY 8

WHAT WOULD THE new year be without a quote from John Dewey? In 1900, Dewey wrote in *The School and Society* that the goal of school was not only teaching subject matter but helping the child become a productive member of the community, which is more than an emphasis on specific subject information. The goal of school is not knowledge or information, according to Dewey, but self-realization.

"To possess all the world of knowledge and lose one's own self is as awful a fate in education as in religion," Dewey wrote. "Moreover, subject-matter never can be got into the child from without. Learning is active. It involves reaching out of the mind. It involves organic assimilation starting from within. Literally, we must take our stand with the child and our departure from him. It is he and not the subject-matter which determines both quality and quantity of learning."[2]

❧ ARE YOU TEACHING *your students from within? Is your lesson a "departure" from them? How are you helping your students to learn "actively"?*

JANUARY 9

DO YOU REMEMBER the first time your primary school teacher gave you a white sheet of paper and showed you how to fold and cut your very first snowflake? First, you carefully cut a square, then you folded it in half, then half, then half again. With each fold, you carefully smoothed the edge with your finger, or maybe you ran your pencil over it until it was nice and flat. Then you cut, and cut, and cut again, careful little notches and triangles. Cautiously you opened the folds to keep from tearing your masterpiece. And there it was, your very first snowflake!

When you looked around the room, you probably saw that, although all of your classmates had done the very same thing that you had done, no two snowflakes looked alike. Your teacher may have explained that, "Yes, Class, in real life, no two real snowflakes are alike either!" Amazing!

What is even more amazing than snowflakes is that in real life, no two children are alike either! Yet, how many times do we try to teach them as though they were? We try to teach them the same lessons, in the same way, and expect the same results from all of them.

☙ Do you see *your students as individuals?*

January 10

On December 19, we looked at Robert Frost's winter poem, "Stopping by Woods on a Snowy Evening." Another all-time favorite Frost poem, and one that most readers are familiar with, is "The Road Not Taken" which begins with the verse, "Two roads diverged in a yellow wood. . . ."[3]

Choices, that is what education is all about. Being able to make choices using the knowledge we have been exposed to, the decision-making skills we have been taught, and the processes of knowing ourselves. Each of us had, and continues to have, two (or more) roads to choose from in our lives, and many influences on those choices. The fulfilled person is the person who has made the right choice for himself or herself.

☙ DID YOU CHOOSE *to be a teacher? How did you come to make that choice? What do we need to teach the young people in our charge to help them to make the decisions that are best for them in their futures?*

JANUARY 11

ON JANUARY 11, 1935, Amelia Earhart began her first solo flight to cross the Pacific Ocean. Born in Atchison, Kansas, on July 24, 1898, Earhart achieved many "firsts" before her presumed death in the Pacific Ocean in July 1937. She was the first woman to fly the Atlantic, the first woman to fly alone across the Atlantic, the first woman to be awarded the Distinguished Flying Cross, and to fly from Hawaii to Oakland, California. Although her first records were "women's records," in 1932 she set *the* record for transatlantic flight.

Boy, talk about choices! How many of us would choose to pilot a plane (one unlike today's planes) across an ocean? But more than that, how many of us would "buck the norm" and go against what society has pre-ordained as our role in life? A woman piloting a plane across the ocean in the 1930s? Unheard of!

Earhart had a choice of two roads. She married publisher G. P. Putnam in 1931 and could have chosen the road of homemaker (the more traveled and certainly acceptable road), or the "road less traveled by" which made "all the difference."4

☙ IS IT POSSIBLE *to teach courage? The courage to take the road less traveled?*

January

January 12

Is it snowing where you live? Is there enough snow to make a snowman or a snow woman? How about a snow angel?

Do you remember when you gathered a large ball of snow in your mittened hands, packed it hard and round, and then began rolling it through the snow, watching as it gathered that white cover, getting larger and larger? Sometimes you had to ask a friend to help you push it and when it got too large, you stopped and started the next ball for the torso, and a smaller ball for the head. Voilà! A snowman or snowwoman.

Did you ever make a snow fort? Stacking balls of snow one on top of another until you were well protected from the "enemy"? Making little balls of "ammunition" to be well prepared for any confrontation?

How about the game Fox and Geese? Or making snow angels by lying in the clean snow and waving your legs and arms for wings? These are the winter games of the centuries.

꩜ Do you remember *how much fun these winter activities were? When was the last time you made a snow angel? Isn't it time to do it again?*

January 13

Charles Silberman, in his book *Crisis in the Classroom*, writes of the inadequacies of the educational system as we know it. Like many of the critical writers of the 1970s who felt that schools were not doing their jobs for young people, Silberman negatively wrote of the progressive movement of Dewey's time, claiming that "the most fatal error of all" of the progressive movement "was the failure to ask the questions that the giants of the progressive movement always kept at the center of their

175

concern, however inadequate some of their answers may have been: What is education for? What kind of human beings and what kind of society do we want to produce? What methods of instruction and classroom organization, as well as subject matter, do we need to produce these results? What knowledge is of most worth?"[5]

However negative Silberman may have been in his book and in this statement, the questions are valid. Educators throughout the decades and across the country should ask themselves the same questions.

❧ WHAT IS EDUCATION FOR? *What kind of human beings and society do we want to produce? What methods do we need to produce these results? What knowledge is of most worth?*

JANUARY 14

ANOTHER CRITICAL EDUCATOR of the 1960s and 1970s was John Holt, author of the book, *How Children Fail.* In describing how a system not only allows children to do poorly, but encourages it, Holt writes that children begin life on target but somehow are let down by a system that needs changing. "Nobody starts off stupid," Holt writes. "You only have to watch babies and infants, and think seriously about what all of them learn and do, to see that, except for the most grossly retarded, they show a style of life, and a desire and ability to learn that in an older person we might well call genius. Hardly an adult in a thousand, or ten thousand, could in any three years of his life learn as much, grow as much in his understanding of the world around him, as every infant learns and grows in his first three years." But what happens, Holt asks, "as we get older, to this extraordinary capacity for learning and intellectual growth?"

"What happens," he answers, "is that it is destroyed, and more than by any other one thing, by the process that we misname education—a process that goes on in most homes and schools. We adults destroy most of the intellectual and creative capacity of children by the things we do to them or make them do."[6]

Wow, that is pretty strong writing, isn't it? Are things really that bad? Do we really *destroy* the intellectual and creative capacity of children? I am not sure. Although some adults may do this unintentionally, many do not. But it is a worthy question to ask ourselves.

⟫ ARE YOU DESTROYING *the "intellectual and creative capacity of children" by the things you do to them or make them do? If your answer is "Yes," or even "Maybe," what can you do to ensure that you don't in the future?*

JANUARY 15

SINCE WE HAVE BEEN REFLECTING on the old year and on perhaps making some improvements in this new year, let's take a check on how we are doing with motivating students to work productively in our classrooms. The following *Teacher Tips* from veteran teachers may help positively motivate students through positive reinforcement:

• Often, when asking a student a question, we do not give the student time to think about an answer. This is especially important if the question goes beyond simple information. Be sure to give students time to respond. It may take at least ten seconds for some children to formulate an answer, especially if it is a thought-provoking question. Times of silence can feel awkward at first. To go beyond this uncomfortable waiting period, some teachers silently count to ten to give students time to answer.

• As we talked about on October 19, to reinforce learning, keep students informed of their progress either verbally or in writing, at frequent intervals.

• Some teachers find that rewards encourage students to participate in class. They give coupons to their students who participate orally or volunteer. At the end of the period, the students write their names on the back of the coupons and the teacher collects them. This then becomes a participation grade.

• Coupons can also be used for barter to buy supplies such as pencils or paper. They may also be used as restroom passes or as extra credit.

• Praise students as often as possible for accomplishments both inside and outside of your classroom.

• And again, circulate around the classroom regularly. This allows the students to know that you are there and are actively concerned with what they are doing.

☙ IN WHAT OTHER WAYS *can you positively reinforce the students and the type of behavior you want to see exhibited in your classroom?*

JANUARY 16

ON JANUARY 16, 1786, the Virginia legislature adopted the Ordinance of Religious Freedom, guaranteeing that no man could be forced to attend or support any church, or be discriminated against because of his religious preference. Although this very same statute, which had been written by Thomas Jefferson, was voted down by the assembly in 1779, it was passed when reintroduced by James Madison. The Ordinance of Religious Freedom, later became the model for the first amendment to the U. S. Constitution.[7]

It was an innovative measure for its time, allowing freedom that we now take for granted, that we each have a right to believe in the Superior Being of our choice, and practice (or not practice) our faith in whatever manner we so choose. Children, along with making choices, need to be able to make decisions about their own beliefs. Small decisions on simpler matters may encourage students to make major decisions on bigger issues at a later date. It is our right, and theirs.

⅏ HOW CAN YOU *encourage your students to begin making educated decisions?*

JANUARY 17

ONE OF THE RESOLUTIONS that you may have made for this new year is to seek ways to deal with stress a little better. Stress is a part of everybody's life. It is almost impossible to escape from stress in any line of work. Arguably, working with children, parents, and district personnel can sometimes create stresses unknown in other forms of work. The following *Teacher Tips* are from veteran teachers, who have learned to cope with the stresses that are unique to our working world:

• Before being able to cope with stress, an individual needs to be aware of the symptoms of stress. These may include nervousness, upset stomach, irritability, insomnia, and any other form of imbalance in a person's life. (You know when you are stressed.)

• Determining what is causing the stress is the second step to coping with it. Is the little girl you are angry with the reason for your stress, or was it the added bus duty that you were notified about before you started helping her? (For some people, it helps to keep a journal. When I am upset, I find that writing about the problem clarifies it. Sometimes, the event that I write about seems so trivial when I read it back that the stress is immediately alleviated.)

• The next step for dealing with stress is to build a support network of individuals who are in similar situations and therefore can readily understand the problem. There are many pros and cons of teacher's lounge "gossip," but sometimes talking with a peer about a problem can be a lifesaver.

• It may help to remember why you made the decision to become a teacher. Ask yourself if you still feel the same way that you did then. What can you do to help you feel that way again?

• Pamper yourself by learning something new, reading a thought-provoking book or magazine article, going to a show, or taking a walk. Whatever it takes to *get over it.*

❧ WHAT ASPECTS *of your job create stress in your life? What can you do to alleviate future stresses?*

JANUARY 18

WE TALKED ON OCTOBER 29 about the importance of parent participation in the classroom and building their support for your program outside of the classroom. But we all have encountered parents who have created stress for us, yet we needed to deal with the issue for the benefit of the child. A friend of mine often says that a person has to learn to pick his battles, learn which ones are worth fighting for, and which ones are just not worth the effort (the stress).

Another friend has two sayings that help him make the decision to fight or withdraw. The first is from Kenny Rogers's song about the gambler: "Learn when to hold 'em, learn when to fold 'em, learn when to walk away, learn when to run. . . ."[8] The other is the prayer of Saint Francis of Assisi: "God, grant me the serenity to accept the things I cannot change, courage to change the things I can, and wisdom to know the difference."

In working with difficult parents, you may decide, having determined that this issue with the parent or child is not helping the student, that it is in the student's best interest to work together to try to make a difficult situation better. The following steps may help in doing just that:

1. When working with irate individuals, stay calm and try not to get drawn into arguments.

2. Be prepared to understand the other's point of view even when you don't agree with it.

3. Understand that the problems you may be having with the student may not be the child's fault, but may be the result of his or her having been raised in this difficult family.

4. And, most important, be the first to rebuild bridges. This parent comes with a whole history of experiences with teachers and other authority figures which you have no control over. You may be the first school figure who is understanding.

ARE YOU ABLE to "pick your battles," backing away from the ones that are not worth fighting?

JANUARY 19

JANUARY 19 nicely lends itself to the issues of minorities in America because, not only is it Martin Luther King Jr.'s birthday (born in 1929), but on this day in 1869, Susan Brownell Anthony was elected president of the American Equal Rights Association, the beginning of an organized women's movement.[9]

Many of your students are acquainted with King's "I Have a Dream" speech (and if not, introduce it). In comparing the social difficulties of African Americans with the social difficulties of others, such as women, Native Americans, or Jews, you may want to have students rewrite Martin Luther King Jr.'s "I Have a Dream" speech as if written by one of these groups historically or today.

What will your students need to know about various minorities in order to rewrite this speech? What is your dream?

JANUARY 20

TO EXPAND ON your celebration of Martin Luther King Jr.'s birthday and the birth of the women's movement, the following *Teacher Tips* may give you some suggestions for activities that will enhance your instruction on diversity:

• Have your students research a minority member of Congress. Subjects may be a Native American, Hispanic, African American, Asian American, Pacific Islander, or other ethnic group represented in your student body. Students can then assume the role of their subjects in mock debates, stressing their political and socioeconomic views as well as their cultural and religious views.

• Bring in minority business leaders, scientists, authors, or artists as guest speakers. Ask your guests to discuss how they achieved success and the difficulties they faced as minorities entering their fields.

• Ask your students to choose one professional athlete and research that person's heritage, what his or her nationality is, and how that helped or hindered his or her achievements. Be sure that women athletes are represented equally as are men.

• Arrange for your students to write to pen pals from other cultures.

• Have your students make (sew) full-sized flags of the countries of their heritage. Hang these flags from the ceiling, making the room wonderfully colorful.

꩜ HOW ELSE *can you introduce diversity and the need for understanding in your classroom?*

JANUARY 21

HERBERT KLIEBARD WRITES in his book *Forging the American Curriculum* that teaching is "supremely contextual," and because of this it is important that teachers are taught in education classes, "not recipes for what to do under particular circumstances; rather . . . the ability to use whatever 'intellectual instrumentalities we are able to acquire . . . in order to make wise judgments and sophisticated choices in those unique contexts.

"This means that teachers are not simply the compliant beneficiaries of research findings . . . they are compelled by the nature of their work as teachers to reinterpret those findings in the light of situationally determined characteristics."[10]

There is much information available to teachers and a large amount of research being done that will enhance our practice. What is important is to take this good information and to use it wisely within the right contexts, making "wise judgments and sophisticated choices" to enhance learning.

꩜ DO YOU KEEP UP *on the research that is being done to improve instruction and learning? How might you be better informed?*

JANUARY 22

TODAY WOULD HAVE BEEN my father's birthday, but he passed away during the writing of this book. I would have liked him to see it. My dad was always so supportive of me that I know no matter how it turned out, he would have liked it. When I wanted to join our school band, he bought the saxophone; when I left for college, he helped me move in; and when I decided to get married, he liked my husband. Once, when I was twelve or thirteen years old, and I could not decide if I was grown up or not, he bought me a football and high heels on the same shopping trip.

I would have liked him to be here to see the finished book. But he lived to see me graduate from college and receive my Ph.D. He saw my children born and grow, as well as the birth of my first grandson. We were able to spend many years together, so I have been blessed.

Having people who support you in life is so important, especially in your position as a teacher—mainly, because you give so much to others.

❧ DO YOU HAVE ANYONE *in your life who supports you? (If you don't, find someone!)*

JANUARY 23

AT ONE TIME OR ANOTHER, you may use videos in your classroom to enhance learning. Using videos can enhance classroom instruction or waste precious instruction time. The worst scenario is the teacher who gains the nickname "Captain Video" by students who understand (and resent) the overuse of this medium. The following *Teacher Tips* may help you with the decision "to video or not to video":

January

• Make sure that the video you are showing is an appropriate addition and enhancement to the lesson that you are teaching.

• Along with deciding whether to show a video, make the decision of how much to show. It may not be necessary to show the whole movie. If a ten-minute section shows enough to make your point, that's enough. (One of my son's teachers showed to her eighth graders a whole Civil War series that had been on television. No only did it take two weeks to show it, the information was inaccurate, and in some cases inappropriate for thirteen and fourteen year olds. It wasted precious classtime when the students could have been doing more pleasurable activities and learning more accurate information about this time in history.)

• Make sure that everyone in the room can see the television properly. This is not as easy to do as with the old movie screens because of the size of the TV screen. Television has a relatively small visual area, and often students will not speak up when they cannot see.

• An occasional "reward" video is appropriate as long is it is entertaining and has language and content that is appropriate for young people. (As a parent, I occasionally resented the movies that my children's teachers selected as rewards because they were movies that I did not want the children to see.) Remember, too, a reward does not happen every week. Teachers who show movies every Friday are cheating their students out of a good education.

• And last, but certainly not least, be aware of copyright laws. Many school districts have rules about showing rented videos in the classroom that pertain not only to the rating (G, PG, PG13, R) of the video but to whether it is legal to show videos at all. Check with your district about copyright infringement.

⋙ FOR WHAT PURPOSES *do you use videos in your classroom? Is it appropriate? Is it legal?*

JANUARY 24

JANUARY 24 is Bodhi Day, the Buddhist celebration of the enlightenment of their founder Shakyamuni Buddha around the year 596 B.C. Buddhism was a religious sect that arose in India during the sixth century B.C. and exists there and in other countries today. The core of the teachings of the Buddha are the search for, and the achievement of, enlightenment.

Enlightenment as a concept seems like an achievement that we all should wish to attain. Helping our children and others gain enlightenment may well be as much of a goal of education as it is of religion.

❧ ARE YOU ENLIGHTENED? *How can one become enlightened and teach others to be likewise?*

JANUARY 25

A POPULAR BOOK of the 1970s was Robert Pirsig's *Zen and the Art of Motorcycle Maintenance,* a thought-provoking essay on Pirsig's ride with his son across the countryside, trying to discover who he was and where he was going in life. It is an interesting insight into self-education and enlightenment through mindfulness.

At one point in his book, Pirsig relates the importance of *awareness* in even the menial tasks we do. "So the thing to do when working on a motorcycle, as in any other task, is to cultivate the peace of mind which does not separate one's self from one's surroundings. When that is done successfully, then everything else follows naturally. Peace of mind produces right values, right values produce right thoughts," he continues. "Right thoughts produce right actions and right actions produce work which will be a material reflection for others to see of the serenity at the center of it all."[11]

January

Wouldn't it be wonderful if the work produced by your students would be productive of right values, right thoughts, and right actions? According to Pirsig, it is possible when done with peace of mind and connection.

⚘ DO YOU ACCOMPLISH TASKS *throughout the day with peach of mind and full concentration on the task at hand? How can you be more "mindful" in the future?*

JANUARY 26

IN BUDDHIST TEACHING, the follower is taught the importance of "mindfulness" in every action that is attempted throughout the day. That is, keeping the mind attentive to the task and not letting it wander to former problems or future possibilities. It is important that the individual pay attention to what is happening in the "here and now."

A saying that you will often come across in these teachings is the importance of being "awake and aware"—awake and aware of what you are doing at this very moment—being a part of the moment, experiencing the moment, and savoring the moment.

Being awake and aware also allows the individual an opportunity to go with the moment and perhaps learn something new that may have been missed in the rush to get on to the next task.

If you are like me, you waste a lot of time reliving the past and worrying about the future. None of this reliving and worrying changes anything. Being "in the moment" relaxes the system and allows us to live this moment, right now.

⚘ HOW MIGHT *your students and others around you benefit from your mindfulness—your being fully with them, in the moment,* right now?

JANUARY 27

OK, TIME FOR a little memory recall. Think back to your education classes, because today we are going to review Bloom's Taxonomy. (Actually, it is Benjamin Bloom and Co-authors' Taxonomy.) Bloom writes in *Taxonomy of Educational Objectives Handbook* that there are levels of thinking which we experience that exist on a hierarchical continuum and enhance our thinking and understanding as we move through these levels. Beginning with knowledge, thinking moves through comprehension, application, analysis, synthesis, evaluation, problem solving, and finally creation. (Is it coming back?) In order for students to pass through these thinking abilities, it is important for the teacher to ask questions and allow experiences that will give students opportunities to be successful at higher levels.[12]

The importance of learning the Taxonomy is for teachers to develop ever higher forms of questioning, to move students from the ability to answer questions at a simple knowledge level to being able to evaluate problems, problem solve, and ultimately create knowledge through thinking.

To do this, teachers must go beyond the simple questions that ask students to repeat information given by the teacher back to the teacher, and move on to a deeper level of thinking.

    ☙ AT WHAT LEVEL *are most of your students located on Bloom's Taxonomy? How can you move them on to another level?*

JANUARY 28

MY ALMANAC says that today is not only Chinese New Year, but Vietnamese New Year as well. Within the last year we have celebrated new years in many different cultures: Jewish, Vietnamese, American, Chinese, and others.

Why do we have New Year's celebrations? There seems to be more to a new year than a simple change of the calendar. Cultures seem to want to celebrate a new opportunity to start anew, with fresh beginnings. If you think about it, doesn't it seem as though we have more in common with other cultures than we originally thought?

To all of our Chinese and Vietnamese friends, happy new year!

What is there that is significant about a new year? *Is there some way we can experience new years more often? How can we use these celebrations to teach diversity, tolerance, and similarities among cultures?*

JANUARY 29

WHEN WE THINK OF the new year, we often think of the goal (or resolution) of "to take better care of ourselves." Hence the resolutions to go on a diet (ugh), exercise, and to give up bad habits such as nail biting, negativity, and smoking (absolutely). It has been three weeks now since you started any plan to make changes in your life. How is it going? Have you been able to keep it up? If so, how? If not, what did not work?

Experts know that losing weight has more to do with nutrition and exercise than it has to do with giving up favorite high-calorie foods. The bad news is, and the fact remains, most diets fail. We also know that many people often tend to gain more weight back after a diet than they originally had lost. I can vouch for that, having been one of those statistics. The sad truth is that, for real weight loss, the individual must *use* more calories than he or she *expends*. To lose weight in a healthy way, the individual must pay careful attention to nutrition to continue to be healthy. Obviously, the individual who is exercising to lose pounds must be even more careful of the fuel he or she is putting into his or her body.

And last, most individuals who pay attention to nutrition and eat the right foods are not only more healthy, but they *feel* better as well.

꩜ How are you doing *with your New Year's resolutions? Congratulations if you have been successful. If you have not been, today is a new day. What can you do to get started again?*

JANUARY 30

YESTERDAY WE WERE TALKING about the importance of good nutrition, not only for weight loss and exercise, but for well-being in general. In his important book, *Democracy and Education,* John Dewey wrote about education as the "nutrition" of the social life.

"What nutrition and reproduction are to physiological life, education is to the social life," he writes in *Democracy and Education.* "Education," the Tanners paraphrase Dewey in their book *Curriculum Development: Theory into Practice,* "not only is the means through which a culture is transmitted but also the means through which it is transformed."[13]

In this respect, what you are doing as a teacher is *feeding* children the education that they need to transmit the culture from one generation to the next, but also the ability to *transform* the culture for constant improvement. What a wonderful responsibility has been entrusted to you.

❧ ARE YOU *"feeding" your students the educational nutrients they need to be healthy and ensure a healthy society?*

JANUARY 31

WHAT BETTER WAY to end January than with a quote from John Dewey's *Democracy and Education.* "Life is a self-renewing process through action upon the environment."[14] There are two important elements here: Life should be self-renewing, and the self-renewing process is through action.

Life is not, as some say, what happens to us when we are not looking, or busy doing something else. Life is the looking and the doing. Believe it or not, no one is as much in charge of our lives as we are, thank goodness. Dynamic living and dynamic teaching involves a reflective mindfulness that requires being awake and aware.

We spend the days before New Year's Day reflecting on the old year, looking to the new year, and making resolutions about the things we will do that will change our lives. In essence, every day should be New Year's Day, because it is.

❧ HAVE YOU MADE *a resolution to reflect on your life and teaching daily? What "self-renewing process" will ensure that this happens?*

FEBRUARY

FEBRUARY 1

ON FEBRUARY 1, 1865, the Thirty-eighth Congress proposed the Thirteenth Amendment to the Constitution, abolishing slavery in the United States. Ratified on December 6, 1865, this amendment made it a law that "neither slavery nor involuntary servitude, except as punishment for crime ... shall exist within the United States. ..." Although the law abolished slavery, unfortunately, it did not abolish the prejudice carried in the hearts of some people against minorities. The abolition of prejudice has, and will, take years of education to overcome.

Teachers have for decades been instrumental in attempting to teach tolerance to students who come from a variety of home settings. Often it appears to be an uphill battle to convince children to let go of the hatred that they have learned from adults who have influence over them. The following *Teacher Tips* on dealing with prejudice may be a beginning:

• According to some researchers, tolerance is better learned through interaction than through information. Teaching tolerance seems to be more effective when students are given opportunities to communicate and exchange ideas among themselves and their teachers.

• Understanding how it feels to be a minority sometimes allows students better to understand classmates of other races. A nonthreatening way to teach sensitivity is to ask students to write a song about what it is or might be like to be a member of a minority group. Songs should be factual and can be written to the tune of any popular song.

• We have all experienced prejudice in our lives. A good example for young people is the prejudice that they experience every time they go to the mall to shop. Ask students to write about this experience, or another incident in which they experienced prejudice or were discriminated against, and how they responded to the situation.

February

• Students can also write about an incident in which they observed discrimination or prejudice. Ask them how they responded or should have responded.

• A fun (and educative) game to help students identify how stereotyping can affect the way people feel about themselves is "The Headband Game." Students wear prepared headbands that have characteristics written on them that the wearer cannot see. Some examples might be, "I am overweight" (underweight, well-developed, blind, black, white, Asian, attractive, unattractive, handicapped, athletic, smart, dumb, rich, or poor). Observe how students react to the characteristics, then discuss the game with them, asking questions about how they felt about the way that they were treated or why they treated others in a particular manner.

❧ WHAT CAN YOU DO *to teach tolerance to your students?*

FEBRUARY 2

FEBRUARY 2, Groundhog Day, is the day when the groundhog Punxsutawney Phil comes out of his burrow, checks his shadow, and predicts how much longer winter will last.

Have you ever seen the movie *Groundhog Day*, which stars Bill Murray and Andie McDowell? Murray stars as a smug television weatherman who is trapped in the same twenty-four hours; each day is a repeat of the previous day, over, and over, and over. . . .[1]

There are probably times when we feel like we are caught up in a version of *Groundhog Day*, when every day seems to be a carbon copy of the day before. Sometimes the day before was not such a good day to begin with; some of us may feel like every

195

day is Groundhog Day, and like Murray's character, we cannot escape from the repetition of the day before.

❧ How can you *keep each day fresh, free from becoming Groundhog Day? If you are already stuck in Groundhog Day, how can you get out?*

FEBRUARY 3

IN 1942, Albert Hatcher wrote a poem called "The Challenge," which appeared in the *New Republic* magazine. Although it may be difficult to obtain, this short poem is an excellent introduction to a discussion on discrimination. It is also well worth reviewing occasionally for your own awareness.

In a section titled, "Negro Youth and College," Hatcher wrote that there are many things that he can change about himself—his behavior, his appearance, and even his lack of education—but he adds, "if you discriminate against me because of my color, I can do nothing" because "God gave me my color."[2]

❧ Do you discriminate *against any of your students for something over which they have no control (gender, skin color, weight, et cetera)? Do you try to help students work on areas in which they do have some control?*

FEBRUARY 4

FEBRUARY IS THE MONTH of Valentine's Day, when we send cards, candy, and flowers to people who we care about. But it can also be a month when we care about all of man- and womankind, as well. (Actually we should do so every month, but we will start where we can.)

One of the things we discover as we delve deeper into tolerance and diversity is that, although we are separate individuals, we are often very much alike. The purpose of tolerance education is that we learn that it is OK to be individuals, too. The following *Teacher Tips* will help us as we continue our conversation on tolerance and diversity:

• Allow your students to design and produce masks or shields that show their individuality and that also identify them as members of a group. By drawing symbols that identify them with a sport, music, scouts, or other group (not gangs), students are challenged to express symbolically their identities by bringing them together in a unified design. Have students discuss, or better yet write, why they chose the symbols, colors, or emotions (such as anger, happiness) that they did.

• Ask your students to take the perspective of a minority in an historical situation such as the Native Americans on Lewis and Clark's expedition, or the African American view of slavery. Have them conduct a council on their feelings and what they will do about the situation.

❧ WHAT WILL YOU *draw on your mask or shield? What group do you strongly affiliate with? How might that affect your teaching?*

FEBRUARY 5

YOUR STUDENTS have probably been taking tests for some time now, but the following *Teacher Tips* from veteran teachers

197

may help test-taking time be a little less stress-producing or at least less *un*pleasant for you and your students:

• Rarely, if ever, are tests that are made by textbook publishers appropriate for classroom use. You are teaching students, not the book. Unless you have emphasized the main points of the book and followed it exactly, you will find that students are unable to do well on these tests. Teachers should test what *they* taught.

• It may make your test-making experience easier if you have a computer in the classroom with a test bank of questions that you have made up. When it is time to make a test for your students, you have questions to choose from, and test making is quicker.

• Be sure to vary the *types* of questions you use. Some students do better with essay questions, still others prefer multiple choice, true or false, or matching. Using a variety of types of questions allows all students an opportunity to achieve. The point is to find out what the students have learned. If your students know the information, but have difficulty with certain types of test questions, you will not discover whether they have learned the material.

• Along with varying the types of test questions, remember that it is unfair to try to trick students on exams. The objective of taking a test is to see if the students learned the material that was taught, not to see if you can fool them. Keep in mind that if your students all do poorly on an exam, it may be a good indication that the subject was not *taught* well.

• At the end of a quiz, offer extra credit questions with trivial details that were mentioned in class. If the student gets the extra credit right, that tells you that at least he or she was listening to the discussions. It may also be an incentive for students to stay alert during classtime discussions.

February

꒰ꕀ HOW ELSE *can you make test taking, and test making, less daunting for you and for your students?*

FEBRUARY 6

REMEMBER HOW YOU FELT in school and in college when it was time to take a test? Were you a little nervous? Did you hope (and perhaps, pray) that you studied the right material? As you may recall, during the Reagan administration there was an ongoing discussion about the possibility of reinstituting prayer in the public schools. If you were teaching, or a student during this time, you may have also recalled that many people felt that prayer had never *left* public schools—just ask any student before a test!

Yesterday we discussed ways to make test making and test taking less daunting for you and your students. Today we will continue with a few more suggestions:

- Obviously, in order for students to do well on exams, they need to have learned the material in the first place. Learning, like most difficult tasks, is more easily accomplished if it is broken into smaller segments, which allows students to learn difficult information gradually. (For example, rather than learning all of the parts of the body, ask the students to learn two bones a week.)

- If you want to ensure that your students do well on exams, allow them to have an opportunity to retake the exam. You may want to give a test on Thursday, and if students do poorly allow them to retake it on Friday.

- When you give a written test, have another activity ready for those students who finish early, such as a word search or a crossword puzzle. (A good idea may be to have the extra activity relate to the upcoming lesson, introducing words and information.) You may also want to have two activities for advanced students.

⁐ IN WHAT OTHER WAYS *can you make tests meaningful for your students?*

FEBRUARY 7

OK, THIS IS an unpleasant topic, but it seems to follow any discussion about test taking, and because the problem exists, it is a necessary addition to the conversation. That is, how can you keep students from illegally helping each other (cheating) on an exam? Knowing that students cheat is upsetting to teachers who take time to prepare tests to see what students have learned. It is also frustrating for students who do not cheat to have their grades compared with those who do.

An interesting situation, which is troublesome to me even as I write about it today, occurred in my junior high classroom a few years ago. I was teaching a life skills class, in particular a unit on being a successful student. During a conversation on test taking a question arose concerning what should be done if a student knows that another student cheats on exams. Although this discussion generally goes well, in one class the students suggested that it is OK to cheat, and that the fault for cheating lies with the teacher who, in their words, "is *too stupid* to catch it!" If I recall correctly, I was caught completely off guard by this response. I felt blindsided, and truthfully, I felt that I could not trust these *children.* They seemed so cool and calm about dishonesty. This brings us to our first *Teacher Tip* concerning what to do about dishonest test taking:

February

• In order to do something about cheating, the teacher has to understand what is behind the student's need to cheat. Is it a challenge for the student to see what he or she can get away with? Is it the stress felt by a child whose parents expect too much, or is the student expecting too much from herself? Or is it that the "teacher is too stupid to catch it"?

• Be on the lookout for dishonesty. If necessary, check for writing on hands, desks, erasers, or wherever. Have students place book bags, notebooks, and books in another part of the room, away from the test area.

• Change the exam from period to period, so that the last period of the day does not have an unfair advantage over the first period. Word of mouth about the test travels quickly throughout the day, especially over a lunch period.

• If cheating is a problem, do not give tests. Find some other method of evaluation, such as cooperative learning groups, asking students to express what they have learned verbally to you, or some other test-taking method.

☾ WHAT CAN YOU DO *to ensure that everyone has a fair chance of doing equally well on an exam?*

FEBRUARY 8

THE BOY SCOUTS OF AMERICA was founded on February 8, 1910, having been originally formed by Lord Baden-Powell of England. Designed to develop self-reliance, courage, resourcefulness, and citizenship, the Boy Scouts exist today as a program that develops young men into adults, some of whom have become leaders in Congress and local governments.

You may have some scouts in your classroom. They are not as easily identifiable today as in years past. Few wear their uniforms to school, or talk of the good deeds that they do on the weekends.

Yet, we have all been recipients of some of their good work. Boy Scouts in my neighborhood painted the fence around the community pool. Several of them work in the lookout fire station in the national forest where I am a volunteer. Often the areas around us are cleaner and more attractive because of the work that they and other volunteer organizations have done.

It seems a shame that the title "Boy Scout" has, in recent years, become tinged with negativity, yet it describes someone who is honest and does good things for the community. Maybe it is time to change that connotation and celebrate these young men who stand out in the crowd. Happy birthday, Boy Scouts!

ꙮ Do you have *any Boy Scouts in your classroom? Have you ever asked?*

February 9

OK, this will date some of us. Do you remember when the Beatles first appeared on *The Ed Sullivan Show*? Believe it or not, it was on February 9, and the year was 1964. Four young men from Liverpool excited us, especially young girls like me, and changed music in America, both as a group and in later years as individuals (John Lennon, Paul McCartney, Ringo Starr, and George Harrison).

No doubt about it, music stars influence young people in many ways (not all of them positive, but that is a different topic). Not all of the music is good, and although you may disagree on performers, the lesson for today is, because these groups are so popular, they can be used to motivate students in your classroom. "How?" you ask. These *Teacher Tips* may help you:

• Allowing students to listen to popular music groups (provided there can be some consensus on who will be listened to) can be a great motivation for students to get their work done.

February

- Letting students occasionally write or speak about celebrities in their assignments may encourage them to do their work.

- Last, but not to be underestimated, your knowledge of the music that your students listen to today can make you look "cool" to the young people in your classroom, no matter how old your age (even if you are old enough to remember the Beatles on *Ed Sullivan!*)

♫ How can you *use popular music to motivate your students to complete the tasks you have assigned?*

February 10

On February 7, when we were talking about test taking, the subject of taking tests in cooperative group formations came up. I want to delve further into the topic of cooperative learning. Nearly every teacher knows, and many *use* the techniques of cooperative learning groups to enhance learning. The reasoning behind this is (at least) twofold: 1) Studies show that students learn in groups; and 2) working with your friends in groups is usually more *fun*. Cooperation helps students learn together, gives pupils an opportunity to teach and learn from one another, and encourages collaboration rather than competition.

The following *Teacher Tips* from veteran teachers may give you some ideas for enhancing your students' learning through cooperatively working with one another:

- A sponge activity or focus question given at the beginning of the period may be given to a group rather than individually. When giving a critical thinking problem, allow students to pair up to solve it. If you choose to do so, you can give credit to the individuals in the group for a reasonable effort at solving the problem.

203

- Ask students to read the papers they write aloud to their group members while in their cooperative learning groups. This allows students to hear their own writing errors, and to hone their writing skills by listening to others.

- Vary groupings for different subjects or different units within a single subject. This gives young people an opportunity to work with other young people, learn from others while helping others learn, and getting to know others better. For the same reasons, change groups often.

- Grading groups can be challenging for teachers. A solution might be to use self and peer assessment where the students grade themselves and their peers. (If this is your choice—allowing students to grade each other—it is a good idea to provide a "rubric," or grading guidesheet, to guide students in what you are looking for.)

❧ HOW CAN *cooperative groups be used for the unit you are about to begin?*

FEBRUARY 11

ISN'T IT ABOUT TIME for a Writing Blitz? "What is that?" you ask. A Writing Blitz is an opportunity for students to unleash that creative urge and use various techniques to practice and develop the skills that will make them good writers. This can be accomplished in a variety of ways. The following *Teacher Tips* may give you some suggestions for developing that next John Steinbeck or Mary Shelley (boy, February is beginning to look like *Teacher Tip* month, isn't it?):

- One method of writing that is often fun for students is "Finish the Story." Begin a story or nonfiction writing assign-

February

ment by writing one or two sentences on the board. A student writes the next two or three sentences, then passes the story to the next student, who in turn writes two or three sentences, passing it on to the next person. Continue in this manner until everyone in the class (or group, if the class is too large) has contributed to the writing, then read the story out loud to the class. Compare and analyze stories among groups.

• An activity designed to get the students to know each other is to divide your students into groups of two, and ask them to interview each other. After writing a short biography about the person they have interviewed, students can read the biography to the class.

• Ask students to write autobiographical poems, put their names on them, and then turn them in. After you read them to the class, see if the students can identify the student who wrote each poem.

• To get to know the characters in a novel that you are studying, have your students create a dozen questions they would ask that person if he or she visited the class. Ask students to make note of the questions that they could not answer and to write them down as they find the answers in the coming lessons. (This technique can be used in introducing other subjects as well.)

• Even if you teach a subject that traditionally is not thought of as a writing class, for example math or science, you can still change the pace by having an occasional Writing Blitz. Ask your students to write a creative story about how the topic of your unit came about. For example, how was the Pythagorean Theorem discovered? Who decided the symbol for gold should be Au instead of Go? Then, after a fun time reading these "theories," explain what really occurred.

_____

֎ How can you use *a Writing Blitz to enhance your subject?*

_____

205

February 12

On February 12, 1809, Abraham Lincoln, the sixteenth president of the United States, was born in a log cabin in Kentucky. Known as "Honest Abe," and emancipator of the slaves, Lincoln is remembered as one of our all-time favorite leaders.

Lincoln, as storybooks remind us, was a remarkable leader, and will be a hero for ages to come. It is little wonder that we have a national holiday for this man. Reflecting on this day, on Lincoln's character and accomplishments, one wonders whether any national leader of our time will achieve the status of a Lincoln, especially with the media eager to inform us of the fallacies and dark sides of those in which we have entrusted power. Certainly Lincoln had an advantage in being president prior to television and the information age. One also has to ponder if he would have survived the media onslaught that faces government leaders today?

This also causes us to contemplate just who are our heroes today.

☽ Who are *the individuals living today whom you consider heroes? What have they accomplished? Are they worthy of your admiration?*

February 13

Tomorrow is Valentine's Day, the day when cards are sent, flowers are delivered, and way too much chocolate is eaten (by me), all in the name of *love*. It is the day when Cupid's arrows strike the hearts of many of us and send us straight to the mall, or at least to the greeting card store, for that perfect card (usually written by a complete stranger) that expresses our feelings to a loved one.

February

Rather than cards, candy, and gifts, wouldn't it be better if we gave our most precious commodity—*time*—to those we care about?

One area that we often appreciate but rarely give our time or appreciation to is our school, that place where we spend countless hours, day after day, year after year. How about a little valentine to our "home away from home," our school? A gift of some plants, flowers, a tree, something to beautify the place we inhabit so much of our week. What about the gift of *time* for the beautification of the area around us? Why not ask your students to help?

꩜ HOW CAN YOU *send a valentine to your school? What will beautify a small area where you spend so much of your day?*

FEBRUARY 14

FEBRUARY 14, Valentine's Day, was named after a bishop and martyr of the church who, on this day in the year 270, was put to death for his religious beliefs during the persecution of Claudius II. The custom of choosing and sending valentines on Valentine's Day is a very old one. Probably all of us can remember making and decorating the large envelopes and waiting to see if we would get a valentine from that special person in our heart. Beginning the first week in February, stores and classrooms around the nation begin filling with hearts and sweets for people, both young and old, to give to one another. It is a special day. Do you remember?

In elementary schools around the country, children make or buy valentines for their friends and classmates. In many junior and senior high schools, clubs sell flowers, sweets, and candygrams to be delivered to special people throughout the day.

These tokens of love and friendship make great fund-raisers and are fun for young people to share. But it is important, as teachers, to remember one very important thing, What about the child who does not receive a flower, candy, or card in their envelope?

❧ WHAT CAN YOU DO *to share your heart with* all *of your students today?*

FEBRUARY 15

ON FEBRUARY 15, 1820, Susan Brownell Anthony was born. Noted for her reform efforts, Anthony helped to launch the Woman's State Temperance Society in New York in 1852, published *The Revolution* (a paper dedicated to the emancipation of women) with Elizabeth Cady Stanton and Parker Pillsbury in 1868, was arrested for casting a ballot at the State and Congressional election in Rochester, New York, in 1872, and later served as president of the National American Woman's Suffrage Association.

When we think of women in history, we generally think of Anthony and Stanton, but what of the many other women who have been instrumental during various periods of our history. If you say, "What women?" you are already in trouble, and proof that you were part of an educational system that neglected to teach us about the many women who made outstanding contributions throughout time.

One of the problems with history classes in schools is that instead of focusing on everyday events, they tend to focus on wars—topics that tell the tales of the brave men who fought for their country and exclude those who "fought" other battles during times of peace. We learn of the settling of America, then the Revolutionary War, then the War of 1812, then the Civil War, Mexican-American War, both World Wars, and so on. (I know, I

February

was a history major.) This is not to say that these stories should not be told, but we have many non-war decades when other stories can be told, and women and minorities fit better into these epochs. Do you, or the history teachers that you know, teach history as war?

☯ WHAT OTHER WOMEN *have been instrumental in ensuring equal rights for women? What roles have women played in our history?*

FEBRUARY 16

A FEW DAYS AGO we were talking about Valentine's Day, giving gifts to show that we care about someone. We even talked about caring about our school and sending a valentine to our school. Another group to which you may want to send a valentine is to the community in which your school resides.

This valentine could be done in a variety of ways: by providing a service to the community, or by inviting the community into the school. The following *Teacher Tips* may give you some ideas for your valentine:

• Invite the community to a play, musical program, or a "reading" by your students of the writings that they have done.

• Invite the community to a "literary book party." After students read books and write book reports, invite guests in to learn more about the books that were read.

• Go out into the community for beautification excursions. Clean up areas frequented by students, or plant flowers in parks or along walkways.

• Adopt a community project as a class activity. For example, collect clothes for the Salvation Army, Goodwill, or other charitable organizations, or money for the American Red Cross.

There are so many ways to help the community around your school, and with wonderful results: 1) It is good public relations for the school and for young people; 2) it helps make the area you work in look better; and 3) it helps encourage civic pride and responsibility in your students.

❧ WHAT VALENTINE *can you give to the community that supports your school?*

FEBRUARY 17

LAST MONTH, when we looked at the new year, our discussion on January 17 was on the New Year's resolution of taking care of ourselves. It is important to find time for yourself to reflect and refresh, not only because it is good for you, but because your new, refreshed spirit is good for your students and those around you.

Is it time to remind you again? We talked about February being the month of *love*. We give cards, candy, and gifts to others. Have you thought about doing the same for yourself? This month, starting today, *love yourself*. Pamper yourself, buy yourself candy, buy tickets to a music or sporting event, sign up for golf lessons, buy yourself some new clothes, buy yourself some *comfortable shoes!* Whatever it takes to love yourself, do it now. (And do it again soon!) Give yourself a valentine.

❧ WHAT WOULD YOU *want someone to give you for Valentine's Day? Why not give that to yourself?*

FEBRUARY 18

A PART OF GROWING UP, which can take longer for some of us than for others, is discovering who we are and accepting that discovery. I like the name "Susan" *now*, but that has not always been the case. I can remember, like many children, that I did not like my name for a long time.

By the time I entered junior high school, having been the only Susan I knew, suddenly there were three of us in one class, coming from different feeder schools. So, as many teachers do to eliminate confusion, our names were changed. One girl became "Susie" (the name that I wanted), another became "Susan," and I was stuck with "Sue," a name that I was not fond of. Teachers decided *who I was,* and I remained that person for a long time.

Now I am "Susan" again, and I like my name. I think it has a strong, rich femininity about it that it took many years for me to discover. To some very special people I am "Susie" and hope to stay that way for years to come. Only to a few "old time friends" am I "Sue."

Our students' names (and their pronunciation) are much more important than we adults realize. I will never forget the year I taught at one elementary school in an affluent neighborhood. Two young Asian children, a brother and a sister, both non-English-speakers, were enrolled at our school. The practice at that time, which I hope is no longer the case, was to Americanize foreign students by giving them American-sounding names. Over the years, I have forgotten the little boy's new name, but someone at the school made the decision that the young girl, a fourth grader, would be "Bambi." And so she was. Her beautiful Asian name no longer existed, except on official papers, and probably, today there is a young Asian woman named Bambi living somewhere in the United States.

Names are very important. Ask a child what he or she wants to be called and the correct pronunciation.

〽 Do you make *an effort to allow students to discover who they are? Do you pronounce their names correctly?*

FEBRUARY 19

So, Valentine's Day is over. And if you have any of those little sugar hearts with the sayings on them that you do not want, you can send them to me. I love those little candies and their little notes. And, yes, I believe everything that is written on them. ("You're Super" and "Be Mine." Maybe not "Zoot Suit," since I could never figure out how that was an endearing statement.) Maybe I like them because I am on a sugar *rush* as I am reading them.

My point in referring to those little candy hearts is to show that some of us seek positive reinforcement in our lives (I bet your students do), and pathetic as it may seem, will take it wherever we can get it. Your students seek positive reinforcement from you, so be sure to give it *often.* Not superficially, or in a manner that is meaningless and loses its effectiveness, but genuinely, so they know that you care.

〽 Have you reinforced *your individual students lately? Could they use a little sweetness from you?*

FEBRUARY 20

In 1958, Leonard Covello wrote a lovely book with an equally charming title, *The Heart Is the Teacher.*[3] In this autobiographical book, he tells his story, from his school years as a young immigrant boy through his long career as a teacher and administrator in New York City schools, where he paid particular attention to the special needs of immigrant children.

I suggest that every teacher read this book if it can be found. Unfortunately, like many of the classic older education books, it is out of print, and can be difficult to find except at a university that has a teacher education program. But Covello was right, the heart is the teacher.

There are many classic books by teachers from the past which relate stories that remind us of why we decided to enter this profession. It might be a good idea to read or reread some of these classics when you can. (And encourage bookstores and publishers to keep printing and stocking them.)

⬙ HAVE YOU READ *a good "teacher" book lately? May I suggest Covello's* The Heart Is the Teacher?

FEBRUARY 21

OK, EXCUSE THE PUN, but today we are going to talk about a very touchy subject—touching. To parody a line from Shakespeare, "To touch, or not to touch, that is the question."

So much hoopla has been written and discussed about touching students these days, and whether it is appropriate or inappropriate to pat a child on the shoulder or hug a child. We even have a lesson on it for our pre-service and student teachers at the university where I teach methods classes. Most likely, you heard the same instruction wherever you earned your teaching credential. Your school and district probably have taken a stand on the issue as well, and by all means, you have to do what is right in your circumstances.

For me, however, I need to touch children to feel connected to them and their learning. Usually this consists of a pat on the back or a light touch on the arm. Working in a school district that

213

did not allow teachers to touch students was very uncomfortable for me, and I found myself occasionally—unintentionally—"breaking the law." But I did it because some children, I found, did not have the experience of a hug and seemed to really be crying out for one. Others sent messages that hugging was not acceptable, and so I did not.

Yes, people have abused the principle of touch, but I find an occasional hand on the shoulder, or hand on the forearm, to be very motivating for some children.

The issue of this "touchy" subject is common sense and knowing your students. It also means being aware of the consequences that could arise from touching any child. Use your good sense on this one.

🐌 DO YOU TOUCH CHILDREN? *Do they respond positively? Are you aware of the repercussions of touching your students?*

FEBRUARY 22

ON FEBRUARY 22, 1732, George Washington, the first president of the United States, was born. Did you know that he did not chop down the cherry tree? (Who spread that lie about not lying?) But he did do many other admirable things. And although the date of celebration changes each year, certainly you should be enjoying your day off, no matter what day of the week you celebrate it.

Did you know that 102 years before Washington was born, on this day in 1630, popcorn was introduced to the colonists? Now *that* is a holiday worth celebrating! I don't know about the places where you teach, but in every school I have ever worked in, you could always find your way to the teachers' lounge by the smell of popcorn in the microwave on somebody's prep period.

February

And I am old enough to know that prior to microwaves it was popped in "air pots," and prior to that in electric popcorn poppers. (Ask your grandmother if you have never seen one of these.)

Popcorn is the fifth food group for most school personnel. How about a bowl of buttery popcorn to celebrate George's birthday?

⌘ WHAT ARE YOU DOING *to inform your students about the first president of the United States? Are you telling that "Cherry Tree" story again?*

FEBRUARY 23

ON FEBRUARY 23, 1917, the Federal Board for Vocational Education was created by Congress with the passing of the Smith-Hughes Act, which provided matching funding for states to develop trade and agricultural schools.[4] Since that time, vocational education in the forms of home economics, industrial education, business, and other trades, have been exceedingly popular or unpopular depending on the year's focus on education.

In recent years, vocational education has found it difficult to survive during periods of budget cuts and limited resources. Keeping vocational education classes stocked with modern supplies has been a challenge for vocational education teachers.

Most recently, teachers in vocational programs have found themselves defending their programs when asked what they are teaching their students to do and whether they can keep up with modern technology. In essence, are they teaching their students skills that will be obsolete by the time they graduate from high school?

A more flagrant and perhaps justifiable complaint against these programs is that they are sometimes labeled as "tracking":

programs for the poor, minorities, and less-gifted students—preparing a labor force for business.

Having been a vocational teacher, I do not see these accusations as a problem, nor do I see the need to defend the skills that I teach. The solution is to modernize the courses for today and tomorrow's expectations. The skills taught in these classes can be used for personal enhancement and leisure activities as well as for job skills. Young people will still need to understand good nutrition even if the future predicts that Americans will eat out more and more at fast food restaurants. Learning how to type, build something, prepare a resume, and repair equipment are useful skills for everyone. And some of the activities taught in these classes are downright *fun!*

Does all learning have to be academic? Do the schools in your district use vocational education classes to "track" students?

February 24

Along with hearts and love, February is also the month for celebrating the Mardi Gras, or Pancake Day, or Shrove Tuesday, the last day before Lent. Mardi Gras is celebrated in many cities, in theme parks, and on cruises, among other places. Although it is a religious holiday, we often associate it with irreligious behavior. Hummm! Interesting, isn't it?

Mardi Gras is generally celebrated with processions, masquerades, and fun activities. When we think of the Mardi Gras we usually think of bright colors and costumes. What a great day to make your room brightly colored, and maybe keep it that way for a while.

⚬ HOW CAN YOU *incorporate the Mardi Gras into your day?*

FEBRUARY 25

COOPERATIVE LEARNING, as we discussed earlier on February 10, is based on the theory that students will more easily comprehend difficult concepts if they can work on lessons with one another. It incorporates the belief that learning is social in nature and that students working with their peers model for each other appropriate learning and ways of thinking. Students working in cooperative learning groups, according to this theory, are better able to understand difficult concepts, experience higher achievement, and feel better about learning.

Cooperative learning methods include the use of student learning teams, team-assisted individual learning, cooperative grouping, learning together, and group investigation.[5]

⚬ IN WHAT *different forms can your students learn together—cooperatively?*

FEBRUARY 26

ONE LAST VALENTINE. Often, when an individual becomes a teacher, it is because he or she enjoyed school, possibly did well in it, or had a teacher who in some way impacted their lives. You impact children's lives everyday, and as a result, some of them may become teachers someday, too.

Wouldn't you like to know if you have impacted someone's life? Maybe you have been around long enough to know that you did. Some of you have, and have received notes of thanks from those former students. Others of you have motivated students to become successful adults but have not heard from those busy individuals. After all, how often have we thanked those teachers who were an influence in our lives? (And we *are* teachers.)

Have you ever thanked your teachers? Have you written a letter to them explaining how they were an inspiration to you?

I try to do this occasionally, and I know that it has been important for those recipients of my letters to know that someone is thinking of them after all these years. Several have written back, building my ego as well. What goes around comes around, or so they say.

Is there *an individual, a teacher, that deserves a "thank you" from you? Isn't it about time that you told him or her so?*

FEBRUARY 27

IN THE SONG "Frozen," Madonna sings of her wish to "melt the heart" of someone she cares about, so that the individual can experience the love that she feels. The lyrics read, "If I could melt your heart. . . ." Have you ever loved someone who had difficulty in opening up to you, so that you wished that you could "melt" their "frozen heart"?[6]

We are not talking here about the love you may have experienced for another adult. We are looking at the child whose heart has been frozen by the cruelty of people who should have known better.

Have you ever taught that cold child who will not open to your love, and therefore your teaching, because of previous hurts? How can you "melt the heart" of such a child?

February

꩜ HOW DO WE *melt the hearts of children who have experienced pain so that we can open the door to the educational experience?*

FEBRUARY 28

TODAY IS my mother's birthday. What better time to talk about moms than on her special day. Yes, I was like most other teenagers and young adults and went through a period when my mother was a difficult person. (It couldn't have been me who was difficult then, during those teen years, could it?) But prior to that time, I thought my mother was one of the most beautiful women in the world, and after that time—those teen years when "she" went completely out of date—I have felt the same. Mothers, my mother, are some of the most beautiful people on Earth, and although your older students may not admit it, the younger ones will agree with this.

Moms can be wonderfully supportive of you and your classroom, if you take the time to invite them to be a part of their children's educations. Invite them in and see how beautiful they really are. (And dads, too.)

꩜ HAVE YOU *taken the time to see how beautiful your students' moms are? How will you find out if you don't invite them in?*

FEBRUARY 29

EVERY FOURTH YEAR, an amazing phenomenon occurs on our calendar: We get one extra day!

In actuality, every year is not 365 days long, but 365 and a quarter days long. Leap year is the name given to that fourth year when a day is added to make up for the accumulation of quarter-days. Someone (supposedly Julius Caesar) decided to add that day to February, possibly because February was shorter by a couple of days than the other months of the year.

If this is leap year, then you are blessed with one more day to accomplish many things, one added twenty-four hours to encourage growth in your students, an extra 1,440 minutes—surely you can eke out some time for yourself.

☙ HOW WILL YOU *spend this extra day of the year?*

MARCH

MARCH 1

MARCH IS ONE of "those" months. Students and teachers have been in school for more than six months, and the holidays are over (especially the anticipatory ones where children receive gifts, candy, and special activities are taking place). The weather is often unpredictable; sunny one day and snowy or rainy the next. When the morning arrives, it is difficult to know how to dress for the day.

March is windy, cool, warm, cold, rainy, snowy, blustery, and nice. It is also a long month, usually without a day off or special occasion to celebrate except St. Patrick's Day. So what is good about March?

For one thing, it is the official beginning of spring, the "over-the-hump" month for school, and summer sports like baseball, soccer, track, and tennis begin their seasons. It is the end of winter, good kite-flying weather, and time to watch for crocus to sprout through the dirt or snow (depending on where you live). It is a great time to splash in puddles.

It is the month in which we celebrate Women's History Month.

It is also the time when "a young man's fancy turns to love. . . ." Why else would I have had my first date with the man in my life, married him in March three years later, and conceived our first son in a later March? (These were not planned as March activities, honest!)

There is something more to March than first meets the eye. March is not just one of "those" months. Let's look at it.

꩜ CAN YOU RECALL *anything special about March? If so, what? If not, maybe now is the time to make it memorable. How can you make March something other than one of "those" months?*

March

MARCH 2

WE HAVE BEEN IN SCHOOL for several months now, and some teachers may be finding that the original enthusiasm of their students is on the wane. Part of this lack of spark can be attributed to the difficulty, to paraphrase Dewey, of seeing the "end in view." Also, as mentioned yesterday, March tends to be one of the few months when there are no vacations, no end-of-semester breaks, and no three-day weekends. Other than St. Patrick's Day (which comes with no gifts attached), few fun activities occur unless it is that rare year when Easter is early.

It looks like it is a good time to get both your students and yourself back on track for the next few weeks. The following *Teacher Tips* are helpful hints, collected from other teachers (who have "been there, done that . . ."), which may help you through this long time:

• If you have not already, have your students keep a "planner" that is checked daily to ensure that everyone gets the directions and homework assignments correctly. It is easy for students (and teachers) to get a little lazy during this time. Do not dismiss students until they have written their assignments and directions in their planners.

• Although you may have done so earlier, make it a point to walk around the school grounds during breaks and at noontime, to talk and visit with students. This gives your students an opportunity to get to know you outside of the classroom and helps with discipline inside the classroom.

• Remember to continue sending home weekly progress reports that require a parent signature. Remember that this reduces the number of surprises (and possibly phone calls) at report card time.

• Don't let misbehavior get to you. Remember that if you lose your temper, you have lost the situation. You may need to remind your students of your standards (or maybe reevaluate them), be consistent, and calmly deal with the offender and the offense.

• Be flexible with interruptions from the office, counselors, principals, and students. Be a model to your students of what a calm adult looks like.

❧ ARE THERE *any other areas that need to be worked on or reevaluated because it is March?*

MARCH 3

PLANNING CURRICULUM is so much more than teaching a subject to a child or adolescent. It requires that the various elements involved in their learning must be taken into account. Dewey called these learning elements the subject, the child, and the society in which we all live.

According to Jerome Bruner, developing curriculum involves knowing the child as an individual and includes knowing the educational psychology behind the individual. He wrote in 1966, "a theory of instruction seeks to take account of the fact that a curriculum reflects not only the nature of knowledge itself but also the nature of the knower and the knowledge-getting process. It is an enterprise par excellence where the line between subject matter and method grows necessarily indistinct." Bruner concludes, "Knowledge is a process, not a product."[1]

When you think of knowledge as a process, it is easy to see that the process of knowledge includes that of being a lifelong learner. We are not developing curriculum as an end product, and therefore not all learning is "testable." Instead we are giving young people the tools to go on learning. Wow! What a mission!

✍ DO YOU DESIGN *your curriculum as an end product or as a process which encourages learning to continue?*

MARCH 4

DURING HER LIFETIME and after her death, Hilda Taba (1902–1967) continues to have a major influence on curriculum theory and practice. In a similar vein to Jerome Bruner, who considered education as a process, Taba wrote, "Since no program, no matter how thorough, can teach everything, the task of all education is to cause a maximum amount of transfer."[2]

To *transfer,* according to the dictionary, is to send or carry something or someone to another place. Isn't that what we are trying to do with young people? Although Taba is writing of the transfer of knowledge, isn't education about the transference of an individual to somewhere else, to a higher plane of knowledge?

✍ DO YOU PLAN *your curriculum for maximum transfer, not only of information but for transference to that higher plane?*

MARCH 5

JOHN DEWEY, too, wrote of the necessity of knowing the nature of the learner (as did Bruner) and the transferability of the information (like Taba). Dewey believed that "if the subject-matter of the lessons be such as to have an appropriate place within the expanding consciousness of the child," it must grow out of his own past "doings, thinkings, and sufferings," and grow "into application in further achievements and receptivities." If a teacher utilizes the child's interests and thinking, "then no device or trick of method has to be resorted to in order to enlist 'interest.'" The result is transfer of learning.

So often we view curriculum as something to give (teach) to the child rather than teaching the information as part of their own experiences. That is why it is not transferable, because, as Dewey writes, it is not "psychologized . . . that is, placed in the whole conscious life so that it shares the worth of that life."[3]

◐ HOW CAN YOU *find out what experiences and "thinkings" are active in your students lives to further enhance transfer?*

MARCH 6

DEWEY ALSO BELIEVED in the importance of *play* in a young person's life. He once wrote that "play is not to be identified with anything which the child externally does. It rather designates his mental attitude in its entirety and in its unity. It is the free play, the interplay, of all the child's powers, thoughts, and physical movements, in embodying, in a satisfying form, his own images and interests."[4]

Isn't it interesting that so often we are afraid to use play as a method of teaching and learning, especially as children get older. Our fear seems to stem from the idea that someone may visit our classroom and see that our students are having "too much fun." Yet, if you think back to the learning experiences in your childhood, weren't many of the "fun times" the most memorable?

When I think back, I realize that not only were some of my own play experiences in school the most long-lasting educationally, but in my teaching experience, when my students were learning and having fun, I was having fun, too.

꩜ How can play *be used to make learning fun and meaningful for your students?*

March 7

Yesterday we talked about making learning fun, and today we are going to investigate how to do that. There are many behaviors that you want your students to learn along with subject information. The following *Teacher Tips* from veteran teachers may help you to devise some meaningful play experiences for your students:

• One of the first behaviors that you want your students to learn is how to follow directions. To do this in a fun way, divide the students into groups of four. Give to each group a large piece of butcher paper, crayons, markers, and a list of instructions telling them what to draw. When the group is finished drawing, compare pictures to see how well each group followed directions.

• On February 11, we gave an example of a "Finish the Story," an activity which helps students to overcome their fear of writing. This time we will vary the pattern by *hiding* previous sentences from the writer. If you recall, in Finish the Story, the teacher begins a story with one line and a student writes the next line. But this time the student folds the first sentence under so that the next student sees only the second sentence. That student writes a third sentence based on only the second and folds the previous sentence under. The process is repeated until each student has added one sentence to the story. The resulting work is often quite humorous.

• Teachers can also teach the parts of speech with the use of *Mad Libs*. These books were popular in the 1980s. A story is developed with blanks throughout the paragraph. The reader was asked to fill in the blank by using a noun, verb, adverb, adjective, or other part of speech. The results, which required a knowledge of the parts of speech to complete, were also quite humorous.

• Students can also study serious information in a fun way using food. In a science class, students can construct a model of DNA, elements of chemistry, or the solar system using multicolored marshmallows.

⋙ How can you *make important information in your subject area fun for your students?*

March 8

Continuing with our theme of "*Fun* in the Classroom" or "The Use of *Play* to Make Learning *Fun,*" factual information can also be learned through play in content-specific classrooms. The following *Teacher Tips* will show you how:

• In social studies classes, one teacher I know uses music to help her students relate to the subject being studied. Her students sing "Dixie" during the Civil War, ballads, and even spirituals, to discuss how music was relevant to the individuals during this period.

• Certainly in English classes, but also in other subjects where vocabulary words are learned, a teacher can write the vocabulary word on the board and see how many words the students can make from it. The students are then asked if the words that they made are related in meaning to the vocabulary word.

• At the end of the class, if there are a few minutes remaining, have big flashcards with the unit's vocabulary on them. Ask the students to define the word or explain its relevance to the topic that you are studying.

• Some teachers have students make their own business cards, license plates, flags, or shields, when studying various topics or as a method of getting to know the students better.

☙ Is your classroom *fun for your students?*

MARCH 9

NOT ONLY can games and play be a meaningful learning experience for your students, sports, too, can encourage learning and increase information for your students. The following *Sporting Teacher Tips* may be fun for you and your students. They are also excellent ways to study for tests:

• Baseball Jeopardy. Mark "bases" on the floor using masking tape. Then develop questions from your subject area organized into four levels of difficulty representing a single, double, triple, or home run. Divide the class into two teams. Students "come up to bat" asking for a single, double, triple, or home run question. If they are correct, they take their base. If the answer is incorrect, they are out. (Unless you are nice and give them three chances/strikes.) The game continues until everyone has a turn, or longer if you are having fun.

• My students often enjoyed a game of basketball before a test. I had a wastebasket basketball net that I brought out for just this occasion. I divided the class into two teams. Each student had a wadded piece of paper (a good way to use up scrap paper) that they could try for a basket if they answered the question correctly. The point only counted if they made the basket.

• Often physical education teachers will develop new sports by combining the rules of existing sports. (For example: volley-tennis or basketball-bowling.) This not only teaches the rules of the original games, but "levels the playing field" as students get older, allowing those who have less experience in athletics to have a fair chance with those who have more.

• Students can learn math by following the statistics of teams and individual players using the sports sections of the newspaper. Assign a player or team to each student or allow students to select their own. Bring in the newspaper each day, and have students keep track of their player's or team's performance and calculate their statistics.

Using sports for learning is not only fun but allows students to learn *actively.*

☙ How can *your students learn* actively?

March 10

Although we often think of television as being a detriment to learning, television game shows have worked their way into the classrooms with some positive and fun methods for learning. Because young people watch so much (too much?) television and are familiar with the games, many of the popular TV games lend themselves to teaching facts with very little preparation. The following games have been modified for various subjects:

• *Jeopardy.* Divide students into groups (instead of individual contestants). Students can select a category for a number of points, then try to answer the questions.

• *Wheel of Fortune.* Groups can spin a wheel and answer questions to gain points.

• *Concentration.* Have students make one stack of index cards containing only a word and another stack of cards containing the definitions of those words. When they come in the classroom they may play *Concentration* with a few other students.

March

- *Tic Tac Toe.* Groups are asked questions to "earn" a square.

- Create a talk show where the characters of a novel or historical figures are interviewed.

Remember, you don't have to do all the work. To save time, have students make up the questions and/or the games!

❧ SINCE TELEVISION *plays such a major role in young people's lives, in what ways can you piggyback on its success?*

MARCH 11

ASIDE FROM TELEVISION, young people often spend a considerable amount of time playing board games that can also be used to enhance learning. The following are some *Teacher Tips* for transforming these games into learning-rich activities for your students. (Again, ask your students to help with developing the game as well as playing them. Keep this year's questions for next years students.):

- Boggle is a game played with letters on "dice" where the players make up words from the letters that are rolled. For our purposes, the teacher selects his or her own letters and writes them on a Boggle grid on an overhead transparency before class begins. As the bell rings, the letters are uncovered and students have a predetermined amount of time to find as many words as they can.

- Pictionary is another fun game that can be adapted for the classroom, with the students drawing the vocabulary words while other students try to guess the word by the drawing.

- Bingo has been adapted in many forms for use in the classroom. Students can play Vocabulary Bingo where students write their vocabulary words in each box, marking off the box as the teacher calls the definitions. Variations of the game can be played with math (multiplication, division, fractions, et cetera), geography (using capitals and states), history (significant dates), and science (elements). The list of possibilities seems endless.

• Board games can be made by the teacher or the students to teach a variety of subjects. Or allow students to teach a subject *and* select the game they will use to do so. End the topic by playing the games.

• Teachers can also use existing games to teach a subject, such as board game math. Split into groups of three or four, having each group select a different board game such as Monopoly, Life, or other game. After each group has selected a game, then ask how math is being used in the playing of the game.

Whew, I think we have covered enough games for the month of March.

꽃 IS THERE *any other way that you can think of to use board games to make learning fun?*

MARCH 12

ON MARCH 12, 1912, the Girls Scouts of America was founded by Juliette Gordon Low in Savannah, Georgia. Its aim was to help girls grow into happy, useful women and good citizens through democratic participation in group activities, community service, creative arts, and outdoor recreations. The group's divisions include Brownies, Intermediate Scouts, and Senior Girl Scouts. Similar to Boy Scouts, Girl Scouts earn badges, do good deeds, and learn outdoor skills. In addition, they sell great cookies.

Having been a Brownie Scout and Girl Scout, I can personally vouch for the fun these young ladies experience and the citizenship and leadership skills they are taught. Why not see if you

March

have a few Girl Scouts in your classroom and utilize these responsible young women in your class?

❧ HAVE YOU *bought your Girl Scout cookies this year?*

MARCH 13

SINCE MARCH IS Women's History Month, and we just celebrated the Girl Scout's birthday, maybe it is time to look at the topic of "women's work." As part of my responsibilities as a college professor, I occasionally have to supervise student teachers, encourage them to be high-quality teachers, and sometimes point out where they need improvement.

I have been blessed with some very strong young (and middle-aged) students who will be fine teachers one day. But one area that I constantly have to work with them on is reminding them not to squelch a young girl's future successes with an outdated view of what is "women's work."

For example, just the other day, one of my better students gave a beautiful lesson on "tools" to accompany a story she was reading to second graders. She spoiled it by asking what tools would be found in their *father's* garage, and what tools do their mothers use for *cleaning house.* This job-specific thinking reminds students of their roles in life and may be the determining factor in discouraging a young woman from becoming an astronaut and a young man from becoming a nurse. We also need to remember that many of our students live in one-parent households where it is indeed *mother's* garage or *father* does the cooking and cleaning. Is there any such thing as "women's" or "men's" work?

❧ DO YOU MAKE *an extra effort to ensure equality by keeping traditional gender-specific references to a minimum?*

233

MARCH 14

WHILE WE ARE ON the topic of equality, it is important to review the stories we select for heroines as well as heroes. We need to be aware of the examples we use to our impressionable young men and women. According to the *Publication Manual of the American Psychological Association,* the definitive style manual for writing in educational journals and books, "Sexist bias can occur when pronouns are used carelessly; when the masculine pronoun *he* is used to refer to both sexes, or when the masculine or feminine pronoun is used exclusively to define roles by sex (e.g., 'the nurse . . . *she*')."[5] We need to think about this as we write, read, and discuss people in our classrooms.

The *APA Manual* adds, "The use of *man* as a generic noun or as an ending for an occupational title (e.g., *policeman*) can be ambiguous and may imply incorrectly that all persons in the group are male. . . . Use caution . . . to avoid stereotypes."[6]

ᗞ DO YOU MAKE an effort to avoid sex bias in your discussions? How do you do that?

MARCH 15

MARCH 15, the "Ides of March," the day of Julius Caesar's death in Rome in the year 44 B.C. "Beware of the Ides of March," according to Shakespeare. But what is there to beware of? Maybe it is to be *aware* of the Ides of March. It seems like any other day doesn't it?

But that is exactly why we should be aware of it. As we discussed on March 2, it is easy to become complacent during these days because it appears that not much is happening. These are the "Dog Days" that we talked about on August 4. Do you remember? The time when the season has been going on too long and

March

the end is still a good distance away. The time when "players" are getting nicks and bruises. And yet, what else is happening? That's right, you remembered, "the good players rise to the top."

Now is the time to get out those activities that you planned for the Dog Days of School—the field trips, good behavior trips, contests, and special activities—that will keep your students *and* you motivated for the days ahead.

WHAT WERE the activities that you planned for the Dog Days of School? What are some new activities that you have thought of since?

MARCH 16

BECAUSE MARCH IS Women's History Month, we have focused on gender issues and equality in teaching to encourage full growth and future success for all of our students. Treating girls equally means giving equal responsibility and having equal expectations as well.

A situation occurred last spring in the classroom of one of my student teachers where boys were treated unfairly, thus reinforcing the idea that girls should be treated differently. The story goes like this:

Some fifth-grade boys were playing basketball and a girl asked to play, too. When one of the boys kept blocking her shot, the girl became angry and shoved the boy out of the way. When the boy shoved back, the girl reported the incident to my student who punished the boy for shoving the girl, responding that boys do not treat girls this way.

She was right in one respect—boys should not shove girls, *but* girls should not shove boys either. *And* shoving is not allowed in basketball. So, both players were wrong. Therefore, if one is punished, then both should be in trouble. This incident allowed a girl to get away with something *because she is a girl!*

For equality to be equitable, punishment as well as rewards are equal in school and elsewhere.

⊃ DO YOU GIVE *equal correction when it is due to both girls and boys?*

MARCH 17

EVERY YEAR, on March 17, we celebrate the one March holiday, St. Patrick's Day, named for Patrick, the patron saint of Ireland, and thus the "wearing of the green." Saint Patrick was born in western Britain in the early fifth century and died in Ireland around A.D. 492. Although there appears to be some discrepancy in his life story, he did serve as a bishop in Ireland with some satisfaction to the Irish.

In America, in Boston, the first municipal celebration of St. Patrick's Day was held by the newly established Charitable Irish Society in 1737. Until that time it had been celebrated only within its religious context. Municipal celebrations of the holiday were initiated in Philadelphia in 1780, and in New York in 1784, where their joyous activities were jointly sponsored by Catholics and Presbyterians.[7]

Today St. Patrick's Day is generally celebrated with parades, parties, shamrocks, and wearing green. No gifts please, but it does break up the month.

⊃ CAN YOU THINK OF *any fun activities for students for St. Patrick's Day that celebrate diversity? That focus on the color green?*

March

MARCH 18

CONTINUING ON OUR THEME for March—Women's History Month—I mention again the book *Failing at Fairness: How Our Schools Cheat Girls,* by David and Myra Sadker, which we first discussed in August. Many other good books and pamphlets are available that should be required reading by teachers and students in teacher education programs.

A worthwhile series of booklets have been written and published by the members of the American Association of University Women (AAUW), such as *How Schools Shortchange Girls* and *Growing Smart: What's Working For Girls in School.* These articles consist of reports researched and written by professors at universities.

Another "must read" book is the 1982 publication *In a Different Voice: Psychological Theory and Women's Development* by Dr. Carol Gilligan, a psychologist and Professor of Education at Harvard University. Gilligan, who worked and researched with Lawrence Kohlberg (remember Kohlberg's "Theory of Moral Development"?), discovered that the theories of development that were being written in educational psychology books, and read by teachers throughout the nation, had been developed by researchers who studied boys and not girls. Could it be, thought Gilligan, that the development of females is different and therefore we do a disservice to them by expecting them to fit into the theories of *normal* development that we see in males?[8]

❧ DO YOU EXPECT *boys and girls to develop the same in school? What differences can you see in the development of the males and females in the age group of students that you teach?*

237

MARCH 19

ON THIS DATE in 1860, Elizabeth Cady Stanton appeared before the New York State Legislature to promote the cause of women's suffrage. What an interesting spectacle that must have been! Stanton, a woman without voting privileges, addressing a room full of men to gain the right to vote for women in the state of New York.

Thirty-two years later, in 1892, at seventy-seven years old, Stanton addressed the rights of women again and said, "If we consider her as a citizen, as a member of a great nation, she must have the same rights as all other members. . . . Her rights and duties are still the same—individual happiness and development."

She continued, "The strongest reason for giving women all the opportunities for higher education, for the full development of her faculties, her forces of mind and body; for giving her the most enlarged freedom of thought and action; a complete emancipation from all the forms of bondage, of custom, dependence, superstition, from all the crippling influences of fear—is the solitude and personal responsibility of her own individual life.

"To throw obstacles in the way of a complete education," Stanton wrote, "is like putting out the eyes; to deny the rights of property is like cutting off the hands. . . . Who, I ask you, can take, dare take on himself the rights, the duties, the responsibilities of another soul?"9

   WHEN STATED *that way, do any of us have the "right to take the rights of another's soul" by not giving equality to every one of our students?*

March

MARCH 20

MARCH 20, the first day of spring. Do you see a difference? Have you taken the time even to look? If you look closely, you will probably see at least a minor indication that spring may be on its way.

Spring is a time of growth, birds, and love. The beginning of the pre–baseball season and other new beginnings. The days are getting longer, and we hope (at least occasionally) the days are a little warmer. It is time to open the windows, if only for a short time, to let the fresh air in.

This time of year often reminds me of my childhood when springtime meant spring cleaning, a yearly ritual when floors were waxed, walls were washed, and freshly washed curtains were hung out on the line to blow in the breeze. I remember coming home from school and knowing it was spring because the house had a fresh, bright, open-aired look, and the smell of paste wax on wooden floors was fresh in my nostrils. Just thinking about it brings the sights and odors back to me with fond memories.

---

๑ HAS SPRING ARRIVED *in your classroom? Is your room full of fresh air? Can you bring a breath of fresh air into your classroom?*

MARCH 21

REMEMBER ON March 18 when we talked about Carol Gilligan's work on the developmental psychology of girls? Gilligan promoted the rights of young girls to be accepted and taught according to their form of development. Not to be accepted in a boys' world (assuming that boys are the *norm*), but to be accepted in the educational world as *both boys and girls being the norm.*

Gilligan writes in *In a Different Voice*, "Psychological theorists have fallen. . . . Implicitly adopting the male life as the norm, they have tried to fashion women out of masculine cloth." The result is that, in the life cycle, according to Gilligan, as in the Garden of Eden, "the woman has been the deviant."

She continues with a discussion of the various theorists that we study in educational psychology:

"Freud considered women to be deprived by nature of the impetus for a clear-cut Oedipal resolution. Consequently, women's superego . . . was compromised." In "Piaget's account (1932) of the moral judgment of the child, girls are an aside, a curiosity to whom he devotes four brief entries in an index that omits 'boys' altogether because 'the child' is assumed to be male." And Kohlberg's (1958, 1981) six stages that described the development of moral judgment from childhood to adulthood are "based empirically on a study of eighty-four boys" whose development Kohlberg had followed for a period of twenty years.

Gilligan concludes, "Yet herein lies a paradox, for the very traits that traditionally have defined the 'goodness' of women, their care for and sensitivity to the needs of others, are those that mark them as deficient in moral development."[10]

❧ Do you allow *your female students to be female, while allowing "female" to be OK?*

MARCH 22

TO ME, ONE OF THE most unique things about spring is that so much is happening *outside*. Trees are budding, plants are sprouting, bulbs are growing, the sky seems clearer, the sun brighter, and nature appears to be in its most creative form. Because of this, today seems to be a good time to discuss creativity in our classrooms.

When I think back on my time as a teacher, whether in elementary, junior high school, senior high school, and perhaps even college, I do not recall encouraging any of my students to be creative in their endeavors to fulfill the requirements for the course. I do not recall being encouraged to be creative in my own schooling either.

It seems, with our need to test for recall, and our rubrics for achieving high grades, our students are continually reminded to stay within the guidelines and give us the responses we seek to move on to the next step. When a budding Picasso or Monet recklessly colors outside the lines, we show them the *proper* way to do better the next time. Musicians must play the written notes, young authors must write a proper paragraph, and we end up with students just like ourselves who earned good grades because they followed directions. But where has the creativity been "taught" or encouraged in our daily lives?

Rollo May writes in *The Courage to Create* that "there is a special point" he would like to make "about preoccupation in the United States with 'behavior.' . . . Practically all of us as children have heard: 'Behave yourself! Behave! Behave!'" What this focus on behaving does is threaten the "creative freedom of the artist."

May adds, "We cannot escape our anxiety over the fact that the artist together with creative persons of all sorts, are the possible destroyers of our nicely ordered systems. For the creative impulse is the speaking of the voice and the expressing . . . and this is, by its very nature, a threat to rationality and external control."[11]

ᗝ Do you encourage *students to be creative? How can you allow freedom of expression within your subject?*

MARCH 23

IS IT TIME for a new wardrobe? Have you had your sweaters and woolens out long enough? It is spring now and time to freshen up the environment with some transitional dressing. It is time to do what my mother-in-law calls, "go shopping in my closet."

When is the last time you saw the back of your clothes closet or the bottom of your drawers? If you are like me, these areas can be scary places as I find sweaters from my high school days (and I am not young), shoes that have been out of style for several seasons (and were never comfortable to begin with), and outfits that have been the wrong size for some time (but I am sure I will fit into one day, when they will no longer be in style).

One advantage of "shopping in your closet" is that you have an opportunity to run into that outfit that you bought on a whim last year, forgot about, and that is perfect for that upcoming conference or special activity.

It is time. Go through that closet and those drawers. Not all at once of course; go through maybe one drawer a week. Try on a few things and get rid of the items that you will never wear again. (Box them up, give them to a charity, and you will be helping someone else *and* yourself.)

⚘ HAVE YOU BEEN *"shopping in your closet" lately? Did you find anything interesting?*

MARCH 24

ON MARCH 24, 1883, telephone service was put into operation between Chicago and New York. Isn't that amazing? That connection allowed people to talk, for the first time, to friends and relatives hundreds of miles away from one another. It seems

March

strange that it has only been a little more than one hundred years since that long distance service that we take for granted was established. Few of us reading this book can recall a time when we were unable to just pick up the phone and, provided the individual we wanted was home, talk to anyone in the United States. In our lifetimes, we have arrived at a time when we can call almost anyone in the world, leave a message if they are not available, and access an almost incomprehensible amount of information through the Internet using the phone lines in our home and at work.

Thank goodness for those creative individuals who developed inventions that made our daily lives easier. Do you suppose they were students who "stayed between the lines"?

☺ Why not celebrate *the connection of the phone lines in the last century by calling someone special and saying hello? Who will you call?*

March 25

We have been talking about spring housecleaning, and, by the way, have you found any new outfits in your closet shopping spree? While you are at it, why not clean out those cabinets in your classroom too?

Although it may sound a little strange, one of the most successful classroom cleaning sprees I experienced was the year that my building burned in an arson-set fire at my school. I was fortunate, in that although the structure was badly damaged, the contents of the room suffered only smoke damage. However, if you have ever experienced a fire, you know that that is quite a mess. The contents of the room—books, supplies, bulletin boards, personal belongings—were permanently stained, and smelled for years after of smoke. But this was a great opportunity to throw away unused, no-longer-needed items, if for no other reason than to improve the smell of the room. It was difficult to decide what to throw away and what to keep, but it was a cleansing experience after all.

As you have at home, maybe it is a good idea to take one closet or supply cabinet at a time. Warning: Do not attempt to clean closets at school and at home at the same time. It will be frustrating and you will soon lose interest in completing the job.

If you have supplies that you are not planning to use again soon, why not donate them to a colleague? In the process of cleaning, you may find something in the back of that cabinet that is just what you needed to enhance your teaching. Good luck!

When was the *last time you cleaned a school cabinet, closet, or your desk? Where will you begin?*

MARCH 26

ONE OF THE THINGS we can predict about March is its certain *unpredictability*. March is one of those "cusp" months that can be springlike one day and cold and wintry the next. Sort of like that saying I used to hear often when I lived in the Midwest: "If you don't like the weather, stick around and it will change." This time of year you may experience spring in the morning and winter by nightfall. March may have good days or maybe not. Like life, some days are good ones and some are not.

Your students may be affected by the weather, too. I used to do a secret survey when I taught. My theory was that people, no matter their ages, tended to wear dull, somber colors on gray days and brighter colors when the sun was shining. I was rarely proven wrong.

March

So, you say, what is the big deal about these results? The *deal* is that gray weather encouraged gray clothes, which seemed to influence gray attitudes!

You may want to do your own survey. See what clothes your students and colleagues wear on the various days. See what happens when you break the trend and wear bright clothes on a dreary day.

❧ HAVE YOU TRIED *the survey? What did you discover?*

MARCH 27

"WHY DON'T YOU go fly a kite!" Has anyone said that to you recently? I mean it in the good sense of the saying. When is the last time that you have flown a kite?

Kite flying can be fun and educational as well. To begin with, how do you build a kite that functions as it should? Does it need a tail? What are the aerodynamics of getting the kite off the ground and keeping it in the air once you do so?

Do you remember the tissue kites, box kites, and tails of torn sheets? Do you remember running to get the kite up in the air, splashing through puddles of melted snow, the discouragement of having your kite nosedive and crash to the ground, the teamwork involved with one person holding the kite while the other let out string, or deciding on the best open field to begin the process?

I think you should go fly a kite, splash in puddles, and have a great day.

❧ HAVE YOU FLOWN *a kite lately? Do you remember how?*

245

MARCH 28

SPRING, WHEN A "young man's (or woman's) fancy turns to love." At least it did for me. I started dating my husband in March of our senior year of high school. What is it about March that does this to young (and older) people?

Don't be surprised if your students, too, are being influenced by spring and falling in love, and don't make any less of their experiences than you would have others do about your affections. I am sure that the teachers who saw Paul and me holding hands outside the classroom, walking to the buses after school, and looking longingly into each other's eyes had no idea that we would end up together, have children, grandchildren, and many years of happiness together.

꙯ DO YOU MINIMIZE *the feelings of your students because of their youth?*

MARCH 29

IN THE EARLY 1970S, Judy Collins sang a song about clouds titled "Both Sides Now," which included the line, "I've looked at clouds from both sides now...."[12] Have you ever looked at clouds from both sides? Sitting on the ground or lying in the grass we can see clouds as wisps of white or billowy fluffs. They can be light with air or ominous with angry shades of gray. But from the top, these very same clouds appear entirely different. Flying in an airplane at 20,000 to 30,000 feet, clouds can seem stringy or dense and bumpy.

Children, too, can appear different depending on our angle of view, and which side we are seeing. We can affect our view of our students depending on which angle we want to see.

⏵ How do you *see your students today? Can you vary the way they appear to you by changing your angle? Can you see a better side of them?*

MARCH 30

THIS MONTH WE SPENT a lot of time on making learning fun through the use of games, sports, and play, and selecting subject matter for our students. On subject-matter selection, John Dewey wrote, "Abandon the notion of subject matter as something fixed and ready-made in itself, outside the child's experience; cease thinking of the child's experience as also something hard and fast; see it as something fluent, embryonic, vital; and we realize that the child and the curriculum are simply two limits which define a single process."[13]

Too often we think of "curriculum" as subject matter to be taught while students sit and listen. Implementing fun into the curriculum allows for students *and* their teacher to enjoy one another's company and accomplish the job we are hired to do.

⏵ Did you incorporate *fun into your classroom this month? Did you enjoy it?*

MARCH 31

DEWEY ALSO WROTE that curriculum should not be packaged materials and "preset frameworks carved in stone." Nor should it be text-driven planning or practice for standardized achievement tests. Curriculum is the living, instilling activities that children do in school which encourages them to become lifelong learners capable of knowing how and where to find the answers to their questions later in life.

According to Dewey, planning curriculum requires a teacher who is aware of the present needs of his or her students, and who also has the foresight to see into the future and predict the needs of the generations which follows. A teacher doesn't prepare a child for the future by teaching what he or she needs to know for that time, but by equipping him or her with the abilities to know in the future "how and where" to find the answers on their own.

❧ How are you *equipping your students to find answers in the future?*

APRIL

April 1

THE FIRST DAY of April is commonly known as April Fools' Day, a holiday "celebrated" (if we can use that term) in many countries around the world. On April Fools' Day, practical jokes, fun, or cruel tricks are played on the unsuspecting. Whom among us has not been the butt of or played such a joke on our friends and family members? April Fools' Day can be fun for everyone, except for the "fool," of course. Unfortunately, teachers are often the brunt of these jokes.

Sometimes as teachers we are afraid to look foolish or participate in the joke, but children respect the teacher who can be a part of the joke and laugh with the class. So often we want to be seen as the flawless expert, and for some of us this means not being able to accept our own imperfections. But, some teachers, often the well-loved ones, actually "set themselves up" to be imperfect, and their students benefit from the game.

One young student teacher I recently taught was just such a person. I admired her courage in facing her high school English students, putting her knowledge on the line and actually encouraging them to test her knowledge in a game she called "Stump the Teacher." "Stump Miss Rupe" was an activity she played with her students during vocabulary lessons, when she encouraged her students to use the dictionary and to try to find a word that she did not know. To stump her, they had to pronounce the word correctly, and she would try to guess the meaning or spelling of the word. If she did not know the word, students received candy or points toward their Preferred Activity Time (PAT). Her ability to show that she "did not know all the answers" allowed her students to see a "real" human being, a model of the lifelong learner. Would you be so brave?

    荤 DO YOU ALLOW *your students to see you as a human being? How can (or do) you do that?*

April

APRIL 2

UNLESS THIS WAS A YEAR when Easter was early, in March, it must be getting close to Easter time, which gives teachers a wealth of ideas to use to usher in the season. If we just set aside a few moments to think about Easter, aside from its religious connotations, Easter time is ripe with activities—pastel colors, Easter bonnets, coloring eggs, and so forth.

Did you know that on this date, April 2, in 1877, the first Easter Egg Roll took place at the White House, and it has been an Easter tradition to roll colored eggs across the White House lawn ever since? The numerous activities available that just use eggs alone can keep a teacher quite busy for the rest of the month. Using eggs as the center of discussion, they can become a biology lesson (the embryo), a science lesson (What happens to eggs when they are boiled?), a history lesson (the significance of eggs in spring rituals), a cooking lesson (What can a hungry person make with all of those hard-boiled eggs?), a farming lesson (What is involved to get the eggs from the farm to the market?), an economics lesson (early settlers bartering using farm produce), a dyeing lesson (What does vinegar do to the colors in the dyeing process?), a coloring lesson (What happens when two dyes are mixed? For example, blue and yellow makes green), and on and on.

Even if your school district does not allow religious discussions, and, like many districts, celebrates spring break (rather than what we old-timers knew of as Easter vacation), the season is "embryonic" with ideas for meaningful (and fun) activities.

᠑᠊ CAN YOU USE *the symbols of the season in your lesson planning? How?*

April 3

WHEN WE THINK of Easter time we often think of eggs, especially the colorful eggs that we dye for Easter egg hunts or that we place in Easter baskets. Eggs are used at Easter time because they are a symbol of the "new beginning" of the season. The religious symbolism of the egg can be seen as a new beginning of life with the resurrection of Jesus Christ, who had been nailed to the cross, died, was buried, and came back to life.

Do you dye hard-boiled eggs and decorate them for the season? I can remember years when I carefully decorated the eggs with crayon drawings, times when I glued stickers purchased just for the occasion, and even as a child, poked a hole in the egg on both ends, blew out the insides, decorated the shell, and hung it on an "Easter tree." In other busy years, I would quickly drop the hard-boiled eggs in egg dye, and that was the extent of my decoration, but they were still colorful in the bowl on Easter morning.

My husband always hid the eggs for our children the night before, and we would watch them hunt for the colored eggs on Easter morning. One year they miraculously appeared in the basket before any of us got up (apparently); one year we forgot about the dog and found no eggs on Easter morning; and in other years I hoped and prayed that they had all been found so that there would be no smelly "surprises" at a much later date.

Do you remember on January 9 when we discussed snowflakes and how each snowflake is different and unique? Do you recall that the discussion continued with the uniqueness of every child? Eggs allow us to expand on this conversation because they, as do snowflakes, remind us that students come in many forms, sizes, colors, and stages of development; but children, like eggs, can be fragile. Even the hard-boiled ones. If forgotten in some hidden spot, they too can "go bad."

April

Do you have *some students who have been ignored, left unattended for a long period of time? What can you do to "find" them?*

April 4

Three days ago, on April Fools' Day, we discussed the importance of appearing human to students, allowing students to see us as maybe a little less that perfect. Lest I give the wrong impression, and before we move on to other topics, I was not insinuating that we allow ourselves to appear to be "fools." Teachers need and deserve respect from their students and the community in which they work.

Part of that respect, as we discussed on August 24, is earned by the appearance and demeanor with which we carry ourselves. Obviously, teachers should not appear foolish to their students by wearing revealing or ridiculous clothing, by not being careful with hygiene, or by ignoring bad habits. Part of teaching is role modeling.

But being a good teacher, according to Thomas L. Good and Jere E. Brophy, also includes having what they call "with-it-ness," sometimes described as "having eyes in the back of one's head."

Good and Brophy write in *Looking in Classrooms* that "successful classroom managers display with-it-ness—their students know that they always 'know what is going on' in the room." This requires that teachers position themselves so that they are able to see all students and that they continuously scan the room to "respond to problems effectively and nip most of them in the bud. Those who fail to notice what is going on," they add, "are prone to such errors as failing to intervene until a problem becomes disruptive or spreads to other students. . . . Teachers who regularly make such errors convince students that their teachers do not know what is happening."[1]

253

Teachers who appear to be "with it" to their students, appear to be "un-foolish" as well.

⁂ How can you *appear to be "with it" and "un-foolish" to your students?*

April 5

Speaking of eggs . . . OK, you did not really think that you would be able to get through a whole month without a quote from John Dewey, did you? And the quote that follows seems to be fitting for April, since we have been discussing the many uses of eggs.

Dewey often used the school as a symbol of an "embryonic community," necessary for nurturing the young into our society. He wrote in *The School and Society* (in 1900) that it is important to "make each one of our schools an embryonic community life . . . that reflect[s] the life of the larger society.

"When one thinks of the child or student living in an embryonic condition within the school," Dewey continued, "one sees the true character of the school as nurturing sustenance for the undeveloped individual. School, therefore becomes the element in which the child can be nourished, protected and given an atmosphere to grow."[2]

⁂ Is your classroom *or place of activity an embryonic state for the young? How can it become so?*

April 6

The new growth and beginnings associated with spring and the colors of the Easter season bring to mind the wonderful opportunities for art, music, and creativity that seem to be a part of the season (or any season for that matter). As most teachers are aware, art can be used in many subjects, and should not be relegated to elective classes alone. The following *Teacher Tips* may give you some ideas for using art and music in the core subjects, no matter what the age of the students that you teach:

- Ask your students to "Color a Song." At the beginning of class, play a classical, modern, or other song that is related to your topic. (For example, a Native American flute or drum piece, a campaign song, or music that is reflective of the season.) Give your students a set of felt pens, crayons, coloring pencils, paints, or some other medium. It is their task to draw images that come to their minds as they are inspired by the music.

- Play classical or other music and ask students to draw lines with the flow of the music. See if they can "feel" the music. This also introduces students to forms of music that they may be not be familiar with from the radio.

- Pick a particularly expressive piece of music (preferably one without lyrics), and have the students close their eyes and imagine a place with something happening. Let them listen for about three minutes, then go around the room and ask each student to tell what they "saw" while listening to the music. This can be a starter activity for demonstrating an understanding of the expressive and figurative nature of poetry.

- Ask students to draw pictures of the topic you are studying. This allows those "artistic-but-not-good students" to have an opportunity to succeed in your class, too.

- Last, but not least, doodle. Yes, doodle. You, doodle. Doodling helps us relax after a long day. It is mind-clearing and you may even be surprised at your own creative skills.

255

⊃⟩ IN WHAT OTHER WAYS *can you use music or art in your subject to encourage creativity in your students? (P.S. Did you doodle today?)*

APRIL 7

BESIDES USING music and art, there are many other ways that students can express their creativity. Encouraging students to create may open an avenue for personal satisfaction for your students (and for you) for years to come. The following *Teacher Tips* will give some suggestions for the use of creative expression in your classroom:

• "Design your own word." Ask your students to create their own word, including a definition for the word. Students should be able to define it, tell its part of speech (whether a noun, verb, adjective, or other), and use it in a sentence. Remind students that it cannot be a word that already exists in the dictionary. Slang words are OK, as long as they are appropriate and nonoffensive.

• Have students draw their favorite scenes from the textbook or other book that they are reading. Students may also design bookmarks, placemats, maps, or make other creative objects as long as the end result relates to the story.

• Have an "Artist's Opening." Students can either create the artwork that you will display or bring art from garage sales or home. If they bring in artwork that they did not do, have the students pretend to be the artist and discuss the merit of "their" work. Students can design and prepare brochures for their guests, and refreshments can be served after the "show."

• Design and decorate T-shirts, or have a student-created work printed on them. The results can be shirts that are worn during the studying of the topic, as gifts for others, or they can even be used as a fund-raiser. (Used men's dress shirts make good "artists' canvasses" also.)

- Scavenger hunts can also be fun for the students. Choose a topic and let the students "find" the items that are related to the topic. For example, during a library visit ask students to find the distance between New York and Los Angeles (atlas) or an author's birthplace *(Who's Who in America)*. Better yet, let the students create their own lists relevant to the subject.

❧ WILL ANY *of these "creative ideas" work for you in your classroom? If so, which ones and why?*

APRIL 8

ONE OF THE hot topics for schools in the last decade has been the theory of "Multiple Intelligences" and its use in the classroom. Multiple Intelligences (MI) as a theory proposes that there are many "types" of learning styles, or "intelligences," that are experienced by individuals, and the knowledgeable teacher will vary his or her teaching methods so that all students have an equal opportunity to learn in the method that best suits their learning style.

Howard Gardner is perhaps best known for developing this theory. In his works he writes of seven intelligences and the characteristics of each of these learning types, including: 1) "logical/mathematical," the ability to handle long chains of reasoning; 2) "linguistic," a sensitivity to the sounds, rhythms, and meanings of words; 3) "musical," an appreciation of rhythm, pitch, timbre, and musical expressiveness; 4) "spatial," the ability to perceive the visual-spatial world and transform perceptions; 5) "bodily/kinesthetic," the ability to control body movements and handle objects skillfully; 6) "interpersonal," the capacity to discern and respond to other people; and 7) "intrapersonal," the

257

ability to access one's own feelings and the knowledge of one's own strengths.[3] (Later research has included the possibility of at least two more types of learning.)

The creative lessons from yesterday and the day before were good examples of teaching to the "musical" and "spatial" intelligences.

⊃⟩ THINK OF *one lesson you will be teaching soon. How can you reach a greater number of "intelligences" by the lessons that you choose?*

APRIL 9

IF YOU REMEMBER your U.S. History, you know that the Civil War ended on this date in 1865, when the Confederate General Robert E. Lee surrendered to the Union General Ulysses S. Grant at Appomattox Court House, following the Battle of Five Forks on April 1. Although this surrender officially ended the War, unfortunately, because of poor communication, the battles continued for several weeks after Lee's surrender, and more soldiers died needlessly.

We spend a great amount of time in history classes teaching and learning about the Civil War, books and movies have been made about it, and Civil War aficionados reenact the battles in full garb at historical sites around the nation. It seems that we glorify and romanticize a completely unromantic era and a black mark on our nation's history. Never before, or since, has our country experienced the turmoil and divisiveness of that one era in our history, where states, factions, and even families fought one another.

Did you know that England and other countries ended slavery in their countries without war?

⟫ WHAT CAN YOU *tell your students about today's date that reflects the actual experience without glorifying and romanticizing the situation?*

APRIL 10

ALONG WITH THE COLORS of April and the creativity of springtime, this month also allows us an opportunity to use nature to enhance learning in our classrooms. Many of the lessons that we relegate to science classes can fit equally well with other subjects. The following *Teacher Tips* from veteran teachers may help your students learn important information for their good health:

• Bring in goldfish for students to observe. Give each student a goldfish in a glass or bowl and ask them to count the number of breaths the fish takes in a minute. Then change the temperature of the water (just a little), and see how the fish's breathing rate changes. Inform them that the effect of temperature on humans is similar.

• Bring a chameleon to class, place it on various colored surfaces, and watch it change colors. Explain to your students that chameleons change colors to hide from predators. Discuss how (and why) people can sometimes be "chameleons" too.

• Bring a variety of objects that are living and nonliving into your classroom. After observing the characteristics of the objects, ask the students to identify the various characteristics of the object's life (for example, seashells, fossils, herbs, et cetera). Ask your students to determine if the objects are or were alive, and how they can tell.

• Give each student a straw, and ask them to attempt to breathe in and out of the straw while they perform some physical activity such as stepping or walking quickly. This will give your students some idea of what a smoker feels like when he or she exercises and we hope discourage them from smoking.

• Remember, when using animals in your classroom, treat them fairly and carefully. This will be a good lesson for your students on how to treat pets and other living beings.

ॐ WHAT OTHER OBJECTS *from nature will help your students learn important and healthy information?*

APRIL 11

WHEN WE DISCUSSED earlier the significance of April Fools' fun, the necessity of enjoying the fun without appearing foolish, and the need for teachers to be "with it," we also included the importance of appearing "human" to your students. Anna Quindlen once wrote, "A good judge remembers what it was like to be a lawyer. A good boss remembers what it was like to be an employee. A good parent remembers what it was like to be a child."[4]

To this, I might add, "A good teacher remembers what it was like to be a student."

It is interesting to watch the graduate students in my master's degree classes. These men and women teach all day, expect proper behavior from their students, and have rules about tardiness, talking, and turning in papers on time, yet they are the very same people who whisper throughout the class discussion, come to class ten minutes late, give the same excuses as their students for late paperwork, squirm in their seats when it gets close to break time, and start packing their book bags before the class is over. If you ever want to remember what it was like to be a student, become one.

April

❧ IN WHAT WAYS *do you "remember what it was like to be a student"? Shouldn't you think about it now?*

APRIL 12

EVERY YEAR, either the week before Easter or the week after, members of the American Educational Research Association meet for five days, each year in a different major city across the United States and Canada, to present information relevant to educators from research that has been completed at colleges and universities around the world. This weeklong annual meeting draws thousands of members, including authors, professors, graduate students, and other notables in the field of education. It is one of the most exciting conferences that I attend each year, and one that I look forward to going to every year because I meet so many fascinating people and learn so much about my field.

You may not be able to attend the AERA Annual Meeting (although you are welcome to do so), but there are hundreds of conferences held yearly throughout the United States for teachers and others who work with young people. Probably every subject taught in schools has its own conference for disseminating information to those who need it.

Subject-matter conferences can be enlightening and a boost to those who attend. Not all conference speakers are wonderful, but a conference attendee will probably gain something of value by going to at least one conference whenever possible. Most often what attendees find valuable about these meetings is the information gathered outside of the actual workshops and presentations—information on lesson ideas, or where to get free or reasonable supplies. Information gleaned from other attendees is often as valuable as the planned session.

If you do not receive information on conferences, ask your principal or district personnel clerk to keep you posted on promotional flyers that may be of interest to you.

❧ WHAT CONFERENCES *are available for your subject or grade level? Why not plan to attend?*

APRIL 13

THOMAS JEFFERSON, the third president of the United States, was born in the town of Shadwell, Albemarle County, Virginia, on April 13, 1743. In 1787, he wrote in a letter to James Madison (who was serving in the Virginia Assembly at the time, and who later became the fourth president), "Above all things, I hope the education of the common people will be attended to; convinced that on their good sense we may rely with the most security for the preservation of a due degree of liberty."[5]

It was Jefferson's hope that the American people, who had only recently gained their freedom, would be able to make wise decisions for themselves and their countrymen. Only through education could the electing body make the decisions necessary for a young nation to survive and maintain freedom. Today, too, education ensures an electorate that is knowledgeable and able to use critical thinking to make decisions that affect all of us.

❧ ARE YOU PROVIDING *your students with the critical thinking skills that will maintain our heritage of freedom?*

April

APRIL 14

ON THIS DATE IN 1614, Virginia planter John Rolfe married Pocahontas, who was the daughter of the chief of the Chickahominy tribe, Powhatan, who had been openly hostile to the new settlers. Although it was hoped that his daughter's marriage to a settler might bring peace to the two nations, Powhatan continued his hostility even after his daughter's marriage. Most of what we learn in history classes about this young woman is the story of her daring rescue of Captain John Smith, a story that has since been considered as doubtful of ever having occurred.

Whether it is true or not that Pocahontas fell across Smith to save him from decapitation is not the highlight of her story. What is more important and certainly more memorable is that she undoubtedly rendered many services to the colonists that were paramount to their survival in the new land: supplying the starving inhabitants of Jamestown with provisions and preserving peace between the two warring factions. Pocahontas was converted to Christianity in 1613 and given the baptized name "Rebecca."[6]

So many times in history we romanticize stories (such as Pocahontas's saving John Smith) when the actual story was "just as good." Pocahontas is the story of a brave woman who reached across cultures to bring peace to her community and welcomed strangers to her land.

᎐ DO YOU RESEARCH *"romanticized stories" for their veracity or do you continue to misinform students with the stories you were told?*

263

April 15

OK, TODAY IS Income Tax Day, probably the most dreaded day of the calendar year. I hope that you have completed your paperwork. And I hope just as much that you have money coming back in the form of a refund. But, whether you have money coming back to you or you had to pay this year, remember that the good thing about tax money is that it pays for your salary.

Income tax in the United States is a relatively recent development—a twentieth-century enactment—meaning that our ancestors in the 1700s and 1800s, although they paid taxes on material goods, did not have to pay taxes on the money that they earned. The income tax as we know it was a product of the Sixteenth Amendment that was signed into law in 1913.

Although it may seem painful to pay more money to a government who has already taken a large portion from our paychecks, the benefits we receive are well worth the percentages that we have to pay. We all benefit from the collection of tax money that pays for schools, jobs, military protection, services, police protection, and Social Security, to name only a few benefits.

If you do not like paying taxes and feel that the government is taking too much, be sure to investigate the possibilities of lowering your tax liability. Check with a qualified tax preparer, or read the myriad of books on the subject to see if there are legitimate deductions that you are eligible for as a teacher. Discuss with your retirement planner the possibility of setting aside more money in a retirement account to avoid taxable income today.

When all is said and done, and the forms are in the mail, rejoice that you have a job and that some of that money you spent will come back to you next payday.

❧ HOW CAN YOU *reduce next year's tax payment with legitimate deductions?*

April

APRIL 16

ONE OF THE THINGS that I have learned as I get older is the importance of staying healthy; including eating right, thinking right, and staying active.

Although I have always enjoyed participating in sports, and up until a few years ago played basketball with some coworkers, I recently learned a new activity that I enjoy doing daily—roller skating.

Although it took some getting used to, and an initial outlay of money for the proper equipment, I have learned that for me a day without roller skating is a day that seems unfulfilled. When I am in the park, in the fresh air, rolling along at a comfortable pace, I not only see nature in a beautiful setting, I can think about the day, what I will write, what I will teach, and even what I will wear to work to look my best. I think I look better having experienced the outdoors first thing in the morning before my work day begins.

Fortunately I live where the weather is generally sunny and comfortable, so I can maintain my sport. Having an avocation, especially one that requires physical activity, can be that motivation that jump-starts the day. It can be something to look forward to doing, something that gets you outside in the fresh air. Roller skating required that I learn something new, something that keeps me young.

WHAT ACTIVITY have you found that helps keep you healthy and emotionally wise? Do you have an activity that you enjoy doing outside? What are the benefits of doing it?

APRIL 17

WHEN I FIRST DECIDED to take up roller skating, I found that my first task, after buying the appropriate equipment, was to get over my fear of falling. This required buying the right equipment, a piece of information I learned the hard way. In one of my first attempts to skate I fell backward, landing on my back, scraping my elbows, and barely missing hitting my head on the cement. Although I missed hurting myself seriously, I severely bruised my ego, as the neighborhood children were playing nearby.

To keep fear from stopping my learning before it even began, I readily purchased a helmet, knee pads, elbow pads, and wrist guards, and began again. The result is, although I still have a fear of falling, it is not as great because I know that I am protected from head to toe from that oh-so-hard pavement.

It is easier in life to learn something if we know that we are protected from that fear of falling, or equally as painful, the fear of failing. Protective gear does just that. Children need that protection from falling (failing) too, and we provide that by teaching in a manner that allows for mistakes as part of succeeding, not failing.

❧ HOW CAN YOU *provide the protection that allows your students to try something new?*

APRIL 18

YESTERDAY WE DISCUSSED the importance of providing protection to students when they are attempting to try something new that may be a little frightening. Lev Vygotsky's theory of cognitive development emphasizes the importance of the interaction between the teacher and the student in what is known as the "sociocultural" nature of learning.

Vygotsky's voluminous writings, many of which were unknown to the Western world until the opening of the Soviet Union, detailed the learning that takes place when a child works within his or her "zone of proximal development." Put simply,

April

this means that these tasks within this "zone" are ones that the child cannot do alone, but can do with the assistance of another person who is more competent in the task, whether a teacher or a peer. The assistance is called "scaffolding." Learning is enhanced, according to Vygotsky, with "scaffolding," or providing a child with support while he or she is learning, and then diminishing the support (taking away the scaffold, so to speak) as the child becomes more able to accomplish the task. Sounds similar to providing protective gear for the next physical challenge.

Vygotsky also believed that higher mental functioning usually exists with the conversation and collaboration among individuals before it exists within the individual—again, the sociocultural nature of learning.[7]

☙ IN WHAT WAYS *do you provide "scaffolding" for your students to give them a safety net in trying something new?*

APRIL 19

WHEN I BEGAN roller skating, once I learned the importance of the right safety equipment, the next thing I learned was the importance of continually looking ahead, looking far enough in front of me to see where I was going, yet keeping my head down to pay attention to the cracks in the sidewalk directly in front of me. Cracks and uneven pavement can be the bane of skaters. A small ridge in the cement can cause one to lose one's balance and come crashing down on the (very hard) cement.

Water on the pavement can also be a problem for roller skaters and bicyclists (I know, having fallen doing both), because it is slippery, and can cause wheels to slide sideways.

As unbelievable as it may seem, a good way to hit an unlevel piece of sidewalk is by heading straight forward, even speeding up a bit. By going slowly, the beginning skater cannot get enough

267

speed going to get over the bump adequately and therefore stops just before the crack or on it. When slowing down, he or she is more likely to trip and fall.

Learning is a lot like skating. Sometimes it is important to go at a regular pace and not stop at an uneven area, and sometimes it is important to speed up our learning, to project ourselves right over the rough spot and into the new area. No loss of pace, no tripping up. And sometimes it is equally as important to stop before the "bump" and evaluate overtaking it—reviewing the situation ahead to better understand it.

And finally, as with any bump, whether in skating, bike riding, or learning, sometimes we hit the bump, fall down, and have to pick ourselves up and try again.

ᗌ How do you *encourage your students to face the "bumps" they run into on the way to learning? Do you stop, proceed slowly, or hit them head on? What are the benefits of each of these methods?*

April 20

Before we leave the metaphor of skating for learning, I want to leave you with a few *Teacher Tips* from a veteran teacher/beginning skater—me:

• When people see me out in the park—a grandmother with knee pads, elbow pads, wrist guards, and a helmet—they may think I am an amusing sight to behold. But I like challenges, especially those of a physical nature. Challenges keep the mind and body younger than our chronological years. Try new things whenever you can.

• Don't overcompensate for fear. One of the painful mistakes I learned in roller skating is the importance of skating at a fluid

April

pace. When I approach a challenging surface, if I hesitate and go too slow, or if I speed up to take the area too quickly, either way, I wobble and sometimes fall. Take new and challenging experiences in stride, carefully aware yet smoothly focused. When making a commitment, follow through.

> ☽ I HAVE FOCUSED *on the metaphor of skating for learning. What metaphor can you use to denote your philosophy of learning?*

APRIL 21

FRANCIS WAYLAND PARKER, who John Dewey called the "Father of Progressive Education," in 1894 wrote a book called *Talk on Pedagogics.* In it he stated the importance of teaching for learning, a novel idea considering that he wrote this book during the era of the one-room school house, where desks were bolted to the floor, and rote memorization was the popular teaching method of the day.

Parker wrote in his book that the business of an instructor begins where the reading of a book ends. Teaching is the action of mind upon mind. It is exciting and awakening. Teaching shows by example the power of reasoning and the value of generalization. It renders it impossible for the pupil not to think. Therefore the role of an instructor is noble and ennobling.[8]

What a powerful thought for the time, and what a powerful thought for today!

> ☽ DO YOU *make it "impossible" for your students to "not think"? How can you ensure that thinking happens?*

269

APRIL 22

IVAN ILLICH, writing at the height of the 1960s and 1970s protest movement, advocated in his book *Deschooling Society* the abolishment of schools, suggesting that they be replaced by some less formal method of educating young people, for instance, a mentoring system. John Holt, writing in the same era, advocated a less radical approach than the abolishment of schools, advocating instead a change in the methods by which students are taught. Holt wrote that "we cannot know, at any moment, what particular bit of knowledge or understanding a child needs most, will most strengthen and best fit his model of reality. Only he can do this. He may not do it very well, but he can do it a hundred times better than we can." He continued, "The most we can do is try to help, by letting him know roughly what is available and when he can look for it. Choosing what he wants to learn and what he does not is something he must do for himself."

As a result, according to Holt, to provide for the interests of young people, "the school should be a great smorgasbord of intellectual, artistic, creative, and athletic activities, from which each child could take whatever he wanted, and as much as he wanted, or as little."9

Although we may disagree with Illich on whether schools should be abolished, we can certainly agree with Holt that students should be allowed to have the responsibility for their learning.

☙ SHOULD SCHOOLS *provide a "smorgasbord of intellectual, artistic, creative, and athletic activities" for young people? Should children be able to choose what they want to learn? Why or why not?*

April

APRIL 23

ON OCTOBER 29 and January 18 we discussed the importance of parents' involvement in their student's success, and I hope that you are encouraging and invite parents into your classroom. But much of parental involvement occurs outside of the school, at home, where teachers hope that parents are encouraging their students and supporting what we do in the class. Many parents want to help their children be successful students, but they may be reluctant, unsure if they know how to help their children with homework or if they have the necessary information to understand what their child is learning from you.

Teachers can reassure parents and help them become advocates for their program by giving parents information on how to help with homework (looking to see if it is done, not just asking about it), by encouraging them to ask specific questions about school (rather than the popular, "What did you do in school today?"), and by providing periodic messages to parents on what is happening at school and what home lessons can support your program.

⏵ HOW DO YOU *help parents become supporters of your program? What can you do to encourage their success?*

APRIL 24

ALTHOUGH APRIL 24 is not a national holiday, it is the anniversary of several important events in American history. On this date in 1649, the Toleration Act was passed in Maryland under the administration of a Protestant deputy governor, William Stone. Although it did not include toleration of non-Christian religions, the Toleration Act provided for religious freedom for all Christians and included freedom for Catholics, too.

271

On April 24, 1800, the Library of Congress was founded, providing "for the purchase of such books as may be necessary for the use of Congress." This library has grown tremendously over the last two hundred years to include outstanding collections, and provides many services to citizens and libraries across the United States.

Last and maybe least, today is American Martyrs Day, as we recall those who died for individual causes, and we remind ourselves not to appear to be martyrs to our students and our loved ones.

❧ WHAT WOULD BE *a good way to celebrate these holidays today? Have you shown toleration to others? Have you thought about reading a good book?*

APRIL 25

JOHN DEWEY WROTE in *The Child and the Curriculum* (1902) that "the fundamental factors in the educative process are an immature, undeveloped being; and certain social aims, meanings, and values incarnate in the matured experience of the adult. The educative process is the due interaction of these forces."[10] So many times in our day-to-day interactions with young people it is easy to get caught up in the complexities of the job and fail to recall why we originally chose this position. It is at times like these that it becomes important to remember that the position's requirements include the responsibility of being that mature adult who will induce the immature, undeveloped being into the society in which we adults live. Working with young people may not pay what we would like in material goods, but it certainly pays us societally. It is a most, if not *the* most, noble profession, and worthy of praise for all who do it well.

April

꩜ IN WHAT WAYS *are you representative of a mature member of society?*

APRIL 26

WILLIAM SHAKESPEARE, the third eldest of eight children born to John and Mary Shakespeare, was born in Stratford-on-Avon, on April 26, 1564, and died on April 23, 1616. Although historians have questioned the origins of some of the works credited to Shakespeare, he has catapulted through history as the writer of plays, poetry, sonnets, and some of the most quotable lines known to humankind. Shakespeare's works included comedy, romance, tragedy, and histories (some of which have made colorful the actual events that were written about).

In celebration of William's birthday a discussion of his varied and greatest works might be in order for your students today. Ask your students to list from memory the many plays and sonnets they can recall that Shakespeare wrote. See if any can recite lines from memory.

꩜ WHAT IS *your favorite Shakespeare quote, play, or sonnet? Can you recite it from memory?*

APRIL 27

IN 1859, Herbert Spencer, noted philosopher and author, asked the curricular question that has been examined by educators since that time: "What knowledge is of most worth?" Spencer continued, "Before there can be a rational *curriculum,* we must settle which things it most concerns us to know."[11]

273

Often, beginning teachers believe that reading and completing their subject textbook from cover to cover fulfills the needs of the students in their charge. It is left to district curriculum specialists, textbook authors, and state politicians to answer the questions of what to teach. But deciding what you want your students to know, or what knowledge from your subject matter is of most worth to your students, requires much more than letting outside resources guide the curriculum. One must take into account the student's age, abilities, and needs, and make a decision about what portion of the total knowledge needed for the student to become a functioning adult can be taught at their current level and understood by their age group.

ꙅ WHAT KNOWLEDGE *is of most worth to the young people in your charge?*

APRIL 28

HELEN KELLER ONCE SAID, "The highest result of education is tolerance."[12] Teaching tolerance requires that students have access to critical information that will allow them to understand the feelings of others, imagine what it would be like to be in someone else's shoes, and feel what it would be like to be discriminated against. The following *Teacher Tips* may help your students understand what it feels like to be someone else:

• The "AIDS Simulation Activity." Have each student pull a piece of paper from each of three bags that are marked *gender, sexual orientation,* and *ethnicity.* In the appropriate bags are papers that are labeled *male, female; heterosexual, homosexual,* or *bisexual; African American, Caucasian, Asian,* or *other minority.* From a separate bag, students pull out a paper on which is written the number of sexual contacts they have had. A student pulls out one candy from a bag of M&M's. If he or she pulls out a pre-specified color (for instance blue), the student is considered to have AIDS. This teaches that AIDS is not picky. As in real life, everyone, even heterosexuals, has a chance to get it.

- "Discrimination." Using Monopoly, Life, or any other money-oriented game, prepare cards that contain information that would make it difficult for a woman, an African American, or individual from another minority to get ahead, get a position, or earn a good salary. Select which students will be men, which will be women, African American, Caucasian, or other, and have them play the game using the cards you have prepared. This shows students the unfairness some people experience when they are kept from succeeding because of who they are rather than because of their capabilities.

- Teach the Golden Rule—Do unto others as you would have them do unto you.

ꙮ WHAT OTHER GAMES *or methods can you think of to teach important lessons to your students?*

APRIL 29

HAVING DEBATES in your classroom can be an informative and important way to share information and teach sensitive subjects to your students. But often teachers shy away from debates, because their students do not benefit from the lesson, or worse yet, the debates turn into shouting matches rather than controlled debating situations. In order for debates to be successful, students must have researched the topic and have the information readily available so they can logically discuss the topic. Because of the necessary preparation, many teachers believe that debates are too time-consuming.

The following *Teacher Tips* from veteran teachers may help make your debates more successful:

• For debates to be successful, topics must be clearly stated. Assign each of your students a topic, but do not tell them until the day of the debate whether their position will be pro or con. This way they have to research all sides of the issue, giving them more accountability for preparation.

• Topics for debates can include, but are not limited to political issues, sports teams, historical events, proper attire for students, school rules, and current events.

• Remind students that the important lesson to be learned from debates is not who wins, but that the individuals stay alert to what their opponent is saying, clearly state their sides, and stay cool throughout the process.

Teaching debating is not teaching the art of arguing; it is teaching how to discuss an issue in a logical, calm way. It also shows your students that there are two (or more) sides to most issues, and imparts some very important information about the subject.

---

๑ WHAT LESSONS *that you teach can be enhanced by having your students debate the topic?*

APRIL 30

ON APRIL 30, 1803, during the administration of Thomas Jefferson, the third president of the United States, the Louisiana Territory was purchased from France, giving the new nation the largest area of land acquired at one time. For the sum of $11,250,000 (which excluded $3,750,000 in debt owed by France), this "Louisiana Purchase" gave the U.S. government the land west of the Mississippi, not including the land owned by Mexico. The acquisition of this land doubled the land area of the United States by adding approximately 828,000 square miles. What a deal!

The Louisiana Purchase was a big chunk of land, and much needed to be done to explore, colonize, and govern that new area.

As we end April, and enter into the last full month of school, it is important to reflect on what is left to be accomplished before your students leave your classroom. Is there a big chunk of knowledge that needs to be explored and governed before the end of the year?

❧ WHAT DO YOU *have left to teach your students before the end of the school year? How can you organize that information to make it more meaningful?*

MAY

May 1

FOR CENTURIES, May Day, or the first of May, has been celebrated throughout the world as the arrival of the season for new vegetation. As a result of the need for "appeasing the god(s) of spring," remnants of ancient agricultural and fertility rituals are enacted around the world, complete with elaborate festivals, bonfires, wreaths, maypoles, and many other ways of celebrating the occasion.

When I was growing up, when May Day arrived, we used to make paper baskets filled with any kind of flowers we could find (most often dandelions) on the way home from school, and give them to our mothers. In kindergarten I grew marigolds, from seeds planted in a little clay pot, and gave them to my mother on May Day. Sometimes we would pick wildflowers from the fields around our house, set them on the porch and ring the doorbell, then run to hide until our mother spied the flowers on the doorstep, gathered them up, and took them into the house to place in a small vase for display in the kitchen window.

Do children still give flowers to their moms on May Day? I do not recall my own children doing that for me. Maybe it is not as popular as it once was, but I still recall that it was fun to do and a good lesson in giving joy to others.

❧ DO YOU CELEBRATE *May Day, celebrating the arrival of fresh vegetation and new growth?*

May 2

IN MARCH we talked about cleaning closets and drawers both at school and at home and how the process is made easier by portioning the one big job into several smaller ones: instead of cleaning the whole closet, clean only one shelf; instead of the entire desk, clean one drawer at a time.

Portioning the work eventually leads to the whole job being done and means that you did not have to look at the mess of the whole closet's contents strewn all over the floor. When we tackle big projects in little pieces, it just seems to make the job easier.

When I teach my graduate students at the university how to do their master's theses, I often get phone calls from students who are having difficulty with their final master's projects because the task of writing book-length papers has become overwhelming to them. The students, who are otherwise successful teachers, will make appointments seeking advice on how to get started with the task at hand. Some students actually get frustrated and give up, and we never see them again. After all of the course work is completed, they cannot figure out how to write a thesis that is possibly one hundred pages long.

What I try to teach them to do to get a handle on the writing is to break the big project into small chunks of no more that three to five pages of writing per day. I tell them that when they have written their assigned pages, they must put the paper away and they may not work on it again until the next day. I tell them that I write this way too (which is true); what happens is that we get into the habit of looking forward to the next day to begin again because we stopped writing when we still had something to say.

☙ IS THERE SOME TASK *that you are having difficulty finishing? Can you break it into small sections that are easy to complete?*

MAY 3

YESTERDAY WE TALKED about "chunking" your work into small, reasonably sized pieces in order to complete big tasks,

281

which encourages us to look forward to working on the project the next time. Your students can benefit from this information, too, if you teach them how to divide large projects into smaller tasks that can be more easily managed in a short time.

For some students who are younger, or unable to comprehend portioning their work, you may have to help by assigning smaller assignments (pieces) at a time. For example, if you want a science fair project to have a certain number of steps, you may need to assign a sequence of dates for the different steps to be due, and the total project due at a later date. (Parents will most likely appreciate this too, because it will alleviate the last-minute, late-night work on the day before the project is due.)

Remember, learning is like chunking; it takes place a little bit at a time until finally the whole of the information is learned.

∂ WHAT LARGE PROJECT *or task do your students have difficulty in completing? How can you divide the steps for them so that they can manage the project better?*

MAY 4

IN FEBRUARY we investigated ways to help our students do better on teacher-prepared content tests to determine whether the students know the information that we have taught to them. (These content-area tests are referred to as "criterion-referenced tests" in the educational psychology world, because they test whether the student has learned the information, or criteria, necessary to move on to the next level.)

In May, we will look at criterion tests and "norm-referenced" tests, which show how well your students have answered questions or understood certain information compared to students across the nation, and how well they fit within the "norm" of students who are at the same age and grade levels. Examples of norm-referenced tests include achievement tests such as SAT, CAT, ITBS, and ACT, and aptitude tests such as IQ, Wechsler, and Lorge-Thorndike, to name only a few.

Unfortunately, while your students probably have little difficulty with criterion-referenced tests (if you have adequately taught the material), students often can have difficulty getting good scores on norm-referenced tests because it is more difficult for teachers to help students do well on them. Also, you may recall, a major problem with norm-referenced tests is that these test scores are posted in the newspapers and compared to other districts and/or schools within your district (often without taking into account the level of the students that you are teaching, or the socioeconomic level of the community in which you teach). Because of this, norm-referenced tests become frightening for teachers and school districts, and appear to provide the worst ammunition for politicians and others who may be negative toward schools.

⚘ HOW CAN YOU *counteract the negative press of norm-referenced test scores?*

MAY 5

MAY 5, CINCO DE MAYO (which, in Spanish, means "the fifth of May"), is commonly misrepresented as Mexican Independence Day, but it is not. (Mexican Independence Day is September 15). Cinco de Mayo is the celebration of a Mexican victory that occurred on May 5, 1862, in a war against France; in actuality it is celebrated in the United States more than it is in Mexico! But that is OK, because it gives us one more reason to celebrate diversity.

In our house, May 5 is the celebration of our daughter-in-law April's birthday. April is a truly wonderful young woman—a hard

283

worker, a good daughter and daughter-in-law, *and* she is also a teacher (hooray!) who teaches at a private religious school nearby.

An interesting fact about April is that she was raised as an only child; her one sibling had passed away when she was very young. I bring this up for one reason: to show how the stereotypes we have of young people can influence our prejudgment of them, and I will use my prejudice to make the example. My experience and *stereotype* of "only" children was that they were spoiled, demanding, and difficult to get along with. Fortunately, however, I had that stereotype disproved when April came into our family, for not only is she unspoiled, but she is giving, loving, and a wonderful addition to this previously male-oriented family.

As the mother of sons and the sister of brothers, the addition of another female into our family was interesting. Perhaps I was the spoiled, demanding, and difficult one. Having both sons marry within a year brought two young ladies into our lives, and I have learned what it is like to have a daughter twice over. What a joy to have added to the family.

> Do you have *a stereotype of particular individuals that needs to be broken?*

May 6

Two days ago we discussed the difference between criterion-referenced tests and norm-referenced tests: the first are the tests you give to your students to determine whether they have learned the material that you taught, while the latter tests compare your students to others around the country.

Although it is probably impossible to teach your students everything they need to know to obtain a high score on norm-referenced evaluations, there are ways that you can help your

May

students to improve their scores. The following *Teacher Test Tips* may help you not only add points to your students' scores on achievement tests but improve your district's scores as well:

• Familiarity breeds confidence. Occasionally give your students tests that are written in the same manner as the achievement tests that they will be given. That may mean using more multiple choice tests or tests that require students to fill in bubbles.

• Maximize critical thinking skills and problem solving. If a student does not immediately know an answer, he or she may be able to "figure it out."

• Teach your students the "tricks" to answering tests ("All of the above" or "None of the above," if used for the first time, are probably good indications that they are the correct answers; the words *never* and *always* often indicate incorrect answers).

• Emphasize the importance of reading questions carefully.

• Encourage your students to use their time wisely.

• Also, encourage your students to get a good night's rest, eat a sensible breakfast, and take the test seriously.

✑ WHAT ELSE *should your students know that will help them to score higher on norm-referenced tests?*

MAY 7

ACCORDING TO GEORGE MADAUS, "The idea that any testing technique, be it a new test design or a national test system, can reform schools and restore America's competitiveness is the height of technological arrogance and conceals many of the negative possibilities of such a move under the guise of a seemingly neat technological fix. . . . It is the teachers," he concludes, "not test or assessments, that must be the cornerstones of reform efforts."[1]

That is reassuring, but not likely to make the testing situation, nor the repercussions of poor test scores, go away. By the time that norm-referenced test scores hit the papers, it is too late to convince the community that the schools are satisfactorily teaching their children, or that teachers are doing their jobs. The important thing to do is to beat the test scores to the papers by being *proactive* and filling the news with school activities and the successes of the young people in your classroom.

- Call the newspaper, write a newspaper article, or send pictures to the local press to ensure that the positive story of what goes on in classrooms has been told.

- Maintain good public relations with your community so that negative test scores, should they occur, will not be "just one more thing" that the school is doing wrong.

- And try to raise those test scores by teaching to encourage learning and thinking.

➥ IN WHAT WAYS *can you counteract the possible negative effects of published test scores?*

MAY 8

ON THIS DATE, May 8, in 1785, the U.S. Congress passed legislation known as the Land Ordinance of 1785. If you recall from your history, this ordinance provided for a survey which divided the northwestern territories into six-mile-square townships, which in turn were to be divided into thirty-six lots of 640 acres each to be sold for $640. In this enactment was also included legislation that would set aside one of these lots in each township for a school or to finance public education. A motion to set aside

May

another lot to support the religion of the majority of the residents was narrowly defeated.

Our predecessors realized that in order for a nation to be free, it had to include a citizenry that was educated and able to make decisions. Setting aside 640 acres in each of the six-mile squares was a generous and thoughtful thing to do.

---

๑ IF YOU *could set aside land for a school, what would that property look like?*

MAY 9

ALTHOUGH IT MAY SEEM as though national tests create more problems than they are worth, there is a positive aspect to these tests. The results of these tests can give teachers information about their students that can help in planning future lessons. According to Laurel and Daniel Tanner, in their textbook, *Curriculum Development: Theory into Practice*, "Many teachers understandably feel personally threatened by standardized tests for assessing student progress. They do not know that a major purpose of testing is to provide them with information about students that they can use in instructional planning."

On the other hand, the Tanners also support the dilemma of teachers who are held accountable for test results. They write, "It must be remembered that standardized tests provide only a very limited perspective of what is learned in school, and even the most sophisticated analyses will not compensate for the inadequacies of standardized tests." Unfortunately, according to the Tanners, "too many district officers measure program success only on the basis of student performance on standardized tests and college entrance. One might well ponder the reasons for this narrow-minded approach."[2] Although standardized tests "provide only a very limited perspective of what is learned," that

287

perspective can provide information we can use in making future plans. The point is not necessarily to blame ourselves for poor results but to use whatever is available to improve the education our students receive.

〽 HOW CAN YOU *utilize the information gained from standardized tests to help your students?*

MAY 10

SOMETIME AROUND THIS DATE (the second Sunday in May), we set aside a day to celebrate as Mother's Day, to pay special recognition, and rightfully so, to our mothers who have done (and continue to do) so much for us. Mothers sacrifice careers, sleep at night, and opportunities for other activities to be with us. They take care of us when we are sick, praise our accomplishments, and listen to us whether we are three or twenty-three years old. It is only fitting that they have at least one day out of the year to be celebrated.

Often, especially in the elementary grades, we take the week before Mother's Day to allow our students to make something special for their moms. This is a lovely idea, as long as we take into account that there are children who do not live with their mothers, which may complicate the Mother's Day gift project. We should not want something that is meant to be thoughtful to become thought*less*ly painful to our students.

〽 HOW CAN YOU *make Mother's Day gifts in your classes and not hurt some of your students?*

MAY 11

BECAUSE WE HAVE BEEN looking at testing, and in particular those norm-referenced tests that schools districts give to their students for comparison with the scores of students in other schools in the area and across the nation, perhaps it is time to look within our classrooms and remind ourselves that it is our students' total accomplishments, not their one-time scores on a nationwide test, that are important. At these times it is important to ask ourselves, "What is the BIG picture that we are trying to accomplish in school?"

Too much emphasis on tests, whether norm-referenced or criterion-referenced classroom tests, can bend our and our students' focus from what schooling is all about. The Tanners write in their textbook, *Curriculum Development: Theory into Practice*, that "teachers tend to overlook the importance of collateral learning. Pupils may receive a grade of A in a literature course, but if they have learned to dislike good literature it is doubtful that they will be impelled to read such literature on their own."3 This is also true with teaching toward a test.

It is not that test scores are unimportant, or should be taken lightly, but the big picture is that these scores do not indicate abilities to do many things, such as paint a picture, play a musical instrument, write a creative story, enjoy reading, or learn how to get along well with others.

In California, as in other states, teachers are required to pass a test of basic skills, the CBEST test, and then they are allowed to teach in public schools, *even if they do not have a teaching certificate*. In their effort to get educated, intelligent individuals teaching in the classroom, state legislators have overlooked the fact that a CBEST test does not indicate that a person is a good teacher, knows how to teach, or even likes children.

The big picture is the knowledge, skills, and interest in learning that your students have gained in your presence this year. The big picture is also having a teacher that can *teach* what he or she knows to young people.

꩜ Do you keep *the big picture in the forefront of what you do? What is the big picture that you have for your students this year?*

MAY 12

SINCE YOU PROBABLY have less than a month left of school, and if you teach high school, your students may be graduating, or at least looking for part-time summer work. Now may be a good time to give your students an opportunity to look into careers. Even younger students can benefit from looking ahead to employment one day. The following *Teacher Tips* may help your students, no matter what their age:

• *Career Detective.* Ask your students to research a career that they may be interested in doing someday. What are the requirements for the job? (Is it college? Vocational school? No training?) What might be some of the benefits and/or problems with pursuing and attaining that career?

• *Your Own Business.* Ask students to decide what kind of company they would like to have if they could own their own company. What would be some of the requirements for beginning their company and keeping it running? Ask them why they think that people might need a company like theirs?

• *Brainstorming Careers.* Ask your students to write down as many jobs as they can think of that would use the skills that they are learning in school. Next to the job title, ask them to briefly explain how or when the skill might be necessary. Have the students explain how they think the topics being studied are relevant to their life now or will be in the future.

• *Building Your Resume.* Show your students how to write a resume, and the importance of convincing an employer that you are the right person for this type of job.

May

- *Practice Interviews.* Have your students dress up and practice interviewing for jobs in groups and in front of the class. Discuss what questions are typically asked at an interview, the importance of dressing appropriately, and the etiquette that is considered appropriate during an interview.

꘎ IN WHAT OTHER WAYS *can you help your students plan for their futures now?*

MAY 13

ALONG WITH HELPING your students plan for careers comes helping them to plan for their adult lives, when they will be finally on their own. This includes learning to budget, allowing for food, clothes, entertainment, extracurricular activities, and other monthly and yearly expenses. The following *Teacher Tips* will help you to prepare your students for the time when they will be on their own:

- Ask your students to discuss with their parents what *types* of bills an adult has to pay (not the actual bills that their parents have, because some parents may find this too personal). This gives many parents the opportunity to open a discussion on bills, finances, and budgeting with their children.

- Discuss with your students, or invite a guidance counselor to talk to your students, about the cost of college. Many students are not aware that there is money available to them in the form of scholarships and financial aid for students who want to earn a higher degree but cannot afford it. Often students mistakenly give up on the idea of going to college because they do not think that they can afford it, even though the money may be available for them.

- Give your students a fictional budget in which an individual is spending more money than he or she earns. Ask them to identify the areas in which the person could cut down expenses or save money.

⋙ WHAT ELSE *do your students need to know for adulthood?*

MAY 14

IN THE PAST FEW DAYS we have talked about giving our students information that will prepare them for adulthood, getting a job, and budgeting so that they spend wisely the money that they earn. Another important piece of information to give young people is that it is often necessary to work for the things that we want in life, whether it is money, material objects, success, good relationships, or happiness.

Bernie S. Siegel once said that the difference between hoping and wishing for something is that hoping is active, while wishing is passive. "Hoping means seeing that the outcome you want is possible, and then working for it. Wishing means just sitting there, waiting for a miracle to happen out of the blue."4

Many times we see our students (and possibly ourselves) confusing the two and wishing for something when they (or we) should be hoping instead.

⋙ WHAT ARE YOU WISHING *for that you should, instead, be hoping to obtain?*

MAY 15

TELEVISION COMMERCIALS have an enormous impact on the buying power of Americans, and students need to become aware

May

of the (sometimes deceptive) techniques companies use in commercials to encourage people to buy their products. Through commercials and advertisements, people are often encouraged to buy products that they do not need or that are more than what they actually desire. To help your students understand how to be a wise buyer, discuss the various methods used by companies to trick consumers into buying their product by analyzing the propaganda and rhetoric these companies use. The following *Teacher Tips* may help your students become wise consumers:

• Ask your students to watch television for an hour or so. (They will like this assignment.) What types of products are advertised during the different kinds of shows (sports, adult viewing, cartoons, et cetera)? What images are being used? (For example, the beautiful woman during the beer commercial.) What is the image saying? (Drinking "brand name" beer will make you popular with the opposite sex.)

• In the past few years home shopping shows have become increasingly popular on TV. What is an advantage of shopping this way? What is a disadvantage? What types of products are generally being sold on these shows? Who is the market?

• Have students design their own product and make an advertisement for it. What are they selling and who is their market? Allow them to make a commercial using a video camera.

___

⟫ WHAT ELSE *do your students need to know to become wise consumers?*

___

MAY 16

TODAY IS Armed Forces Day on my calendar, a day when we thank those men and women who have made countless sacrifices for the rest of us. On November 11 and December 7, we discussed the role that these servicemen and servicewomen have played in our history and, in particular, the emphasis on military confrontations in our social studies courses.

History is more than the memorization of facts and the studies of wars and battles. John Dewey wrote in *The School and Society*, "History must be presented, not as an accumulation of results or effects, a mere statement of what happened, but as a forceful, acting thing. . . . To study history is not to amass information, but to use information in constructing a vivid picture of how and why men did thus and so; achieved their successes and came to their failures."

On this topic of the aim of history in school, he wrote that, rather than studying a confrontation or a mere memorization of facts, "the aim of historical instruction is to enable the child to appreciate the values of social life, to see in imagination the forces which favor and allow men's effective *co-operation* [italics are mine] with one another, to understand the sorts of character that help on and that hold back. . . ." Adding that, "the essential thing in its presentation is to make it moving, dynamic."[5]

Once again, history is not an accumulation of dates and facts, but a lived experience. We are as much a part of it as those we read about in our textbooks.

☙ Do you make *history a living experience for your students? If not, how can you?*

May 17

The New York Stock Exchange was created on this date in 1792, organized by twenty-four brokers who gathered at the Merchants Coffee House in New York. Investigating the stock market can be an interesting and meaningful project for your students to participate in and gives them knowledge that may be useful in their futures. Even if they do not play the stock market when they are older, many companies have retirement programs that allow employees to participate in "growth" plans that invest in stocks with a portion of their money. The following *Teacher Tips* may give your students information for future stock market deals:

- Play the Stock Exchange. "Give" your students $20,000 dollars to invest in stocks, allowing them to invest it in any way they prefer. Ask your students to follow their stocks in the newspaper or on the Internet.

- Discuss the various options adults have for investing money. If you are unfamiliar with this information, ask a financial advisor to visit your class. (You may learn some important information, too!)

- Newspapers often have special lesson packages for students to learn how to play the stock market, and they will provide your class with a set of newspapers to follow the market.

Keep in mind that playing the market has risks as well as gains.

WHAT RISKS do your students need to know about while playing the stock market?

MAY 18

THROUGHOUT THE YEAR we have looked at diversity and multiculturalism and the celebration of the many varied holidays of cultures other than our own. We have also looked at the uniqueness of individuals in other races and ethnicities, and the importance of knowing about others in order to get along. Today we are going to close the discussion of diversity and multiculturalism by focusing not on our differences, but on our similarities—to see how, as human beings, we are more alike than we are different.

What are some of the ways that different races, religions, and ethnic groups are alike? Some similarities that I can think of are:

1. We want to be loved, appreciated, and accepted for who we are.

2. We want to be comfortable. We want to have enough money and material goods to feel comfortable, regardless of what we consider comfortable to be.

3. We want to achieve and feel successful in the activities in which we participate.

4. As parents, we want our children, and ourselves, to be happy.

There are many other similarities between cultures. A good exercise may be to ask your students to pursue this topic.

❧ IN WHAT OTHER WAYS *are people of the world more alike than different?*

MAY 19

ON MAY 19, IN 1806, New York City introduced the Lancaster Method of teaching students into its schools. The founder of the Lancaster System, an Englishman named Joseph Lancaster, developed this method to help those schools that had large classes by helping instructors in the teaching of large groups of students. With the Lancaster Method, students were trained by more advanced students who had been taught the necessary information by the master teacher. The concept was widely accepted in large schools, and especially in cities, because of its low cost.

Although it makes sense for older children to teach younger ones, and we often do this today in what we call "cross-age tutoring" programs, the problem with the Lancaster Method was the degree to which it was used. While today, older children tutor younger children and therefore reinforce what a teacher has taught, in Lancaster Method schools, children were taught by children, encouraging the use of rote learning and few critical-thinking activities. Although it may have benefited the older children by reinforcing what they had already learned, it is doubtful that the younger children were better off when it was used.

Do you use *older children to help teach the younger children in your classroom? Does it benefit both the younger and the older child?*

MAY 20

MOST LIKELY, in every classroom there is at least one chalkboard or dry-erase board for teachers to fill with important information. These classroom standards can be great learning devices if they are not abused by teachers. In my days of observing teachers and student teachers, I have seen the range of use for chalkboards vary from never being used, to the worst extreme, being filled with information that is never allowed to be erased. The following *Teacher Tips* from veteran chalkboard users may help you in getting the most use out of these devices:

- Use the board as much as possible. It is an important visual display for visual learners.

- Erase the board often so students are not confused by the clutter. Notes that are left unerased can be distracting or cause confusion.

- If you are having trouble writing in a straight line on the board, project lines on the overhead when no one is around and write the information ahead of time, or draw lines on the board that are not visible from a distance. (Or, if you do not mind your students knowing that you need lines, make them more visible.)

297

- Check occasionally, at the end of a lesson, before erasing the board to see how visible your writing is to your students. Is it high enough, large enough, legible?

- Be heard as well as seen—do not talk to the board while writing on it. If you find it necessary to write and talk at the same time, stand sideways so your students will be able to hear you.

- Give your pupils an opportunity to write on the board. Most students, especially younger ones, enjoy writing with chalk.

ᔥ IN WHAT OTHER WAYS *can a chalkboard or dry-erase board enhance your teaching?*

MAY 21

CHARLES SILBERMAN, writing of the education that the children of today—who will be in the work force in the year 2030—will need for the future, stated in his book *Crisis in the Classroom*, "To be 'practical' an education should prepare them for work that does not yet exist and whose nature cannot even be imagined." Since one cannot predict what young people will need in the future, he writes, to do this "means that the schools must provide a liberal, humanizing education."[6]

Since Silberman's book was written in 1970, we can add even more years onto that year 2030 figure and ask, "What will children need to know in the second half of the twenty-first century, to be in the work force for the year 2050, 2060, 2070 . . . ?" More important, how can you prepare them with a "practical" education that "should prepare them for work that does not yet exist and whose nature cannot even be imagined?" If you think for a few moments what knowledge has been gained in the past century, it is impossible to know what the inhabitants of the next century will be experiencing. Perhaps it is best to provide your students with, as Silberman points out, an education that is both "liberal" and "humanizing" as well.

> How can you *provide your students with a "liberal, humanizing education"? How can you prepare your students for the next century?*

MAY 22

IF YOU THOUGHT that yesterday's question ("How can you prepare your students for the next century?") was not complicated enough, we continue today in a similar vein. Although it is important that young people be prepared to earn a living as adults, and there are people who argue that one of the most important reasons for gaining an education is to become employable, there is much more to preparing for the twenty-first century than gaining skills for the workplace.

The Tanners write in *Curriculum Development: Theory into Practice*, "In this quest it is not enough to prepare oneself for an occupation but one must also develop a vision of the good person leading the good life in the good society. In a free society, the citizen is expected to develop the ability to think reflectively, to communicate thought, to make intelligent judgments, to discriminate wisely among values in coming to grips with problems and issues that are common to all citizens."

"General education," they continue, "in a free society, then, is intended to develop the independently thinking, socially responsible citizen."[7]

The task of teaching invariably gets more complicated, doesn't it?

299

꩜ HOW CAN YOU *prepare young people for "leading the good life in the good society"?*

MAY 23

ONE OF THE JOYS of grandparenthood is not, as we jokingly remark, that we can play with our grandchildren, fill them full of sweets, spoil them, and then send them home (although that is not a negative aspect of the role), but that grandparenthood gives us the opportunity to "parent" once again, with all of the experience and previous knowledge that we did not have while raising our own children. To put it bluntly: Being a grandparent is a whole lot of fun.

I was one of those parents who tried to spend a lot of time in my children's worlds. I enjoyed getting down on my knees and watching a caterpillar (or "pillar-cat" as one of the young ones called it) crawl across the sidewalk. I also enjoyed playing catch with a beginning Little Leaguer and reading my children to sleep at the end of the day. Being a grandmother has allowed me a second chance to enjoy that wonderment with my grandson once again, watching a trail of ants move their goods from one area to another, seeing nature for the first time, and firsthand through a child's eyes. I enjoy reading to him from his father's and his uncle's old books, and someday I will play catch with him to practice for Little League or just to have fun.

We forget these moments as we get older, hurriedly moving about our days, but it is important to STOP and see the world through your students' eyes occasionally, to recall the joy of learning something new and the excitement of doing well at a task that may seem mundane to you but is new to those in your charge.

Today is my grandson's birthday, and I am so glad that he gave me a chance to once again see the world through a small child's eyes.

Do you take the time to see the world "through a child's eyes"? What have you "seen" lately?

MAY 24

ON MAY 24, IN 1607, the first colonists landed at Jamestown, Virginia, under the patent of the London Company. During the first seven months they were here, through the summer and late autumn, starvation and disease reduced the original number of 105 settlers to only thirty-two. Fortunately, the dismal situation improved the following year, partly because Captain John Smith was elected council president of the new colony, and also because new provisions had arrived. A very important element in the early settlers' survival was the development of farming, especially crops such as corn. Clearly, those thirty-two early inhabitants of the new land worked very hard to survive the new year.[8]

The lesson we can learn from this is the importance of cooperation and survival skills. We have probably all participated in the various survival discussions that we have been assigned in school. They go something like this:

- "You are on a deserted island, and you have the following materials . . ."
- "You are lost in space, and you have a gun and matches . . ."
- "Your plane has crashed in the ocean . . ."

The purpose of these exercises is not only for critical thinking (why you would select one item over another), but for the cooperation required to arrive at a consensus for the group. After all, as the colonists at Jamestown discovered, cooperation is a very important component of surviving a "dismal situation."

ꙮ WHAT "SURVIVAL" ACTIVITIES *are appropriate for the age group that you teach?*

MAY 25

THIS MAY SEEM to be an unusual time of year (near the end of the school year) to begin a discussion on the importance of knowing child psychology and children's stages of growth. However, any time is a good time to review the information that you learned in your educational psychology classes, because, as you know, children learn best when they are psychologically ready to understand the information that they are being presented. So let's take a look at the various stages that children travel through on their journeys to adulthood, focusing only on school-aged years.

ꙮ WHAT ARE THE STAGES *of growth and development that the children you are teaching are experiencing at this time? Do you remember?*

MAY 26

KNOWING THE developmental stages of the age of the children that you teach allows you to "meet the child where they are." One of my favorite child psychologists is Erik Erikson, who wrote about stages of "psychosocial" development (is it coming back now?). Erikson states that in his or her lifetime, an individual passes through eight stages, each with an element to be either positively or negatively confronted as the individual moves on and takes on new challenges. Unlike other developmentalists, however, Erikson believed that there are those individuals who do not completely resolve their crises, but who nonetheless do pass on to the next stage. You may recall that an individual with an unresolved crisis must deal with the unresolved stage at a later time in his or her life.

Erikson's first two stages, "trust versus mistrust" and "autonomy versus doubt," concern the preschool child, so we will skip over them and begin with stage three, "initiative versus guilt" (children who are three to six years old). As you may recall, the young child who is in this stage continues to grow both in language and motor skills, which allows him to be increasingly active and vigorous in exploring his world. "Being firmly convinced that he is a person on his own," Erikson writes, "the child must now find out what kind of person he may become."9

During stage four, "industry versus inferiority," the six- to twelve-year-old child enters school, expanding his (or her) social world, which now includes teachers and peers who are as influentially important to him as his parents were, while his parents' role increasingly diminishes. In this stage, with success gained by attempting and accomplishing new activities, the child creates a feeling about himself and his abilities to further achieve. The child who is in a negative situation, where he experiences repeated feelings of failure, may learn negative self-images and develop a negative perception of how others see him.

In stage five, "identity versus role confusion" (ages twelve to eighteen years), the young person begins to question who he or she is and increasingly turns away from parents for an identity with peers, experimenting with who he or she is and can be. Some of this identity may be sought in finding himself or herself through a relationship with a significant other.

Erikson's stages give us a glimpse of the child, how he (or she) relates to others, and how his (or her) perception of himself (or herself) is tied in with his view of how others see him. By reviewing this information, it is easy to see how important it is to a child's development that we carefully communicate in a positive manner as much as possible and try to see what they are seeing in us.

ᴥ ARE YOU ABLE *to see what a child sees in your eyes? What do you see?*

MAY 27

ANOTHER IMPORTANT INDIVIDUAL in the field of child psychology was Jean Piaget, the Swiss child psychologist who, with his theory of cognitive development, took a different approach to child development. Piaget's theory had four stages, and unlike Erikson, he wrote that a child would have to pass through one of the stages before being able to attempt the next stage.

If you recall from your educational psychology classes, in Piaget's second stage, the "pre-operational" stage (ages two to seven), the young child develops the ability to use symbols to represent objects that exist in his or her world and therefore enters a time when the child's language and ability to conceptualize begin to occur.

In the third stage, "concrete operational" (ages seven to eleven), the child is able to improve her ability to think logically and is also able to "reverse" operations. Although she has not reached the age of abstract thinking, the child can understand concepts if these concepts are related to known objects in her world.

During Piaget's final stage, "formal operational" (eleven years to adulthood), the child is able to think abstractly and problems can be solved systematically to completion.

What we learn from Piaget's theory is that forcing a child do an activity or understand a concept that is out of his or her range of thinking can be futile.

❧ Do you have *an activity or a concept that you have been trying unsuccessfully to teach your students? Is it perhaps out of their stage?*

MAY 28

ANOTHER CHILD DEVELOPMENTALIST that we often read about in educational psychology is Lawrence Kohlberg and his stages of moral development. In Kohlberg's theory, individuals progress through three levels in their development of moral reasoning (with some individuals never reaching the final stage of his theory). Because individuals pass through Kohlberg's stages at varying times, his theory does not have the ages attached to the levels as did Erikson's and Piaget's.

Kohlberg's first level, one which is often seen in elementary school children, is called the "preconventional level." At the preconventional level, rules are set by others, and children perceive the fear of punishment as the reason to behave rather than any moral notion.

At level two, the "conventional level," the individual begins to adopt the rules of the group and will at times allow the group's rules (whether family, friends, or classmates) to override his individual needs or beliefs about what is right or wrong.

At the last level, the "postconventional level," the individual defines his or her own values according to the ethical principles that he or she has determined to follow, looking to "the right" or "the good" (the "universal good") as the principle to follow.

If we look at our students with Kohlberg's theory in mind, we can see why some young people do the things that they do, depending upon who is important in their lives.

As a guide, they may even be looking at you!

305

🔖 Do your students *look to you as a moral example to follow? Why or why not?*

May 29

BELL HOOKS, who signs her name in lowercase letters, once wrote, "After twenty years of teaching, I can confess that I am often most joyous in the classroom, brought closer here to the ecstatic than by most of life's experiences."[10]

I know what she means. Often, after having completed a long day of meetings and teaching two night-time classes, one from 4 to 7 P.M. and the other from 7 to 10 P.M., I find myself at home, lying in bed and wide awake, not able to come down from the experience of an exciting class where students were *engaged*. And the only word I can think of to describe the class is *awesome*.

Learning is an exciting activity to watch, and it is exciting to be a part of the experience and (especially) to be a cause of it in another individual. I will tell you a secret and I know that you can keep it: It is at times like these that I believe that I would do this job for nothing. (That is right, no pay.) The sheer joy of the experience tells me that it "does not get any better than this." As I sometimes tell my friends, "Sometimes I cannot believe that I actually get paid to do this!"

Now, before you begin thinking that you should quit your job because you do not feel this way, I must tell you that there were years when I did not feel this excitement either. But fortunately I found the age group that I enjoy working with, and that has made the difference.

🔖 Do you feel *"the most joyous in the classroom"? What age students will help you feel this way?*

May 30

IF YOU ARE TEACHING in a traditional situation, *hang in there!* There is less than a month to go until it is *summertime.* This can be a difficult time for you and your students, with loads of activities, paperwork, and correcting to keep up on, and people around you who are weary of being in school. Maybe your students, your coworkers, and even your administrators could benefit from the example of a calm, unaffected individual to emulate just about now.

Albert Schweitzer once wrote, "Example is not the main thing in influencing others. . . . It's the only thing." You may recall that Schweitzer was the medical missionary who, along with his wife, spent years in Africa helping others, and was awarded the Nobel Peace Prize in 1953.

Although this quote is certainly worthy of being quoted (and emulated) at other times, it may help your students and coworkers if you are an example of a calm, productive teacher from now until the end of the year.

   IS THE END OF THE YEAR *beginning to become troublesome? What can you do to be an example for others of the calm, productive teacher?*

May 31

MAY 31 may not be the day that we celebrate as Memorial Day this year, but it is the official holiday, nonetheless. Also known as Decoration Day, this holiday originated in 1868, when General John A. Logan, commander-in-chief of the Grand Army of the Republic, issued an order designating May 31 as the day in which the graves of soldiers were to be "decorated."

307

Another event that occurred on this date happened nearly a century earlier, when President George Washington signed the first Copyright Act to protect plays, books, and maps from being copied for a period of fourteen years, and included the right to renew the copyright for another fourteen years after the first. The passage of this act, it was said, was mainly due to the "unrelenting activity" of Noah Webster on its behalf.[11]

All teachers should know about copyright laws and model good citizenship by not photocopying books, videotaping movies, copying computer programs, or other works for your students. All these activities can violate copyright laws. (If and when you become a writer, you will understand and appreciate getting credit where it is due.)

❧ HOW WILL YOU *celebrate this day?*

JUNE

June 1

IT IS JUNE, the month that some of you have been looking forward to since last September, when you came to the foregone conclusion that this was going to be a difficult year. To those of you who had the class from Hades this year, I extend my sympathy but also my congratulations that a much-needed vacation is about to start.

June is traditionally a fun month, with graduations, family and class reunions, the beginning of summer and the end of the school year. But this fun-filled month requires that a tremendous amount of work get done before the last day of your school session. So, rather than spending the time reading a daily reading, let's get on with the task at hand! Let's make a list and prioritize those activities that are left to do.

৶ WHAT DO YOU *have left to do before the end of the school year?*

June 2

JOHN DEWEY wrote in *Reconstruction in Philosophy* (1920) that education traditionally has been thought of as "preparation," acquiring certain knowledge that will be of use to the individual at some later time. Back on August 16 we read a passage from Dewey in which he said that the view of education as preparation means that "the end is remote, and education is getting ready, is a preliminary to something more important to happen later on." This means, according to Dewey, that "childhood is only a preparation for adult life, and adult life for another life."

Instead of teaching children what is useful at this time in their lives, we resort to a speech in our classrooms, telling students to be sure to learn such-and-such because it will benefit them in junior high, or when they get to high school they will need to know X, in order to get into college, they will need to know Y. And so on.

Dewey continued, "If at whatever period we choose to take a person, he is still in the process of growth, then education is not, save as a by-product, a preparation for something coming later." He concluded by saying, "The best thing that can be said about any special process of education . . . is that it renders its subject capable of further education. . . . Acquisition of skill, possession of knowledge, attainment of culture are not ends; they are marks of growth and means to its continuing."[1]

Teaching should be for *now*. And it should include information necessary for the students to be successful *at this time*. The "by-product" is mastering the skills necessary to be successful at that distant future date.

❧ How often *have you heard just those words, "You will need to know this information when you get to . . ."* (sometime in the future)? *Worse yet, how many times have your heard yourself say it?*

JUNE 3

OVER THE PAST FEW MONTHS, we have often looked at the importance of being a lifelong learner, and the importance of teaching in a way that enables your students to continue to *desire* to learn well past the time that they are in school. For the majority of their lives, in fact. Yet we have not gone into detail on what it means to *be* a lifelong learner.

Certainly life is a learning experience, whether or not we want it to be, and whether or not we enjoy the particular thing that we are learning. Yet making a concerted effort to learn once they have completed school does not often fit into the schedules of many adults who are busy with their own lives. Therefore, maybe the practice of lifelong learning needs to be taught to young people before they leave school.

John Dewey wrote in his book *Experience and Education,* "Perhaps the greatest of all pedagogical fallacies is the notion that a person learns only the particular thing he is studying at the time. . . . The most important attitude that can be formed is that of desire to go on learning."[2]

❧ SCHOOL IS ALMOST OUT; *how can you instill the desire for lifelong learning in your students?*

JUNE 4

YESTERDAY WE TALKED about the importance of teaching the *desire* to be lifelong learners to your students, and you were left with the question of *how* to teach lifelong learning. The following *Teacher Tips* may help you to do just that:

• Introduce a variety of activities to your students, which may whet their appetites for further information. Often activities that are introduced to individuals become later avocations or possible vocations. Art, music, sports, dance, crafts, computers, mechanics, cooking, and sewing are only a few of the activities that adults enjoy.

• Be aware of the negative aspects of collateral learning, that unplanned learning that often takes place alongside the planned objectives. For example, if you force students to read a novel, however good it might be, you may experience the negative collateral learning of students who learn to dislike reading and therefore miss out on the wonderful works of literature available to them.

- Show enthusiasm for your subject. Using the same example of the previous tip, if students are required to read a novel, teach it and assign it in a manner that entices them to want to know more. Making the subject relevant to them also helps; why else would *Romeo and Juliet* be such a popular Shakespearean play?

- Last, and perhaps most important, model what a lifelong learner looks like to your students. If you have learned something new, or are returning to school to further your degree, talk to your students about it. Show your enthusiasm and tell them about all of the wonderful things that you are learning. You will be doing your students and yourself a big favor.

ॐ HOW CAN YOU *model lifelong learning?*

JUNE 5

ONE OF THE ACTIVITIES that I used to enjoy when I was a child, and that I also created for my students when I was teaching elementary school, was to make a calendar of fun assignments for summer—such as read a good book, write a letter to the teacher and tell her what you have been doing this summer, start a rock collection, or a variety of other activities for children to do when the summer gets too long. Kids sometimes get bored in the long, hot summer months, so a list of activities may help them to keep academic activities going all summer long. It may help their parents, too.

Some of the activities that you may want to include are collections, cooking, sewing, craftmaking, reading, writing, helping Mom and Dad, gardening, helping the neighbors and relatives, or going places. The list is endless.

෨ WHAT SUMMERTIME ACTIVITIES *are appropriate for the students that you teach?*

JUNE 6

I OFTEN HEAR older people complain that, with the phone and now e-mail, young people have lost the skill of letter writing, and maybe it is true. When was the last time that you received a letter from a friend, or better yet, wrote a letter to someone? Did you find the experience a pleasant one? The following *Teacher Tips* from a longtime letter writer may help give you some ideas for using letter writing with your students:

• Ask your students to write a letter to themselves as though they were now twenty-one years old. What do they hope to be doing? Where would they like to be? How will they get there? For example, will they have a college degree, a career, a family? After the letters are addressed to their parents' address, ask students to pencil the date on which they will turn twenty-one on the envelopes, then collect the letters, tuck them away, and then send them to your students on their twenty-first birthdays.

• Similarly, write a letter to each of your students describing them as they are today. Place a date on the envelope for five or ten years from now and mail it then.

• One activity that I used to enjoy with my students was done on the last day of school. Each child wrote their name on the top of a sheet of paper. Then they would pass the paper to their right. The person on their right would then write something nice about the person whose name appeared on the top. Then the papers were passed to the right again. By the time the students' papers were returned to them they each had thirty (or however many students were in the class) nice things written about them. The only rules were that it had to be something nice (I checked before I gave the papers back), and a student could not write the same thing on each paper. Students often told me how good it felt to read that paper. Many later told me that they had saved them.

One final note, those people who complain about the lost art of letter writing are wrong. Just look at the number of passed letters you confiscate every day!

What other forms *can letter writing take in your classroom so the skill is not lost?*

June 7

At a recent "Success" conference, the motivational speaker Brian Tracy gave a quote that probably should be tacked on school bulletin boards across the nation. He said, "You are 100 percent responsible for yourself. That means: no excuses, no blaming others, no criticizing others, and no complaining."[3]

How many of our students could benefit from learning that piece of advice early in their school careers and in life? Anyone who has taught school for any length of time has come across the student or the parent who makes countless excuses for work not being completed, irresponsibility, and/or bad behavior. It seems that people want to blame others for what they have or *have not* done in life. If a child learns something in school, *he* learns it. If he does not learn it, it was the teacher's fault. How often do we hear adults blame their inadequacies on their parents when the adults have been on their own for years?

Come to think of it, we all could benefit by tacking this quote where *we* (you and *I*) can see it!

315

❧ WHAT IS HAPPENING in your life that you blame someone else for?

JUNE 8

IT MUST BE getting to be the time of graduation for students in your school district, a memorable time for young people across the nation. I know, I graduated from high school on June 8, a long time ago. But I distinctly remember it to this day! The pomp and circumstance, the flowing robes and mortarboard hats, sitting tearfully with my best friends, walking across the stage, shaking hands with the principal and superintendent of schools, and the graduation parties that followed. What a day (and night)!

So often we see graduation as the end when, indeed, it is the beginning—a commencement. That long-awaited day when school is over. Then what? Have you prepared your students for the beginning? I have been to many graduations in my life and I have noticed, yes, the happiness on the faces of the graduates, but also the *stunned* look of "Now what?"

❧ WHAT WILL *your students be doing after graduation?*

JUNE 9

TV PERSONALITY Joan Lunden once said, "The best predictor of success is to create it." Interesting thought, isn't it? We can create our own success(es). Do our students know this? Do we? I remember a card I received from a friend many years ago. It said, "I am waiting for my ship to come in, but with my luck I will be at the airport."

June

Creating our own success, according to Lunden, happens when we "survey options and select those which work best." And, she continued, "Remove failure as an option."[4]

Waiting for good fortune to come our way goes hand in hand with blaming others for our misfortune. Either way, the power is out of our control and in the hands of someone or something else. Thomas Edison once said, "Genius is one percent inspiration and ninety-nine percent perspiration," and he should know. He was also mighty successful, I might add.

☙ HOW CAN YOU *convince your students (or yourself) that hard work is more likely to make them successful than good luck?*

JUNE 10

DO YOU REMEMBER from your high school or college classes ever reading the works of James Baldwin? Maybe you are a literature teacher and get to introduce his works to your students. We often think of James Baldwin as the twentieth-century essayist, novelist, playwright, and author of *Go Tell It on the Mountain.* But he also wrote and spoke about education, including the following from a speech titled, "The Negro Child—His Self Image," given to New York City teachers in 1963.

At the presentation Baldwin said, "The purpose of education, finally, is to create in a person the ability to look at the world for himself, to make his own decisions, to say to himself this is black or this is white, to decide for himself whether there is a God in heaven or not. To ask questions of the universe, and then learn to live with those questions, is the way he achieves his own identity."

Unfortunately, he added, "no society is really anxious to have that kind of person around."[5]

Maybe no society wants to have the questioning, soul-searching person around, but it sounds like all the more reason

317

to develop them. We need to be able to make decisions and so do our young people. That creates a difficult task for teachers, because it may mean giving up a little power and it may create the potential for students to make decisions that are different from what we want.

ॐ HOW CAN YOU *help children learn to become good decision makers, "able to look at the world for themselves"?*

JUNE 11

JONATHAN KOZOL, author of *Death at an Early Age* and *Savage Inequalities*, more recently wrote the book *Amazing Grace: The Lives of Children and the Conscience of a Nation.* Kozol, perhaps the conscience of education, writes in *Amazing Grace*, "Whatever good things may happen for the children of another generation are, in any case, of little solace to those who are children now and will not have their childhood to live a second time in the next century."[6]

When we read Kozol, we are instantly reminded of the importance of Maslow's Hierarchy of Needs. (Do you remember Maslow from your educational psychology classes?) When studying Maslow's theory we learn that a child (or adult for that matter) cannot become self-actualized, enjoy beauty, or even learn for that matter, if the lower needs of food, shelter, and love have not been met. If we put Kozol and Maslow together, it is easy to conclude that if the child's basic needs are not being met, he or she has little need for an education that prepares him or her for the future.

❧ ARE YOUR STUDENTS' *basic needs being met? If you have been meeting them during the year, who will meet them over the summer?*

JUNE 12

TODAY, JUNE 12, was Anne Frank's birthday. Frank was born on June 12, 1929, and died in a concentration camp in 1945. Most of us have read *The Diary of Anne Frank* at some time in our lives, generally in junior or senior high school. Some of you may have assigned her book as part of the literature you are teaching your students.

I remember the first time I read the book. Well, actually, we had it read to us by that same seventh-grade teacher who read *Hiroshima, 1984,* and other wonderful works of literature to us. I remember that while the book was being read, I felt the sadness for this young girl who was about the same age that I was at the time, who had hidden from the soldiers, and who had been protected by the bravery and heroism of those who would harbor the persecuted in their homes. This was certainly the epitome of caring for the welfare of our fellow human beings.

We are not asked today to risk our lives for our fellow countrymen and women, but we are asked nonetheless to help in those areas that we are able. I know that you are tired after a long school year, but once you are rested, you might want to do some volunteer work in your community to help in areas that you feel particularly strongly about.

At the university in which I teach, we are required to volunteer in the community in order to be considered for promotion or tenure, above the outreach we do for the community as a regular part of our jobs. And although, at first, we may complain about the added burden of volunteering when we are already busy with teaching, preparing, researching, and writing, many of our volunteer positions give us a multitude of benefits that we do not receive in our paid work.

One of my recent volunteer jobs was as a fire lookout in the local national forest. In this position, once or twice a month I drove to the forest, climbed the steps to an old fire lookout tower, and scanned the forest throughout the day looking for fires that could prove devastating to the area. The benefit, other than the obvious ones of being outside and having a terrific 360-degree view, was the opportunity to educate visitors who climbed the tower about the forest, plants and animals, and the equipment used by forestry men and women in the past.

After a "breather," you might want to consider some new and different volunteer position to "give back" to the community and your fellow human beings.

⮕ WHAT UNIQUE *volunteer opportunity might you consider doing this summer (or throughout the year)?*

JUNE 13

FOR MANY university students across the nation, June is also a time for the end of their classes. As we look at today's entry I am sitting in a classroom watching twenty adults who are teachers, parents, husbands and wives, and sons and daughters, writing their final exam for a rigorous course that I just finished teaching to them the previous week. And I am a little in awe of them. Why do they do it? They are such busy people, why do they take the time to gain further knowledge for a job that they already have?

I know that some of them return to school to move over a column on the pay scale, but I wonder, is a year or more of their lives and thousands of dollars in tuition worth the small pay raise that they will be given for the work that they have done? Some students return to school because they realize that they have a gap in the their knowledge, and these students return to school to learn (at least they hope) additional information that will make their teaching easier. Still others, and the ones that I love to work with, are the ones who return to college because they care about their profession and they care about themselves. They want to be with others, to be inspired to return to their classrooms in the fall.

Not all education programs are equal. There are "good" universities and "bad" ones (the ones we call "paper mills" who give students degrees and little else). If you are considering returning to school, I encourage you to investigate a good university and become a part of that environment. It will make your teaching experience easier down the road.

For my students who have completed their course work, their final exams, and their master's degrees, I am happy. I am even happier for their students, who will be taught by a teacher who cared enough to be a lifelong learner.

∾ WHAT WOULD BE *a benefit for you in returning to school or furthering your education?*

JUNE 14

JUNE 14, FLAG DAY, commemorates the adoption of the "Stars and Stripes" by the Continental Congress on June 14, 1777. A bill designating June 14 as National Flag Day was passed by the Eighty-first Congress and signed into law by President Harry S. Truman on August 3, 1949. The thirteen alternating red and white stripes of the United States flag signify the thirteen original states, while the fifty white stars on a blue background represent the individual states presently in the Union.

The pledge to the flag as we currently say it—"I pledge allegiance to the flag of the United States of America and to the republic for which it stands; one nation under God, indivisible, with liberty and justice for all" first appeared, in a shorter version, in *The Youth's Companion* on September 8, 1892. It read, "I pledge allegiance to my flag and to the republic for which it stands; one nation indivisible, with liberty and justice for all." The original pledge was amended in 1923 at the National Flag Conferences, where the words "my flag" were substituted with the phrase "the flag of the United States of America." This remained the official form for thirty years. On June 14, 1954, President Dwight D. Eisenhower signed the bill adding the phrase "under God," which has remained in the official version to this day.[7]

☙ DO YOUR STUDENTS *know the significance of the flag and the pledge?*

JUNE 15

YESTERDAY WAS the birthday of Matthew, my youngest son. He was born on Flag Day and the twenty-ninth wedding anniversary of his paternal grandparents. My mother-in-law, who had been widowed two years earlier, called Matt her anniversary gift, and she still calls him that today.

Now that he is grown and a father himself, if you ask Matt what he likes to do, he will probably answer, "Anything that doesn't involve a desk!" He loves the outdoors, physical activities, and movement. A student with this mindset can spell trouble for teachers.

Fortunately, we had few problems with Matt in school because he is likable, and most teachers found him quick thinking, with a great sense of humor, and a lot of fun. (It helped that he knew when to control what he said.) Although he does not like desk jobs, he loved school, and often had perfect attendance records for the year. He enjoyed the people and liked being with friends in school.

Matt has always been very mechanical. Often, as a small child he would take things apart (whether we wanted them apart or not) and put them back together. If something broke, Matt could fix it, and he could create serviceable items if you told him what you needed.

Often in school we overlook these creative, mechanical students as we look for children who print neatly, give the right answers, and who sit and do correctly what we assign. Yet it is often the active ones, the thinkers, from which society benefits. And some of these (usually) non-A students are a pleasure to have around.

⋙ HOW CAN YOU HELP *the students who have qualities that do not fit into your image of what a student should be?*

JUNE 16

OK, HERE IS A BIT of trivia for you. On this date, in 1895, the comedian Stan Laurel was born as Arthur Jefferson, in Ulverston, England. Laurel, with his partner, Oliver Hardy, was part of the comedy team of Laurel and Hardy, who made Hollywood films for years.

If you are not familiar with this comedy team and the many other comedians of the 1930s, 1940s, and 1950s, you can become familiar with them by watching old movies or renting their classic works from your local video store. Along with Laurel and Hardy, be sure to see the Bob Hope/Bing Crosby "road" pictures, and certainly Bob Hope in *Paleface*. Do not forget Abbott and Costello and their famous "Who's on First" routine.

Comedy can be useful in the classroom if you remember the following rules: Do not *ever* be funny at the expense of a student. It is so easy to be funny by making a quick remark to a student in front of others, but the laughter you receive is not worth the price you pay in a student's eyes. Sometimes the most innocent

323

remarks can be very painful to a young person who wants to be respected by his or her peers. I recall one time I said something to the class that seemed very innocent, but the young junior high student came up to me afterward and said, "You know you hurt me, Mrs. Studer, when you said that." Most students will not be this brave, but they will silently hurt, just the same.

If you are going to use an individual to be funny, use yourself.

ᔔ How can you *interject humor into your classroom without hurting any of your students?*

June 17

ALTHOUGH THERE MAY BE better times of the year than summer to discuss the negative aspects of your students' watching too much television, it may be just the right time for teachers to get "hooked" on what early television reviewers called "the idiot box."

It is not that I am against television as a medium for entertainment. I, like you, have my favorite weekly shows that I look forward to watching, resting with my feet up, and "vegging" for an hour or so *occasionally*. Watching TV provides a great mindless opportunity to relax and let go of the troubles of the day. But I have also had summers where I got "hooked" on a television show and scheduled my day around that special hour. In retrospect, I wasted a summer on (probably) a talk show where I learned little, and could have relaxed in some other fruitful manner.

One of the problems with television and with movies is that we spend so much of our time, as teachers and parents, combating the negatives that our young people learn from the media—shows with mouthy young and older people, sex, violence, and above all the promotion of "getting even."

June

❧ WHAT WILL YOU *be watching this summer on television? How will this (or these) show(s) benefit your day?*

JUNE 18

YESTERDAY WE DISCUSSED the negative aspects of television and movies and how a summer or other period of time can be wasted with mindless television viewing. Today we want to look at the positive models of television and how the use of television in the classroom can encourage students to make wise use of TV time.

• If your class is in session now, discuss the positive and negative aspects of television, and how television can be used to enhance our lives.

• Assign an evening of television viewing (your students will love this) and as part of the assignment ask your students to discuss the plot of the show, the characters, and whether or not they liked the show.

• Next, ask your students about the stereotypes that the show promoted. What were the roles of women, men, minorities, young people, and senior citizens? Who was "in charge"? Is the show "real"? Do people really act the way that the characters act?

• Tape a typical television show for class and ask the same questions as were asked in the previous question.

• Discuss some of the problems with television shows and movies, such as stereotyping and the abundance of "unreal" models to emulate. What happens when people watch too much television? (They have no time for friends, no time for homework, and studies have shown that they tend to be overweight.)

- Discuss what alternatives to television students might have (and how students can help educate their family and friends). What is there to do when the television is turned off?

- Support public broadcasting channels with praise, assignments from these channels, and, if you feel so inclined, donations.

❧ MOST PEOPLE SAY *they do not watch much television, but they do. What do you do for entertainment when the television is turned off?*

JUNE 19

IN THE PAST TWO DAYS we have looked at the pros and cons of television viewing, and today I am offering one solution to the problem. Several years ago, when my children were in elementary school and it appeared that television watching was overtaking our lives, we decided (OK, I decided) to take a "vacation" from television and to turn it off for a month in the summer. Yes, for the whole month of August, the television was unplugged.

Although it was a little difficult for everyone at first, during this month, I enjoyed my children more than I had in previous months, as we worked and played together throughout the days and weeks of August. Some of the activities we participated in, other than the obvious ones of reading, coloring, playing ball, and bike riding, included visits to the library, parks, and museums. My sons helped with chores, helped make dinner, and best of all, spent lots of time talking to me. In the evenings, when their dad was home, we played games, went on armchair vacations (we had a globe that we would spin and then research the country that we landed on), talked, and laughed a good deal of the time.

Although there were times when I am sure that my children visited their friends' houses to watch television, and going without sports in the evening and on weekends was particularly difficult for my husband, they all went along with Mom's "study" to see if life without television encourages communication among family members.

Without a doubt I would encourage families to turn the television off for a prescribed time (perhaps a week, or one night each week) and see if you enjoy each other's company.

☙ HOW LONG *do you think you can go without the television on in your home? When will you try it?*

JUNE 20

LAST MONTH, on May 10, we looked at mothers and Mother's Day and reminded ourselves to be aware of the feelings of those students who do not have mothers in their households. Well, the same is true for Father's Day, which we usually celebrate around this time. In fact, today may be the actual day, Father's Day, if this is the third Sunday in June.

First, let's look at what is so great about fathers. There is the stereotypical view of fathers as providers, builders, repairers, and disciplinarians, the *Father Knows Best* "Jim Andersons" of the world. Then there are the modern-day dads, who may be (serving as) moms to children in one-parent households, who may be weekend fathers, or who may serve in a myriad of atypical roles for our students, our own children, and ourselves. Maybe the person who provides the "father role" in our students' lives is actually their mom. It sure gets confusing, doesn't it?

Whatever the form fatherhood takes for our students, remember, if you are assigning gifts or cards to make for Father's Day, be sure to remember that some of your students may not have a dad in their households.

327

❧ WHAT DO *dads provide? How can it be provided in the non-fathered home?*

JUNE 21

TODAY IS the first day of summer. For some people it is vacation time, time to relax with feet up, broad-brimmed hat, and sun lotion. For some it is time for reading the books set aside during the year. For others it is time for travel. For still others it is yard work or taking classes to get continuing education credits for that master's or doctoral degree. For still others, it is being in the classroom of the year-round school.

June 21 is the longest day of the year, the opportunity to have more daylight than any previous day or any day that follows today.

Whatever you do this summer, do it with lightness, enjoy your air-conditioning if you have it, and make this your best summer yet.

❧ HAVE YOU MADE *any plans for summer yet? What would you like to do?*

JUNE 22

LAST MONTH we looked at testing, and in particular "norm-referenced tests," which compare our students with other students in our district, state, and across the nation. On May 6, we looked at ways we could help students improve their scores by improving their "test-taking" ability rather than having them memorize information that may or may not be on the test. One

June

way we can help our students do better on norm-referenced tests is by helping them develop their critical-thinking skills, and a good way to do this is to ask questions that compare and contrast two similar items.

You probably know from your schooling, or perhaps you have already shared with your students, how the use of Venn diagrams helps us understand how two similar things are alike and different. (Just in case you forgot, a Venn diagram is two overlapping circles, with each outer circle having written in it the uniqueness of each item. The inner, or overlapping area of the two circles holds the similarities, or "alikeness," of the two items.)

❧ WHAT OTHER METHODS *can be used to teach critical-thinking skills?*

JUNE 23

YESTERDAY WE DISCUSSED that critical-thinking skills may help students when they take norm-referenced tests. A method of exercising your students' (and your own) brain power or critical-thinking skills is through the use of "brain teasers" for pushing the mind to think more deeply. The following *Teacher Tips* may help you and your students expand your thinking, which may ultimately help with test taking at a later date:

• Write an idiom on the board such as, "She's burning the candle at both ends," then ask students to explain the meaning and guess its origin. (It was a French expression that came into English in the late 1500s.) Later explain the meaning of this idiom (If one really took a candle and burned it at both ends it would be used up twice as fast; the image refers to people who work hard day and night and use up all of their strength.) You may want to continue the discussion by having your students brainstorm about similar sayings we use today to mean the same thing (for example, to be "burned out").

• Ask your students "thinking-type" questions such as, "If you were stuck in an elevator who would you like to be in there with and why?"

• If you are stuck for ideas to use with your students there are many good books on brain teasers, often available through "book fair" publishers.

ॐ DO YOU RECALL *a favorite brain teaser from your youth? What was it? (Maybe your students would like it too.)*

JUNE 24

IN 1967, Sterling McMurrin, a former U.S. Commissioner of Education, wrote in an article for the magazine *Saturday Review* that discussed the cognitive function of school and concluded that the affective domain was an equally important function. "The affective function of instruction pertains to the practical life—to the emotions, the passions, the dispositions, the motives, the moral and aesthetic sensibilities, the capacity for feeling, concern, attachment or detachment, sympathy, empathy, and appreciation."[8]

Isn't it interesting that education has two sides or functions, according to a former Commissioner of Education, and yet it appears that the only function the community, politicians, and district personnel appear to be interested in is the cognitive or measurable one? This is because the affective domain, however important, is not as easily measured and therefore becomes shortchanged when test scores drive curriculum and teachers are continually reminded of the importance of these tests.

꒱ How can we *ensure that the affective domain gets a fair share of the curriculum?*

JUNE 25

PETER HLEBOWITSH writes in his book *Radical Curriculum Theory Reconsidered* that it is easier to criticize education and educators than to come up with solutions that may help improve what may be wrong. "Radical commentators have written much about how schools fail," he writes. But "they have also left us with little in the way of solutions that might work within the social and political realities of our schools."9

We discussed yesterday the two functions of school—the cognitive function and the affective (nonmeasurable) function—and you were left with the question of how we can ensure that the affective domain gets a fair share of the curriculum. The cognitive domain may be more easily measured, but measuring the affective inevitably misses the point. Because it is affective, involves feelings, empathy, moral and aesthetical qualities, it is immeasurable and should remain so. The point is that we should not even have to measure the affective.

The affective function of schools is the primary quality that ensures that our nation serves as a community and a worthy and wonderful place in which to live. Do we measure our love of our students, our sympathy for those who hurt, or a person's morality? A better question than how to measure the affective domain is: How do we teach it?

꒱ How do we teach *the affective function of school? How do we ensure that it maintains its importance in the school environs?*

JUNE 26

FOR SEVERAL YEARS NOW, there has been an ongoing discussion on the value of having a national curriculum that would uniformly regulate education, ensuring that schools and teachers in classrooms would teach similar, if not identical, curricula throughout the nation. A national standard would take the development of subject matter out of the hands of local control to give students equal access to knowledge nationwide. It would allow (it is presumed) maintenance standards and would create for a transient populace the ability to move to a new school and continue where the student left off. A national curriculum would also allow for the linking of standards and assessment to the curriculum. In short, the curriculum could "teach to the test" and ultimately national test scores would rise.

But, according to Karen Zumwalt, in her article, "What's a National Curriculum Anyway," a national curriculum is "an oxymoron—a phrase that involves contradictory terms." It is an oxymoron because, as we know in education, two or more children sitting in different classrooms, being taught the same subjects by different teachers, are receiving very different experiences and very different educations.

"It is at the classroom level that curriculum comes alive—this is where curriculum has meaning." It is in the classroom where curriculum is "enacted. . . . Curriculum is not just what the class experiences, but it also has individualistic meanings . . . often referred to as the 'experienced curriculum.'"

Zumwalt concludes, "If one thinks of curriculum as that which is enacted and experienced, then a national curriculum could not be nationally enacted or experienced in any meaningful way."[10] An interesting thought, isn't it?

⁐ THINKING OF *one concept of the curriculum that you have taught: how do you think the various experiences of your students may have colored it?*

JUNE 27

HELEN KELLER WAS BORN in Tuscumbia, Alabama, on June 27, 1880, and died in her late eighties in 1968. Helen was born a "normal" child to a wealthy family. She lost her hearing and sight during her second year due to a serious illness. A request to an institute for the blind in Boston brought to her home the teacher Anne Sullivan, who became the governess and teacher of the "wild and uncontrollable" child. The world of language was given to Helen by her teacher, and she later learned Braille at the Horace Mann School for the Deaf. In 1904, she graduated from Radcliffe College in Cambridge, Massachusetts, with honors in English. In order to promote knowledge of handicaps to others, Helen began a lifelong series of lectures, books and writings. She was what Arthur Schlesinger calls "a worldwide symbol of another kind of victory, a victory over crushing personal handicaps, a victory gained with rare grace and determination to help others with similar problems."[11]

Although Helen Keller was a remarkable woman, and she certainly earned the accolades given to her, she succeeded because a *teacher*, Anne Sullivan, opened the world to her and gave her "sight" and "ears."

⁐ ARE YOU REACHING *some "wild and uncontrollable" children? Will the world one day be a greater place because of what you have done?*

JUNE 28

ALTHOUGH WE MAY LIKE to think of ourselves as teachers whose job it is to fill our students full of information, we also know that an important part of teaching is showing students how to think for themselves. The educational metaphors of the pitcher (where we pour information into the pupil) versus the sponge (where students absorb information on their own accord) have long been a part of our teaching curriculum. But there is another spin on the teacher/student relationship that reverses the role of teacher and learner, and gives an example of how the student/teacher relationship has benefits for the teacher as well as for the student.

John Holt writes in *Freedom and Beyond* that there is a problem with the view of the teacher as a curriculum planner who "intervenes" in a child's life in order for that child to grow in knowledge. Holt writes, "The more we intervene in children's lives, however intelligently, kindly, or imaginatively, the less time we leave them to find and develop their own ways to meet their true needs."

But there is more. "The more we try to teach them," Holt adds, "*the less they can teach us.*"[12] [The italics are mine.] Wow! There is more to teaching than giving. There is *our learning* from those in our charge.

꘎ HOW DO YOU *learn from your students? What do you learn from them?*

JUNE 29

YAK, YAK, YAK, do this, do that. It is summertime, which makes me always want to add the line from *Porgy and Bess*, ". . . and the living is easy."

June

If your summer has truly begun, today may be a good day to take the day off, a vacation from anything educational. Do not allow yourself to think about school, students, administrators, curriculum, or anything else related to your job. People who care about their jobs often have a difficult time letting go of them when the time is right to take a break. And this is especially true of teachers, who tend to be very caring individuals. I know that I used to (and still do), when I am on vacation, have a difficult time letting go of thinking about students and curriculum and new ways to teach upon my return. But sometimes we have to let go of it for our own well-being, and today may be just the day to do so.

Think summer! Relax and enjoy your day.

꙳ How will you *enjoy this day?*

JUNE 30

ONE OF THE MANY blessings that I have encountered in my life and in my relationships with others is the privilege of marrying into a family who accepted me from the beginning, and over the years I have had the opportunity to develop a mother–daughter-in-law relationship that is as strong as any friendship that I have experienced throughout the years.

One of the reasons that this relationship has developed is that my mother-in-law makes it a point never to interfere (although there were times that I am sure that she would have liked to) in the way that I directed my life, raised my children, or related to others. She was, and is, a good example of what an "in-law" can and should be.

If you ask Mom why she never interfered in her children's lives, she will jokingly respond that it is because "I like my nose right where it is on my face." But I think there is more to it than that. She trusted her parenting of her children and their ability to make decisions for themselves. That's a good lesson for parents *and* teachers.

Our relationships with others can affect our work as much as our work can affect our relationships. Trusting others may help alleviate some tension that affects both.

✑ IS THERE SOMEONE *(friend, family member, or student) who will benefit from your trusting them to make their own decisions?*

JULY

July 1

JULY, THE MIDDLE OF SUMMER. If you are on a traditional teaching schedule, you have probably been on summer vacation for a few weeks, settled into a summer routine, and may have already taken a vacation somewhere other than your own home. July can be a wonderful month: sunshine, solitude, an opportunity to sit back, reflect, and not be responsible for lesson plans, after-school activities, or even getting up early if you do not choose to do so. That is what makes summertime so wonderful for teachers.

But some of us do not take a vacation during what is traditionally thought of as summer vacation. For some teachers, our summers are spent working on curriculum or special district projects, taking education courses to expand our knowledge, to complete a master's degree, to move toward another position, or simply to move over into a higher column on the pay scale. For still others (often for elementary teachers), July 1 is a teaching day in the year-round schools as the new school year begins, an exciting day for young people and those who work with them.

Whether you are teaching, working, studying, vacationing, or simply enjoying your day, have a good one as we enter July.

☙ WHAT ARE YOU *doing today?*

July 2

JULY 2, 19-SOMETHING-OR-OTHER, is my birthday. I think that birthdays are very important, don't you? I like to celebrate birthdays because a birthday is someone's very special day; it is the day you were born, and what would life be like without you? So I celebrate birthdays, and maybe put more importance into them than most people.

So, here are my reflections on birthdays (and I can say whatever I like . . . because it is my birthday).

On my birthday I like to do something special for myself. I give myself a birthday present that is beautiful. I get my nails manicured, have my makeup done at a cosmetic counter to try a new style, or I go to a spa and lounge in the mud baths and mineral waters. I do something to relax and to make myself feel beautiful. Fortunately, I have a summer birthday, so I usually have the day off.

When I was younger, I did not feel that a summer birthday was so lucky, however. (And this is a good thing to remember for your students, too.) When a child has a summer birthday (in a traditional school year), it means that they miss out on the celebrations that other children have whose birthdays are celebrated during the school year. Families bring cupcakes and classmates sing "Happy Birthday" to children whose birthdays fall during the school year. People are around during the school year for parties. When you have a summer birthday, there are no classmates singing "Happy Birthday"; your classmates are often gone for the summer and unavailable to help celebrate (I got in the habit of celebrating my birthday by myself).

This was even true as a staff member when I taught school and at the university where I teach now. If you have a birthday that falls within the school year, cards are circulated for everyone to sign and there are cakes in the teachers' lounge. This is fun. But the point is, do not forget those summer-birthday students and staff members too!

Here is my birthday gift to you: Be good to yourself and do something wonderful for yourself.

❧ WHAT WILL YOU DO *for yourself to feel wonderful today (and to help me celebrate my birthday today)?*

339

July 3

Tomorrow is July 4, Independence Day. A day when Americans celebrate their freedom. It is a day when families gather at picnics, watch fireworks, and enjoy being outdoors. Schools are just one of the many institutions that close on Independence Day, not only to allow employees to celebrate, but to give everyone the opportunity to relax from the stresses of the other days of the week. Teaching is a demanding job, but July 4 gives us one more day to rest and derive joy from the company of others.

In 1950, the noted historian Henry Steele Commager wrote, "No other people ever demanded so much of education as have the Americans." And this statement is no less true today. He added, however, in the next sentence that, "None other was ever served so well by its schools and educators."[1] Which is also true today.

Thank you for giving to America's young people. What will you do today to have a good day?

July 4

The day before yesterday we looked at birthdays and their importance. OK, we looked at my birthday and how I think that it is pretty important. But today we celebrate a mighty big "birthday"—the celebration of the Declaration of Independence, a significant event in the birth of our nation.

The Fourth of July is a fun time. Probably because it is one of the few summer holidays where families gather; we have picnics, family reunions, firecrackers, parades, and the bright colors red, white, and blue are seen everywhere. With the celebration of Independence Day there is a sense of community throughout the nation. It is a festive occasion!

I love a parade, and the Fourth of July has plenty of them. I enjoy the colors, the floats, the clowns, the flags flying, the veterans in their uniforms, the cars with dignitaries waving to the crowd, and the bands, especially the bands. I often cry during parades, especially during a Sousa march that is well played.

I get a similar feeling when the "Star-Spangled Banner" is played at an athletic event—hearing the music, watching the flag ascend, listening to the spectators sing the words. And I, like you, get annoyed when people are talking, and ball-players are spitting and otherwise acting disrespectfully during this time. I know that many Americans have given their lives so that we can be enjoying that game. It seems only right that we should respect the ceremony of the country that they died to keep free.

I think that one of the problems with these behaviors is that people are not taught to respect the event, nor are they taught the words to the national anthem. It is a difficult song, but I remember how proud I was to learn it when it was taught to my class by my fourth-grade teacher at Quirk Road Elementary School.

❧ HAVE YOU TAUGHT *your students appropriate behavior during flag ceremonies? If you don't, who will?*

JULY 5

DID YOU KNOW that there is a lot more to the flag of the United States than the beautiful colors of red, white, and blue? On April 4, 1818, the Fifteenth Congress decreed an act to establish the Flag of the United States by stating: "Be it enacted by the Senate and House of Representatives . . . that from and after the fourth day of July next, the Flag of the United States be thirteen horizontal stripes, alternate red and white; that the union be twenty stars, white in a blue field . . . that on the admission of every new State into the Union one star be added to the union of

341

the Flag; and that such addition shall take effect on the fourth day of July then next succeeding such admission."[2]

Did you also know that, contrary to popular belief, the stars on the flag represent all fifty states collectively, and that no single star can be designated as belonging to a particular state. All are part of the whole.

No wonder I get a chill when I hear the "Star-Spangled Banner," and see the flag rise on the flagpole.

ॐ WHAT OTHER INFORMATION *about the United States flag might be meaningful for your students?*

JULY 6

TODAY WE WILL CONTINUE with a little more information about the United States flag, the "Stars and Stripes." We all know the story about Betsy Ross, the young Philadelphia widow who supported herself and her children as a seamstress, and who, because of her fine needlework, was called upon by George Washington to construct the first flag of the new country, or so the story goes.

Although this may be a true story, there is little evidence to support that this event actually took place. (Another myth for the new land.) What we do know, however, is that Washington expressed his theory on the flag's design by saying, "We take the star from Heaven, the red from our mother country, separating it by white stripes, thus showing that we have separated from her, and the white stripes shall go down to posterity representing liberty."[3]

Flags are symbolic of a country's views and are meaningful to the individuals who design them. Once made, they are displayed in public buildings, in courtrooms, at sporting events, and while leading men and women into battle. They appear to be something worth fighting to defend.

❧ IF YOU DESIGNED A FLAG, *what would it have on it and what colors would you choose to represent you and your loved ones?*

JULY 7

IN THE PAST FEW DAYS we have been, rightfully, discussing the flag of the United States and its significance to those of us who live in this country. Along with the "red, white, and blue," today may be a good time to discuss the story behind the song which was adopted as the national anthem of the United States by an act of Congress on March 3, 1931.

The "Star-Spangled Banner" was written on September 14, 1814 by Francis Scott Key, a prominent young lawyer in Washington and a member of a distinguished Eastern family. Contrary to common belief (in other words, another myth), Key did not write the poem that later became the national anthem while a prisoner on a ship in the Chesapeake Bay when the British Fleet attacked Fort McHenry at Baltimore. What actually happened was that, as an influential attorney, Key was on board the ship because he had been asked to negotiate the release of Dr. William Beanes, who had been taken prisoner in the "encounter" at Washington. Key did see the "stripes and bright stars" flying above the fort in the early morning mist and was moved to write the now-famous poem that we frequently sing.

The poem, sung to an old tune, was printed in the Boston *American* on September 21 and became an instant success. And "the rest is history," as they say.[4]

❧ CAN YOU RECITE *the words to the "Star-Spangled Banner"? Can your students?*

343

JULY 8

DID YOU KNOW that on this date, July 8, in 1835, the Liberty Bell cracked—a second time? No, it was not during the ringing to celebrate America's independence. It cracked during the ringing, or tolling, for the body of Chief Justice of the Supreme Court John Marshall, who had died on July 6 and was being taken from Philadelphia to his home state of Virginia.

The bell, famous for ringing out the proclamation of the Declaration of Independence (this too occurred on July 8), was originally ordered in 1751 for the new State House in Philadelphia. It was cast in London by Thomas Lister and arrived in Philadelphia on September 1, 1752. It was cracked while being tested, and was recast by Pass and Stow of Philadelphia, who added one and one-half ounces of American copper to each pound of original metal to make it less brittle. Unfortunately, this too produced a defective bell. The third bell was hung in the Philadelphia State House on June 7, 1753, and it is the one that resides there today.

After cracking on July 8, 1835, the bell was repaired for Washington's birthday in 1846, at which time it cracked irreparably. It now hangs in the vestibule of the tower of Independence Hall.[5]

The Liberty Bell has quite a history, but the interesting thing is that it was defective from the beginning and is broken today; seems like a fitting image for all of us less-than-perfect citizens.

⤷ DID YOU THINK *that the Liberty Bell broke proclaiming our independence (another myth we tell our students)? Isn't it better to know that something broken can be a symbol for our nation? (There is hope for all of us.)*

July 9

SINCE IT IS SUMMERTIME, and many of us are on summer vacation, this may be the time to get in some of that important reading that you have been "meaning to do." If you want to feel good about teaching, and if you are tired of the "fallout" from test scores and negative press, a good book to read this summer is David Berliner and Bruce Biddle's *The Manufactured Crisis: Myths, Fraud, and the Attack on America's Schools*.

With the use of statistics, information that is not printed in the press, and common sense, the authors "debunk the myths that test scores in America's schools are falling, that illiteracy is rising," or that teachers are not doing their jobs and therefore hurting our youth and their futures.

Some of the information they provide shows that:

1. "Standardized tests provide *no evidence whatever* that supports the myth of a recent decline in the school achievement of the average American student." (Not in math, science, English language courses, nor in any other academic subject.)

2. Despite greater numbers, "college seniors of today are doing just about as well on the GRE as their parents did a generation ago, and evidence from a GRE analytic-ability subscale suggests that their ability to reason is climbing."

The "Manufactured Crisis," according to the authors, "began on April 26, 1983—the date when, amidst much fanfare, the Reagan White House released its critical report on the status of American schools, *A Nation at Risk* . . . the 'mother of all critiques' of American Education." An interesting side note the authors make is that this adds to what we in education already knew, "the bashing of public education has long been a popular indoor sport in America."[6]

345

❧ HAS THE "CRISIS" *been "manufactured" in American education? Why or why not?*

JULY 10

ACCORDING TO THE AUTHORS of *The Manufactured Crisis,* one of the problems with comparing today's students with their parents, or with the argument that the curricula of today's schools is not in keeping with the objectives of the past, is that "traditional views of curricula have conceived the school as a means for pouring discrete and relatively unintegrated ideas into passive students."

Berliner (Professor at Arizona State University and past recipient of the "Friends of Education Award from the National Education Association," the NEA) and Biddle (a University of Missouri professor and editor of the journal *Social Psychology of Education*) write, "These views have always been suspect, but they are now truly obsolete, given the type of citizens America needs for its evolving, postindustrial society." The new curricula, they add, should be concerned with "developing thoughtfulness . . . knowledge transfer and the social nature of knowledge acquisition."7

In other words, comparisons with education that were designed for a different era and for different students need to be reinvestigated so that today's students are taught what is necessary for *their* futures.

❧ NO ONE LIKES *to be compared with someone else. Why do we continue to do this with our schools?*

JULY 11

IN THE PAST TWO DAYS we have been looking at Berliner and Biddle's *The Manufactured Crisis,* and how a "crisis situation" has been developed that places schools in a position to be "reformed" by those individuals involved in schools; if they cannot reform education, then "outsiders" (politicians and the media) will help them (or do it for them).

Berliner and Biddle conclude, "Our basic concern, however, is not with assigning blame but rather with countering the evil effects that scapegoating imposes on innocent people." They continue, "Educators are *not* responsible for most of the reputed shortcomings of American schools. . . . Indeed, most of the 'shortcomings' of schools suggested by critics are non-existent . . ." Rather, teachers "are coping well with intellectually complex, emotionally demanding, time-consuming, and often dangerous tasks. . . . The vast majority of teachers and administrators run a school system that works well for most American children."[8]

Congratulations!

❧ IN WHAT WAYS *are schools and teachers the scapegoats for what is wrong in society? What can teachers do to counteract that?*

JULY 12

IN MANY of our daily readings we have read the words of John Dewey, perhaps the most prolific of education writers, and certainly one who not only wrote a lot, but said a lot in what he wrote. Lawrence Cremin summarized Dewey's works in a manner that is appropriate as a follow-up to our discussion of Berliner and Biddle's *The Manufactured Crisis.*

347

Cremin wrote in his book, *Popular Education and Its Discontents,* "John Dewey liked to define the aim of education as growth, and when he was asked growth toward what, he liked to reply, growth leading to more growth. That was his way of saying that education is subordinate to no end beyond itself, that the aim of education is not merely to make parents, or citizens, or workers, or indeed to surpass the Russians or the Japanese. . ." The task of education, Cremin continued, is "ultimately to make human beings who will live life to the fullest, who will continually add to the quality and meaning of their experience and to their ability to direct that experience, and who will participate actively with their fellow human beings in the building of a good society."

"To create such an education," Cremin added, "will be no small task in the years ahead. . . ."9

When we worry about test scores, bad press, and the negative comments made by politicians who plan to clean up schools when elected, we lose sight of what education is all about. There is no crisis; continue on.

❧ How will you accept *the "task in the years ahead," to make education meaningful for those young people who look to you for their educational growth?*

July 13

Are you a little tired of being blamed for tests scores? Schnieder and Houston write in *Exploding the Myths: Another Round in the Education Debate,* "As far as we're concerned, many of our political and corporate leaders are using educational reform as a scapegoat for problems schools didn't cause and can't fix. We believe many of these elected leaders and their corporate sponsors are engaging in a conspiracy—a conspiracy against candor with the American people."[10]

Pretty heavy stuff, huh?

I do not know about you, but I get a little tired of society's lack of appreciation for the tremendous amount of work that teachers do. But, complaining and feeling sorry for ourselves is not a productive way to accomplish good results. So-o-o-o, what shall we do? The following *Productive Complainer Tips* may help to change the current use of teachers and education as the scapegoats for today's ills:

• Write an article for the newspaper about something wonderful that is going on in your classroom. Include clear pictures if you can. (Call the newspaper first and ask them if they have a particular format for submitting articles so that they are more likely to accept it.)

• Get involved in the community so that people get to know you, and talk about what is going on in your school and your classroom. Be sure to keep the negative stories to yourself, and above all, never complain about the students to outsiders.

• Send home a newsletter to parents on a regular basis, informing them about all of the wonderful activities that are taking place in your classroom. If you are enjoying a summer vacation, now is the time to think about the format that your newsletter will take. You can even set up the individual months with information now, and fill in the details at a later date.

• We have discussed this before, but it needs to be reemphasized often: *Always* look, act, and be *professional*. (You have a college degree; be smart!)

◢ IN WHAT OTHER WAYS *can you change the image of today's education and the use of teachers and schools as the scapegoats for society's ills?*

349

July 14

YESTERDAY WE DISCUSSED the use of teachers as scapegoats and possible activities that teachers can do to change that image. One of the problems (not really a problem) or issues that used to arise in my home with a nine-and-a-half-month teaching schedule (and a seven-hour teaching day) is that I received little sympathy for a smaller paycheck or other "teacher problems" from my husband and friends who worked forty-plus–hour weeks and had only one week (or possibly two weeks) of vacation each year, or from people who were bound to their work stations or in some other way controlled by their jobs. Having the summer off and long holiday vacations during the year is definitely a positive side of the teaching world.

It is easy to see the negative side of employment in any job or career that an individual may have (and, believe me, I am not overlooking the hours you spend in the evening and on weekends preparing lessons and grading papers). What I am saying is this: Today might be a good day to appreciate those around us who do not have the summers off. Although we may not have the perks that other occupations have, it is important to enjoy the perks that we do have.

And, while you are at it, be nice to your significant other if he or she does not have the summer off!

᠍ WHAT ARE *some of the perks of being a teacher?*

July 15

EARLIER THIS MONTH I complained about the problem of having a birthday in July and not getting cupcakes and "Happy Birthday" sung to me in the classroom. Well, as with most things, there is another side to the story.

One of the nice things about having a summer birthday is that the birthday individual is able to celebrate *twice* a year, evenly spaced for maximum enjoyment. Those individuals who were born on or around Christmas, Hanukkah, Ramadan, Kwanzaa, or other end-of-the-year celebration, risk being shortchanged in the gift-receiving department. I have a son who was born a week after Christmas, and although I felt sorry for him because he had to wait a whole year for the next special day, he seemed to find a positive side to this predicament. He believed that he was lucky because whatever he did not receive for Christmas, he had an extra chance of getting a week later for his birthday. Now that is positive thinking!

I like to think of the Disney version of *Alice in Wonderland,* when the characters have a party and joyfully sing, "A very merry *UN*-birthday to you...."[11] Wouldn't it be fun to have an "un-birthday" for those individuals (or yourself) who have six months to wait until their next big day?

Since July appears to be the month of birthdays, why not have an "un-birthday party" for everyone whose birthday is not in July?

ॐ WHO WILL YOU *invite to your "un-birthday party"?*

JULY 16

THROUGHOUT THE PAST YEAR, we have looked at other countries and their cultures to see how we are diverse, and more important, what we share in common. One thing we all have in common is that we have birthdays, but how we celebrate them may be different. How are birthdays celebrated in the Asian countries? In Europe, Africa, or the Middle Eastern countries? Are they celebrated at all?

Ask your students while they are researching other countries to see how children and adults celebrate their birthdays in these countries. Do they receive gifts? Have parties? Sing "Happy Birthday"? Have a cake? How do you sing "Happy Birthday" in other languages?

Why not have a birthday (or un-birthday) party using another culture's celebrations?

☟ CAN YOU SING *"Happy Birthday" in another language? (OK, let's hear you.)*

JULY 17

ONE OF THE HIGHLIGHTS of having a summer vacation in those rare years when I was not planning curricula or taking summer classes, was the luxury of time to read a few good books. One summer, even when I was busy, I justified the reading by claiming to be cleaning out the garage of all of the old classic books that I was forced to read in high school and college, those books that were difficult to fully enjoy because I "had to" read them.

What a wonderful experience to become reacquainted with *Tess of the D'Urbervilles, Madame Bovary, Of Mice and Men,* and many others. To read these books, *as an adult,* is a truly enjoyable experience. (Which leads me to think that the classics are not really for young people at all.)

If you have time this summer (and even if you do not), why not read a few classics? Or Dewey, or Berliner and Biddle, or the Sadkers, or the many other wonderful education books available through your bookstore.

☟ HAVE YOU READ *a good book lately? Why was it good?*

July

JULY 18

FOR MANY OF US, summertime is the time to go on a vacation, see some new sights, or visit some old relatives or friends. Whether it is cruising, flying, camping, or driving, vacations can be exhilarating, especially when, unlike your non-teaching friends, you do not have to go back to work when you return.

But, another way to take a "vacation" without really going anywhere is to turn off the phone, and take a vacation that will last all year. How can you take a vacation that will last all year? By learning a hobby, taking up a sport, or learning something new that you can repeat periodically during the coming school year when you need to relax and get away from it all.

By taking up something new during the summer you can get deeply involved, learn the fundamentals of the subject in depth, and enjoy it more in the future. Some examples might be golf, tennis, fishing, woodworking, quilting, sewing, music, floral design, and you name it. This summer treat yourself to a hobby, a "vacation," that you can go on all year.

❧ WHAT HOBBY *or sport have you been wanting to try? Why not* do it?

JULY 19

HERE I AM giving you all sorts of things to do on your vacation when what you probably need most is to relax and enjoy the time off. More than that, wouldn't it be nice if you could take that vacation mentality and have it last the rest of the year? The good news is that to some extent it is possible to do just that by using the Zen method of awareness—what practitioners of Zen call "being here and now."

353

When my friends who practice this first told me about "being here and now," I thought it sounded lovely, but found that it is not as easy as it first sounds. In "being here and now," one must only be in the moment, what *is* right now. Focusing on one thought, or better yet, no thought, *non*-mindfulness. That is easy for a moment, but what happens when you are a busy person (and we all are) is that other thoughts soon begin to creep in. What will we do in class tomorrow? What will I do with that student who is being a discipline problem? What will I get my friend for her birthday? What will I make for dinner? And the epitome of non-mindfulness, what will I do when I am finished being "here and now"?

Yet, I can vouch for the fact that it is a wonderful non-experience; it rests the body, the mind, and the spirit, and unfortunately I have to keep reminding myself to do it when I get preoccupied with the trivialities of the day.

A good way to begin is to sit on the floor, close your eyes or focus on the wall, and concentrate on your breathing, in and out, in and out. You will be amazed at the peacefulness that comes over you. You will find yourself doing this while seated at your desk, at your kitchen table, or even at boring meetings (but certainly not while driving). You'll have a momentary vacation, available at any time throughout the year.

꙰ WHEN WILL YOU *take your "vacation" today? How about now!*

JULY 20

WHEN I WAS IN HIGH SCHOOL, we had an English teacher who was the epitome of the learned individual, or so we thought. She was sixty-five years old, had been at the school forever, was the widow of the former school superintendent, and her grandson was in our graduating class. Everyone knew Mrs. Roe, even if you did not have the opportunity to be a student in her class.

Mrs. Roe had sayings such as, "To err is human, to forgive divine." Only she knew the correct pronunciation of *err*. Mrs. Roe said, "To *urr* is human, to forgive divine." She retired the year we graduated from high school, and we elected our class motto to be another of her famous sayings: "A little knowledge is a dangerous thing; drink deeply or taste not." (This is probably a paraphrasing of the original quotation, but you get the idea.) This saying has been steadfastly imprinted on my mind for more than thirty years. It's taught me to learn something deeply before expressing my expertise on the subject.

The last time I saw Mrs. Roe she was gardening in her yard, and she must have been ninety years old. Certainly she drank deeply (of the knowledge) of life.

If you are not already doing so, have you thought about going back to school? One of the most refreshing experiences that I participated in as a teacher was going back to college and earning my postgraduate degrees. It not only allowed me to drink deeply but to be with others who were doing the same. Think about it.

☙ DO YOU DRINK DEEPLY *of the knowledge available to you? If not, how can you do so?*

JULY 21

COMMON ACTIVITIES for summer are the picnics where families gather, or the family reunions for which people travel from all over the continent to see other family members, some of whom they may not have seen since childhood.

Family reunions afford not only great food and fun, but an opportunity to record family history before it is lost. Aside from what I call the "Severe Deprivation Stories" (the exaggerated stories that all parents seem to remember, such as, "I walked six miles to school everyday, in snow, with no shoes"), family reunions give the younger generation an opportunity to seek answers for questions such as, What was school like for the elder members of your family?

Some of these stories are rich with information about schooling in the past. Why not make notes for future generations of family members? Better yet, bring the tape recorder and get the story in the elder family member's own words! While you are at it, why not tape the younger generation for their posterity?

> ARE YOU ATTENDING *a family reunion this year? What would you like to know from your elders?*

JULY 22

NOW THAT IT IS SUMMER, it is easy to relax and enjoy your vacation and accomplish any tasks that you have designed for yourself at a leisurely pace. (At least I hope so.) Is your vacation all that you had hoped it would be? Did you start counting down the days when school would be out beginning after Easter, after Christmas, or after school started last September?

Doesn't it appear that we spend a whole lot of time doing what my mom used to call "wishing our lives away"? Not only do we count down the days until an activity ends ("When I graduate . . . ," "When the kids grow up . . . ," "When I retire . . . ," "When this book is done . . ."), but we even segregate the weeks and days until something "will be better." ("After fourth period . . . ," "After recess . . . ," and so on.) We even have days designated as "hump day" (Wednesday means we are "over the hump" for the week) and TGIF (Thank goodness it's Friday).

July

It seems as though we spend an inordinate amount of time wishing our life away. When do we stop and say, "Right now is good"?

ॐ WHAT TIME OF DAY *or day of the week is it for you? How can you make it "good"?*

JULY 23

AART VAN DER LEEUW WROTE, "The mystery of life is not a problem to be solved but a reality to be experienced."[12] Being here and now allows us the opportunity to experience life as a reality and perhaps solve the problems in our lives as we are partaking in the experience.

As Joseph Campbell says, "People say that what we're seeking is a meaning for life. . . . I think that what we're really seeking is an experience of being alive, so that our life experiences on the purely physical plane will have resonance within our innermost being and reality, so that we can actually feel the rapture of being alive."[13]

Being alive, or being here and now, both relate to *being*. Whatever your definition of being is, or what *being* means to you, I hope you are "experiencing being alive" this summer and that you will continue to do so in the months and years ahead.

ॐ HOW DO YOU DEFINE *"being alive"? How can you experience it?*

357

JULY 24

ON JANUARY 12, we discussed enjoying the season by playing in the snow, looking at snowflakes, making snow angels, and otherwise enjoying the winter weather as you may have done as a child. The summer months have their opportunities to allow you the same childlike experiences.

When I was a child, I used to like staying outside late (which for me was probably around eight o'clock), watching the summer day end, feeling the air cool down, and seeing the stars begin to appear in the sky. The first thing I would do at this time was to "wish upon a star," the first star to appear. (Remember? "Starlight, star-bright, *first* star I see tonight....") After my very thoughtful wish, I would chase fireflies, play "hide-and-seek," and feel the grass as it cooled beneath my bare feet.

Have you done any of these things since becoming an adult? Better yet, have you done them with a child? (Just be careful with bare feet.)

❧ WHAT *childlike opportunities await you this evening?*

JULY 25

IF YOU HAVE TIME (or better yet, take the time), you are probably enjoying activities that are taking place out of doors in the beautiful, hot sunshine. If you are in school, you may be taking children to parks, beaches, or on other field trips. If you are on vacation, you may be going any number of places where the sun is shining hot and bright.

As you probably are already aware, there are many good things about sunshine. It brightens our lives, helps us see, can be harnessed for solar energy, and provides vitamin D for healthy bones and teeth. But as you are probably also aware, the sun's

July

solar radiation can also do damage to your skin that may not show up for fifteen or twenty years. In other words, be careful! If you are going to spend a long period of time (and sometimes even a short period) in the sun, wear a sunscreen. It is probably a good idea to skip the deep dark tans of yesteryear.

☙ ARE YOU PREPARED *for those hot, sunshine activities? How are you prepared?*

JULY 26

ASIDE FROM DEVELOPING a new hobby this summer, this might be just the time to try something new, something a little scary, or something just out of the ordinary, something that others may not have thought of as "being you." I am not talking about anything dangerous, or an activity that will humiliate you, or cause you to have great regret in the future. What I am talking about is something fun, just for fun's sake.

Here is an example of something out of the ordinary I did recently:

I had never been on a train for a trip before, other than a subway or entertainment train such as those they have at museums, but recently I took a train ride for the first time and now I am hooked. I have been on countless plane trips, and certainly many vacations in cars and campers, but the train is an entirely different form of travel.

Not too long ago, my husband was transferred to complete a job in another part of the state, about five driving hours from our home. Since he would be there for a long period, and it was often difficult for him to come home, I found that I could either drive for five hours, take an airplane, or find some other mode of transportation to get to see him.

I am not much of a driver. On long driving trips I often think of the things that I could be accomplishing if I were not sitting in a car. The airport near my house and the airport near his did not use the same airplanes, so a plane trip to see him would be at least two takeoffs and landings, and a trip that would take as long as the drive. So I opted for the train, and I was pleasantly surprised. The trip is no shorter, but it cost considerably less than a trip by air. And instead of driving I could read, write, talk to interesting people, or look out at the beautiful countryside I was passing.

Now, since I live within hearing distance of a train track, I sometimes listen for the whistle of the train as it crosses the railroad crossing near my home, and I have to say that it makes me feel wanderlust for my next trip.

---

๑ WHAT WOULD YOU LIKE *to try that you have never done before? What is stopping you?*

JULY 27

EARLIER THIS MONTH we talked about the Berliner and Biddle book, *The Manufactured Crisis,* and how an appearance of a *crisis* situation allows others to come in to education to "help" eliminate the problem, usually in the form of "reforms." Now, reform is not necessarily bad. But the problem with reform in education is that it creates what we in education call the "swing of the pendulum" from one educational innovation to the next and back again. In many cases the "new and improved" method is not new and is certainly no improvement over the old. We seem to be, using one more well-worn cliché, once again "reinventing the wheel," which as we know, is very frustrating for those of us supposed to make the changes.

I recently came across an H. G. Wells quote that seems to fit a situation such as this. Wells wrote, "The crisis of today is the joke of tomorrow."[14] Enough said!

July

> Is there really a "crisis" in education? If not, why is there the appearance of one?

July 28

John Dewey wrote in 1916, in *Democracy and Education*, that "a society which makes provision for participation in its good of all its members on equal terms and which secures flexible readjustments of its institutions through interaction of the different forms of associated life is in so far democratic." The purpose of schooling is to give citizens equal opportunities to become productive members of society. In order to do this, "such a society must have a type of education which gives individuals a personal interest in social relationships and control, and the habits of mind which secure social changes without introducing disorder."[15]

School gives to students not only equal education, but equal opportunity to have a "personal interest" in making decisions about what society is and what changes need to be made to better the society. And all of this "without introducing disorder." Whew, what a tall order.

> How does one *change society (and change it for the better) without introducing disorder? More important, how do you teach students to do that?*

July 29

Yesterday we looked at the importance of teaching young people to realize the good, and make changes in society where necessary, without "introducing disorder." Dewey continued this discussion in *Democracy and Education.* "Every society gets encumbered with what is trivial . . . with what is positively perverse." Because of this, it is the school's "duty" to do "what it can to counteract their influence in the ordinary social environment."

According to Dewey, "By selecting the best for its exclusive use, it strives to reinforce the power of this best. As a society becomes more enlightened, it realizes that it is responsible *not* to transmit and conserve the whole of its existing achievements, but only such as to make for a better future society. The school is its chief agency for the accomplishment of this end."[16]

During July, we have looked at Independence Day celebrations, parades, the "Star-Spangled Banner," fireworks, and the foundations on which America has stood for over two hundred years. Yet Dewey says that it is not the society's role to train the young; it is the members of the society working *with* the school to ensure that the heritage is transferred to the "better future society."

What a noble cause, and one of which you are a part, if not a leader.

☙ WHAT ARE YOU *doing within your classroom to "make for a better society"?*

JULY 30

IN JULY WE CELEBRATE "Independence Day" as our major holiday, and you may be seeing the remnants of red, white, and blue bunting still hanging in the stores and from small town lampposts. Education is a freedom and *is* freedom, a liberation from ignorance, and the insurance and assurance that independence will survive for generations to come.

July

John Dewey wrote in *Reconstruction in Philosophy* that the purpose of education "is to set free and to develop the capacities of human individuals without respect to race, sex, class or economic status . . . the extent to which they educate every individual into the full stature of his possibility. Democracy has many meanings, but if it has a moral meaning, it is found in resolving that the supreme test of all political institutions and social arrangements shall be the contribution they make to the all-around growth of every member of society."[17]

Education as freeing—what a liberating thought!

☙ HOW DOES EDUCATION *liberate an individual? How do you ensure this through your teaching?*

JULY 31

IT IS THE END OF JULY, and the end of this book of daily reflections. Time to begin the whole process over again. I hope you have discovered in this book the importance of schools and teaching in a young person's life and, more important, the role that you as a teacher play in this process. What you do for society, the future, for you, and for me, is one of the most important careers around. School districts sometimes take it lightly when they hire the unqualified, as do unions who support those who should not be teaching. It is an uphill battle sometimes to get support and continue to do what you know to be right. My hope is that you are carrying the flag of teaching, good teaching, up that hill and planting it deep into the soil.

I hope that as you look to the new school year, you have received ideas from this book and will continue to reflect on your practice. If you are on summer vacation, enjoy the next month. If you are teaching, enjoy your students and take care of yourself.

To end this book in the manner in which it was presented, it is only fitting to end with one last quote from John Dewey: "All that society has accomplished for itself is put, through the agency of the school, at the disposal of its future members. All its better thoughts of itself it hopes to realize through the new possibilities thus open to its future self."[18]

❧ NOW WHAT ARE YOU *going to read every day?*

NOTES

INTRODUCTION

1. Charles C. Carson, Robert M. Huelskamp, and Thomas D. Woodall. (1993). "Perspectives on Education in America," *The Journal of Educational Research* (Special Issue), 86(May/June), pp. 288–297.

2. National Center for Education Statistics. (1997). *Digest of Education Statistics 1997.* Washington, DC: U.S. Department of Education Office of Educational Research and Improvement, pp. 1–13.

AUGUST

1. Barry Levinson (Director). (1987). *Good Morning, Vietnam.*

2. *The Encyclopedia Americana* (Vol. 17). (1957). New York: Americana Corporation, p. 316.

3. John Dewey. (1990). *The School and Society/The Child and the Curriculum.* Chicago: University of Chicago Press, p. 7. (Original works published 1900/1902).

4. Arthur M. Schlesinger Jr. (Ed.). (1983). *The Almanac of American History.* Greenwich, CT: Bison Books Corp., p. 469.

5. Dewey 1990, pp. 64, 75.

6. John Dewey. (1957). *Reconstruction in Philosophy.* Boston: Beacon, pp. 184–185, (Originally published in 1920 by Holt).

7. John Dewey. (1916). *Democracy and Education.* New York: Macmillan, p. 97.

8. Schlesinger 1983, p. 29.

9. Myra and David Sadker. (1994). *Failing at Fairness: How Our Schools Cheat Girls.* New York: Touchstone Books, pp. 6, 1.

10. Sadkers 1994, p. 197.

11. Dewey 1957, p. 186.

12. John I. Goodlad. (1968). *The Future of Learning and Teaching.* Washington, DC: National Education Association, pp. 22–23.

13. John I. Goodlad. (1978). "Educational Leadership: Toward the Third Era," *Educational Leadership, 35* (January), pp. 322–331.

14. Daniel and Laurel Tanner. (1995). *Curriculum Development: Theory into Practice* (3rd ed.) Englewood Cliffs, NJ: Merrill, pp. 294–295.

15. *The Encyclopedia Americana* (Vol. 19). (1957). New York: Americana Corporation, p. 740.

16. Richard Carlson. (1997). *Don't Sweat the Small Stuff... and It's All Small Stuff.* New York: Hyperion, p. 18. Biographical information supplied by *Compton's Interactive Encyclopedia.* (1996). SoftKey Multimedia Inc.

17. Charles E. Silberman. (1970). *Crisis in the Classroom.* New York: Random House, p. 142.

SEPTEMBER

1. Lewis Carroll. *Alice's Adventures in Wonderland.* Many editions are available.

2. Madeline Hunter. (1982). *Mastery Teaching.* El Segundo, CA: Tip Publications.

3. Madeline Hunter. (1985). "What's Wrong With Madeline Hunter?" *Educational Leadership, 42*(5), pp. 57–60.

4. Schlesinger 1983, p. 122.

5. Charles C. Carson, Robert M. Huelskamp and Thomas D. Woodall. (1993). "Perspectives on Education in America," *The Journal of Educational Research* (Special Issue), 86(May/June), pp. 288–297.

6. Daniel and Laurel Tanner. (1995). *Curriculum Development: Theory into Practice* (3rd ed.). Englewood Cliffs, NJ: Merrill, pp. 469–471.

Notes

7. Haim Ginott. (1972). *Teacher and Child: A Book for Parents and Teachers.* New York: Avon Books, p. 15.

October

1. Jerome S. Bruner. (1961). *The Process of Education.* Cambridge, MA: Harvard University Press pp. 14, 40.
2. Bruner 1961, pp. 31, 52.
3. Commission on the Reorganization of Secondary Education. (1918). *Cardinal Principles of Secondary Education.* Washington, DC: U.S. Bureau of Education, p. 22.
4. Albert Einstein. (1950). *Out of My Later Years.* New York: Philosophical Library, p. 32.
5. "People," *Education Week* (1998, June 3). Bethesda, MD: Education Week, p. 5.
6. John Dewey. (1990). *The School and Society/The Child and the Curriculum.* Chicago: University of Chicago Press, p. 29. (Original works published 1900/1902).
7. John Dewey. (1972). "My Pedagogic Creed." *The Early Works of John Dewey 1882–1898.* Carbondale, IL: Southern Illinois University Press, pp. 84–95. (First published in *School Journal,* LIV (January, 1897), pp. 77–80.)
8. Dewey 1972.
9. Lawrence A. Cremin. (1976). *Traditions of American Education.* New York: Basic Books, Inc., p. 37.

November

1. Arthur T. Jersild. (1955). *When Teachers Face Themselves.* New York: Teachers College Press, p. 132.
2. Paul Gray. (1998, June 8). "Required Reading." *Time, 151*(22), p. 108.
3. John Dewey. (1916). *Democracy and Education.* New York: MacMillan, p. 191.
4. *The Encyclopedia Americana* (Vol. 18). (1957). New York: Americana Corporation, p. 466.

5. John Dewey. (1990/1902). *The School and Society/The Child and the Curriculum.* Chicago, IL: University of Chicago Press, p. 14. (Original works published 1900/1902).

6. Anti-Defamation League. (1996). *Memo & Date Book 1996–1997.* New York: Anti-Defamation League, November 17.

7. Robert M. Hutchins. (1963). *On Education.* Santa Barbara, CA: Center for the Study of Democratic Institutions, pp. 1–2.

8. Robert M. Hutchins. (1968). *The Learning Society.* New York: Praeger, p. ix.

9. Arthur M. Schlesinger Jr. (Ed.). (1983). *The Almanac of American History.* Greenwich, CT: Bison Books Corp., p. 155.

DECEMBER

1. Joyce Epstein. (1992). *School and Family Partnerships* (Report No. 6). Baltimore, MD: Johns Hopkins University Center on Families, Communities, Schools, and Children's Learning, pp. 11–14.

2. Alfred North Whitehead. (1929). *The Aims of Education.* New York: Macmillan, p. 3.

3. United Nations General Assembly. (1948, December 10). Article 26 of the Universal Declaration of Human Rights. New York: United Nations.

4. Arthur M. Schlesinger Jr. (Ed.). (1983). *The Almanac of American History.* Greenwich, CT: Bison Books Corp., p. 115.

5. Schlesinger 1983, p. 113.

6. Robert Frost. (1969). *The Poetry of Robert Frost.* New York: Holt, Rinehart and Winston, pp. 224–225.

7. Daniel and Laurel Tanner. (1995). *Curriculum Development: Theory into Practice* (3rd ed.). Englewood Cliffs, NJ: Merrill, p. 189.

JANUARY

1. Nicholas Murray Butler. (1900). "Status of Education at the Close of the Century." National Education Association Proceedings. Chicago: University of Chicago Press, pp. 313–314.

Notes

2. John Dewey. (1990). *The School and Society/The Child and the Curriculum.* Chicago: University of Chicago Press, p. 187. (Original works published 1900/1902).

3. Robert Frost. (1969). *The Poetry of Robert Frost.* New York: Holt, Rinehart and Winston, p. 105.

4. Arthur M. Schlesinger Jr. (Ed.). (1983). *The Almanac of American History.* Greenwich, CT: Bison Books Corp., p. 460. *The Encyclopedia Americana* (Vol. 23). (1957). New York: Americana Corporation, p. 33.

5. Charles E. Silberman. (1970). *Crisis in the Classroom.* New York: Random House, p. 182.

6. John Holt. (1964). *How Children Fail.* New York: Dell, p. 167.

7. Schlesinger 1983, p. 140.

8. Kenny Rogers. (1991). "The Gambler." On the album *Kenny Rogers 20 Greatest Hits.* EMI/Capitol Records.

9. Schlesinger 1983, p. 312.

10. Herbert M. Kliebard. (1992). *Forging the American Curriculum: Essays in Curriculum History and Theory.* London: Routledge, p. 110.

11. Robert M. Pirsig. (1984). *Zen and the Art of Motorcycle Maintenance: An Inquiry Into Values.* New York: Bantam Books, p. 267. (Original work published in 1974).

12. David R. Krathwohl, Benjamin S. Bloom and Bertram B. Masia. (1964). *Taxonomy of Educational Objectives, Handbook I: Cognitive Domain.* New York: David McKay.

13. John Dewey. (1916). *Democracy and Education.* New York: Macmillan, p. 11. Daniel and Laurel Tanner. (1995). *Curriculum Development: Theory into Practice* (3rd ed.). Englewood Cliffs, NJ: Merrill, p. 197.

14. Dewey 1916, p. 2.

February

1. Harold Ramis (Director). (1993). *Groundhog Day.*

2. Albert Hatcher. (1942, November 9). "Negro Youth and College." *New Republic,* p. 612.

3. Leonardo Covello. (1958). *The Heart Is the Teacher.* New York: McGraw-Hill.

4. Susan Studer. (1998). "Smith-Hughes Act/Smith-Lever Act." In Linda Eisenmann's *Historical Dictionary of Women's Education in the United States.* Westport, CT: Greenwood Publishing, pp. 381–385.

5. Robert Slavin. (1997). *Educational Psychology: Theory and Practice* (5th ed.). Boston: Allyn and Bacon, pp. 273, 285–286.

6. Madonna. (1998). "Frozen." On the album *Ray of Light.* Warner Bros.

MARCH

1. Jerome S. Bruner. (1966). *Toward a Theory of Instruction.* Cambridge, MA: Harvard University Press, p. 72.

2. Hilda Taba. (1962). *Curriculum Development: Theory and Practice.* New York: Harcourt, p. 121.

3. John Dewey. (1990). *The School and Society/The Child and the Curriculum.* Chicago: University of Chicago Press, p. 205. (Original works published 1900/1902).

4. Dewey 1990, pp. 118–119.

5. American Psychological Association. (1997). *Publication Manual of the American Psychological Association* (4th ed.). Washington, DC: American Psychological Association, p. 50.

6. American Psychological Association 1997.

7. Arthur M. Schlesinger Jr. (Ed.). (1983). *The Almanac of American History.* Greenwich, CT: Bison Books Corp., p. 85. *The Encyclopedia Americana* (Vol. 21). (1957). New York: Americana Corporation, pp. 402–403.

8. Carol Gilligan. (1982). *In a Different Voice: Psychological Theory and Women's Development.* Cambridge, MA: Harvard University Press, pp. 8–18. *How Schools Shortchange Girls* and *Growing Smart: What's Working For Girls in School* are available from AAUW Educational Foundation, 1111 Sixteenth St. N.W., Washington, DC 20036-4873.

9. Elizabeth Cady Stanton. (1892). "The Solitude of Self." In David A. Hollinger and Charles Capper (Eds.). *The American Intel-*

lectual Tradition (Volume II 1865 to the Present). (1993). New York: Oxford University Press, pp. 48–53.

10. Gilligan 1982.

11. Rollo May. (1975). *The Courage to Create.* New York: W. W. Norton & Company, pp. 74–76.

12. Judy Collins. (1998). "Both Sides Now." On the album *Both Sides Now.* Intersound.

13. Dewey 1990, p.189.

APRIL

1. Thomas L. Good and Jere E. Brophy. (1991). *Looking in Classrooms* (5th ed.). New York: HarperCollins Publishers, pp. 196, 230–231.

2. John Dewey. (1990). *The School and Society/The Child and the Curriculum.* Chicago: University of Chicago Press, p. 29. (Original works published 1900/1902).

3. Howard Gardner and Thomas Hatch. (1989). "Multiple Intelligences Go to School." *Educational Researcher, 18*(8), pp. 6–9.

4. "Quotes Worth Quoting." *1998 Almanac.* Louisville, KY: Lee Almanac Co., p. 6.

5. Thomas Jefferson. (1961). "Letter to James Madison." In Gordon C. Lee (Ed.) *Crusade Against Ignorance: Thomas Jefferson on Education.* New York: Teachers College Press, p. 38.

6. Arthur M. Schlesinger Jr. (Ed.). (1983). *The Almanac of American History.* Greenwich, CT: Bison Books Corp., p. 35.

7. Lev S. Vygotsky. (1978). *Mind in Society.* Cambridge, MA: Harvard University Press, pp. 84–91.

8. Francis W. Parker. (1894). *Talks on Pedagogics.* New York: E. L. Kellogg.

9. John Holt. (1964). *How Children Fail.* New York: Dell, p. 179.

10. Dewey 1990, p. 182.

11. Herbert Spencer. (1890). "What Knowledge Is of Most Worth?" *Education: Intellectual, Moral, and Physical.* Boston: Willard Small, pp. 5–82. (Original work published in 1859).

12. "Quotes Worth Quoting." *1998 Almanac* (36th ed.) Louisville, KY: Lee Almanac Co., p. 6.

1. George F. Madaus. (1993). "A National Testing System." *Educational Assessment, 1* (Winter), p. 23.

2. Daniel and Laurel Tanner. (1995). *Curriculum Development: Theory into Practice* (3rd ed.). Englewood Cliffs, NJ: Merrill, pp. 703–704.

3. Tanners 1995, p. 183.

4. "Quotes Worth Quoting." *1998 Almanac* (36th ed.) Louisville, KY: Lee Almanac Co., p. 6.

5. John Dewey. (1990). *The School and Society/The Child and the Curriculum.* Chicago: University of Chicago Press, p. 151. (Original works published 1900/1902).

6. Charles E. Silberman. (1970). *Crisis in the Classroom.* New York: Random House, p. 114.

7. Tanners 1995, p. 365.

8. Arthur M. Schlesinger Jr. (Ed.). (1983). *The Almanac of American History.* Greenwich, CT: Bison Books Corp., p. 30.

9. Erik Erikson. (1968). *Identity, Youth and Crisis.* New York: Norton, p. 115.

10. bell hooks. (1994). "Ecstasy: Teaching and Learning Without Limits." In Fred Schultz (Ed.). (1998). *Sources: Notable Selections in Education* (2nd ed.). Guilford, CT: Dushkin/McGraw-Hill, p. 232.

11. Schlesinger 1983, p. 157.

JUNE

1. John Dewey. (1957). *Reconstruction in Philosophy.* Boston: Beacon, pp. 184–185. (Originally published in 1920 by Holt).

2. John Dewey. (1938). *Experience and Education.* New York: Macmillan, pp. 48–49.

3. Brian Tracy. (1998, January 27). Speech given at Peter Lowe's Success 1998 Seminar, Anaheim, CA.

4. Joan Lunden. (1998, January 27). Speech given at Peter Lowe's Success 1998 Seminar, Anaheim, CA.

5. James Baldwin. (1963). "A Talk to Teachers." In Fred Schultz (Ed.). (1998). *Sources: Notable Selections in Education* (2nd ed.). Guilford, CT: Dushkin/McGraw-Hill, p. 175.

6. Jonathan Kozol. (1995). "Amazing Grace." In Schultz 1998, p. 358.

7. *The Encyclopedia Americana* (Vol. 11). (1957). New York: Americana Corporation, pp. 316, 324.

8. Sterling M. McMurrin. (1967, January 14)."What Tasks for Schools?" *Saturday Review, 49*, pp. 41–42.

9. Peter S. Hlebowitsh. (1992). *Radical Curriculum Theory Reconsidered.* New York: Teachers College, p. 46.

10. Karen Zumwalt. (1995). "What's a National Curriculum Anyway?" In AREA'S Public Service Monograph, Elliot Eisner (Ed.). *The Hidden Consequences of a National Curriculum.* Washington, DC: AERA, pp. 3–4.

11. Arthur M. Schlesinger Jr. (Ed.). (1983). *The Almanac of American History.* Greenwich, CT: Bison Books Corp., p. 412.

12. John Holt. (1972). *Freedom and Beyond.* New York: Dutton, p. 66.

JULY

1. Henry Steele Commager. (1950, October 16). "Our Schools Have Kept Us Free." *Life, 29*, p. 46.

2. *The Encyclopedia Americana* (Vol. 11). (1957). New York: Americana Corporation, p. 309.

3. *Encyclopedia Americana* 11, 1957, p. 314.

4. *Encyclopedia Americana* 25, 1957, p. 491.

5. *Encyclopedia Americana* 3, 1957, p. 478.

6. David C. Berliner and Bruce J. Biddle. (1995). *The Manufactured Crisis: Myths, Fraud, and the Attack on America's Schools.* Reading, MA: Addison-Wesley Publishing Company, Inc., pp. 34, 40, 139, and the cover.

7. Berliner and Biddle 1995, p. 304.

8. Berliner and Biddle 1995, p. 148.

9. Lawrence A. Cremin. (1990). *Popular Education and Its Discontents.* New York: HarperCollins, p. 125.

10. Joe Schneider and Paul Houston. (1993). *Exploding the Myths: Another Round in the Education Debate.* Washington, DC: American Association of Educational Service Agencies, p. 3.

11. Clyde Geronimi (Director). (1951). *Alice in Wonderland.* Walt Disney Studios.

12. Aart van der Leeuw. (1997). *The Little Zen Calendar.* Workman Publishing, January 6, 1998.

13. Joseph Campbell. (1997). *The Little Zen Calendar.* Workman Publishing, January 5, 1998.

14. "Quotes Worth Quoting." *1998 Almanac* (36th ed.) Louisville, KY: Lee Almanac Co., p. 6.

15. John Dewey. (1916). *Democracy and Education.* New York: Macmillan, p. 99.

16. Dewey 1916. p. 20.

17. John Dewey. (1957). *Reconstruction in Philosophy.* Boston: Beacon, p. 186. (Originally published in 1920 by Holt).

18. John Dewey. (1990). *The School and Society/The Child and the Curriculum.* Chicago: University of Chicago Press, p. 7. (Original works published 1900/1902).